Hazrat Pir-o-Murshid Inayat Khan

The Sufi Message of Hazrat Inayat Khan

Centennial Edition

Volume III
The Art of Personality

Selected titles from Sulūk Press and Omega Publications

Caravan of Souls: An Introduction to the Sufi Path of Hazrat Inayat Khan
Compiled and edited by Pir Zia Inayat-Khan

Gayan, Vadan, Nirtan
by Hazrat Inayat Khan

The Hand of Poetry: Five Mystic Poets of Persia
by Hazrat Inayat Khan and Coleman Barks

The Message In Our Time
The Life and Teachings of the Sufi Master Pir-O-Murshid Inayat Khan
by Pir Vilayat Inayat Khan

The Sufi Message of Hazrat Inayat Khan
Centennial Edition
Volume I: The Inner Life
Volume II: The Mysticism of Sound

The Complete Works of Pir-o-Murshid Hazrat Inayat Khan series
in cooperation with the Nekbakht Foundation

For a complete list of titles please visit
www.omegapub.com

The Sufi Message of Hazrat Inayat Khan

Centennial Edition

Volume III
The Art of Personality

Character Building
The Art of Personality
Moral Culture
Consciousness and Personality
Art and the Artist
The Art of Music

Sulūk Press
Richmond, Virginia

Published by Sulūk Press
an imprint of Omega Publications, Inc.
Richmond, Virginia
www.omegapub.com

Cover background and ornament from Shutterstock.com
Cover design by Sandra Lillydahl

This edition is printed on acid-free paper
that meets ANSI standad X39-48.

Inayat Khan (1882–1927)
The Sufi Message of Hazrat Inayat Khan
Centennial Edition
Volume III: The Art of Personality
Character Building, The Art of Personality, Moral Culture,
Consciousness and Personality, Art and the Artist, The Art of Music
Includes introduction by Pir Zia Inayat-Khan,
biographical note, glossary, index.
1. Sufism
I. Inayat Khan II. Title

Library of Congress Control Number: 2016940929

Printed and bound by Sheridan Books
in the United States of America

ISBN 978-1-941810-27-9 hard case
ISBN 978-1-941810-28-6 paper edition

Contents

Acknowledgments ix

Introduction by Pir Zia Inayat-Khan xi

Character Building 1

- Willpower 3
- The Music of Life 8
- Self-Control 14
- Relationship 20
- Subtlety 25
- Complaining and Smiling 31
- Noiseless Working 38
- Inquisitiveness 42
- Gossip 45
- Generosity 47

The Art of Personality 53

- Gratefulness 55
- The Art of Personality 61
- Gentleness 66
- The Persuasive Tendency 71
- Vanity 76
- Self-Respect 82
- Reconciliation 87
- Word of Honor 94
- Graciousness 97
- Economy 103
- Justice 107
- Ear Training 112
- Attitude 116

Moral Culture 119

- Part I: The Law of Reciprocity 121
  - Reciprocity 121
  - Our Dealings with Our Friends 122

Our Dealings with Our Enemies 123
Distinction of Grades 124
Our Dealings with God 125
How to Take the Dealings of Others with Us 126
How to Take the Dealings of Our Friends with Us 127
How to Take the Dealings of Our Enemies 128
How to Take the Dealings of Others according to Our Own Grade 129
God's Dealings with Us 130
Part 2: The Law of Beneficence 132
Our Dealings with Our Friends 132
Our Dealings with Our Relations 133
Our Dealings with Servants 134
Our Dealings with Masters 135
Our Dealings with Acquaintances 136
Our Dealings with Our Neighbors 137
Our Dealings with Our Fellow Human Beings 138
Our Dealings with Wrongdoers 139
Our Dealings with Enemies 140
Our Dealings with God 142
Part 3: The Law of Renunciation 144
Life in God 144
Renunciation 1 146
Renunciation 2 146
Greed and Generosity 147
The Necessity of Renunciation in Life 148
The Relativity of Gain 149
Renunciation and Loss 149
The Learning of Renunciation 150
The Nature of Renunciation 151
The Final Victory 153
Consciousness and Personality 155
Consciousness and Personality 157
Imagination 159
Thought and Feeling 161
Beauty 165

The Destruction of Ideals	168
The Dream	170
Personality as a Bubble in the Water	172
The Mystery of Shadow	174
Conditions of the Mind	177
The Will	178
Influence and Innocence	179
Influence	179
Innocence	180
Vairagya	182
Are We Masters of Our Destiny?	185
Art and the Artist	193
Art	195
Nature and Art	198
Copying 1	200
Copying 2	201
The Art of Copying Nature	202
Improving 1	203
Improving 2	204
The Art of Improvement	205
The One who Improves	206
Observation	208
Illusion in Art	210
Symbology	213
Art and Religion	215
The Divine Art	221
The Divinity of Art	231
The Art of Music	237
Indian Music 1	239
Indian Music 2	242
Composition	244
Music, Astrology, and Alchemy	245
Improvisation	246
The Effects of Music	249
Inner and Outer Rhythms	252
Dance and Movement	253
The Religion of Harmony	256

The Divine Art of Music 259
The Divine Musician 260

Glossary 261

Sources 265

Biographical note 269

Index 271

ACKNOWLEDGEMENTS

Thanks are due to Anne Louise Wirgman, Director, Nekbakht Foundation in Suresnes, France, who provided invaluable assistance with providing authentic source material for *Moral Culture*, and with editorial suggestions. Thanks are also due to Jeanne Kore Salvato and Nancy Wilkinson, for their editorial work on *Character Building* and *The Art of Personality*, which was published as *Creating the Person: A Practical Guide to the Development of Self* in 2013 by Omega Publications. Additional welcome editorial assistance was provided by Muhasaba Wender and most especially by Cannon Labrie, who also translated "The Divinity of Art" into English from the French transcription.

Sandra Lillydahl, editor

INTRODUCTION

When Diogenes was asked why he walked around with a lantern in broad daylight, he answered, "I am searching for a human being." People are everywhere to be found, but where is one to find a human being? Individuality is a given, says Hazrat Inayat Khan, but personality must be discovered and created. The present volume contains Hazrat's illuminating teachings on the attainment of personality.

Individuality is mimetic; one is what one is by virtue of one's conditioning. Like a mirror—albeit, often, a rusty one—an individual reflects back the impressions that have, by chance, fallen upon his or her mind. Freedom, by contrast, requires an exercise of will. Hazrat says, "If the heart is clear enough to receive reflections fully and clearly, one can choose oneself which to retain and which to repel."[1] This purposefulness marks the advent of personality. Personality is expressive rather than mimetic. In a realized personality, the soul expresses its divine inheritance through its thoughts, words, and actions. Hazrat explains, "Personality is the development of individuality, and in personality, which is formed by character-building, is born that spirit which is the rebirth of the soul."[2]

1 Hazrat Inayat Khan, *The Complete Works of Pir-o-Murshid Hazrat Inayat Khan: Original Texts, Lectures on Sufism,* 1924, vol. 2 (New Lebanon, NY: Omega Publications, 2009), 582.

2 Ibid, 1923, vol. 2 (London and the Hague: East-West Publications, 1988), 509.

Character-building is the very substance of Sufism. The Prophet Muhammad urged, "Qualify yourself with the qualities of God." Sufism accordingly concerns itself with the cultivation of the divine attributes that are inherent in the human soul, but which are ordinarily dormant. Abu Hafs al-Haddad (d. c. 878–9) therefore defined Sufism as spiritually attuned action: "Sufism consists entirely of behavior; every time, place, and circumstance have their own propriety."[3] Abu'l-Hasan an-Nuri (d. 907–8) said, similarly, "Sufism is not composed of practices and sciences, but it is morals."[4]

The first two books in this volume, *Character Building* and *The Art of Personality*, consist of lectures given in Suresnes, France, during the Summer School of 1923. These two works together form an remarkable *futuvvat-nama*, or manual of Sufi chivalry, delineating a series of capacities of mind and heart that, when carefully contemplated and conscientiously enacted, ripen and refine an individual's nature. The insights contained in these two books provide an instructive framework through which to approach the Iron, Copper, Silver, and Golden Rules enumerated in Hazrat's *Vadan*.[5]

The next book, *Moral Culture*, is a compilation of lectures given between the years 1915 and 1920. Its three sections—on reciprocity, beneficence, and renunciation—correspond to stages traditionally designated as the law (*shari'at*), the path (*tariqat*), and the truth (*haqiqat*). By extension, these sections correspond to the contemplative stages that Hazrat names concentration, contemplation, and meditation. Left unelaborated here is the fourth stage, "the renunciation of renunciation," corresponding to wisdom (*ma'rifat*) and realization. Hazrat elsewhere describes this latter stage thus: "Then one finally ex-

3 'Ali B. Uthman Al-Jullabi Al-Hujwiri, *Kashf Al-Mahjub of Al-Hujwiri: The Oldest Persian Treatise on Sufism*, trans. Reynold A. Nicholson (London: Gibb Memorial Trust, 1976), 41–2.

4 Ibid, 42.

5 Hazrat Inayat Khan, *Complete Works: Sayings,* vol. 1 (London and The Hague: East-West Publications, 1989), 320–21.

periences what is called *baqa'*, where the false ego is annihilated and merged into the true personality, which is really God expressing Himself in some wondrous ways."[6]

The remainder of the volume is made up of previously uncollected lectures on various subjects related to personality and aesthetics. For Hazrat, art in all of its forms is the creative manifestation of the unfurling of the human personality. He observes, "Nature is what God makes as God, and art is what God makes as man."[7] Art completes nature.

A powerful piece of art can help us see the natural world around us through new eyes. But the most compelling art of all is not found on brightly painted canvases or in the pages of melodious musical scores. It is discovered, instead, in the personality of a person who has attained the momentous epiphany of self-knowledge. There is a real human being.

Pir Zia Inayat-Khan

6 Hazrat Inayat Khan, unpublished papers.
7 Hazrat Inayat Khan, unpublished papers.

CHARACTER BUILDING

Contents of *Character Building* are taken from a series of lectures given during the 1923 Summer School in Suresnes, France, August 11–27. These lectures have been previously published as *Creating the Person: A Practical Guide to the Development of Self* (New Lebanon, NY: Sulūk Press, 2013). The editors of *Creating the Person*, Jeanne Koré Salvato and Vakil Nancy Wilson compiled the text on the most authentic sources as found in *The Complete Works of Pir-o-Murshid Hazrat Inayat Khan: Original Texts: Lectures on Sufism, 1923*, vol. 2 (London: East-West Publications, 1988).

WILLPOWER

Willpower plays a great part in character building, and willpower becomes feeble when one yields to every little tendency, inclination, and fancy one has. When one fights against every little fancy and tendency and inclination, one learns to fight with oneself, and in this way one develops willpower. When inclinations, fancies, and tendencies have grown stronger than the willpower, then one experiences in life several enemies existing in one's own self, and one finds it difficult to combat them; for inclinations, fancies, and tendencies, when powerful, do not let willpower work against them. If there is anything like self-denial, it is this practice; and by this practice, in time, one attains to a power which may be called mastery over one's self.

In small things of everyday life one neglects this consideration for the reason that one thinks "these are my tendencies, my fancies, my inclinations—and by respecting them I respect myself; by considering them I consider myself." But one forgets that what one calls "me" is not the self. It is what wills that is the self. Therefore, in the Christian prayer it is taught "Thy will be done,"[1] which means "Thy will, when it works through me, will be done"; in other words, "My will, which is Thy will, will be done." It is this illusion of muddling one's possession with oneself that creates all illusion and keeps people from self-realization.

Life is a continual battle. We struggle with things which are outside of us, and so we give a chance to the foes who exist in

1 Matthew 6:10.

our own being. Therefore, the first thing necessary in life is to make peace for the time being with the outside world in order to prepare for the war which is to be fought within oneself. Once peace is made within, one will gain by that sufficient strength and power to be used in the struggle of life within and without.

Self-pity is the worst poverty. When a we say "I am" with pity, before we have said anything more, we have diminished what we are to half, and what is said further diminishes us totally. Nothing more is left of us afterwards. There is so much in the world which we can pity and on which it would be right for us to take pity. But if we have no time free from our own self, we cannot give mind to the condition of others in the world. Life is one long journey, and the more we have left ourselves behind, the further we have progressed toward the goal. Verily, when the false self is lost, the true self is discovered.

* * *

Question: *Why do we find satisfaction in self-pity?*

Answer: The reason is that by nature we find satisfaction in love. And when we are confined to ourselves, we begin to love ourselves; for our limitations we have self-pity. But, therefore, the love of self always brings dissatisfaction, because the self is made to love; and, when we love, the first condition of love is that we forget our self. We cannot love another person by loving our self at the same time. The condition of love is to forget oneself; then one knows how to love. If one says "Give me a sixpence and I will give you a shilling," that is another kind of love.

Question: *Do you mean by the false self, the ego?*

Answer: Yes, by the false self I mean false ego, the deluding ego, someone who has guised himself or herself as the ego. The reason is that the human ego is false ego. What is ego? It is that line which connects God and humanity; that line, one end of which is human, the other is God. Therefore, that end which is the human ego is false, because we have covered it with false ego. The ego is true. It is divine, it cannot be anything else. But a person covers it with illusions and calls it "me," "myself." When that wrong conception is broken by knowledge, love, wisdom, or meditation, then it is just like the clouds which are broken, which cover the sun; and the true ego comes out, the only ego there is.

Question: *Is it easy to say "Thy will be done"?*

Answer: There are two ways of looking at it: the way of the master and of the saint. The way of the saint is "Thy will be done"; the way of the master is "My will be done." In the end both things become one. But to say "Thy will be done" is a resignation.

Question: *Is it possible for an ego to come on earth and never be covered by clouds of illusion?*

Answer: No, the beauty is to come out of that illusion. If one came wise, there would be no joy in coming out of it. The joy is in the unveiling. The question is, what is the ego? It is the ego in us which says "I." It is that ego which says, "This is mine." When we say "I am sorry," what is it in us that says "I am sorry"? It is our ego, not our hand, our eye, our ear.

Question: *The difference between the false and real ego is the difference between selfishness and unselfishness?*

Answer: Yes, the result of the manifestation of the real ego is unselfishness. It is a natural outcome of it. And the more one is absorbed in the false ego, the more selfish that person is.

Question: *To say "I am sorry" is an act of compassion. How then can the false ego say this?*

Answer: The real ego does not know sorrow; it is happiness. We long for happiness because our true being is happiness. God is happiness. There are many people who do not long for God, but they long for happiness. It is the same thing. For instance, an atheist says there is no God, but longs for happiness. God is happiness.

Question: *What really is character?*

Answer: Character is, so to speak, a picture with lines and colors we make within ourselves. And it is wonderful to see how the tendency of character building springs up from childhood, just like one sees the instinct of building a nest in a bird. The little child begins to note everything in the grown-up people and begins to adopt all that seems to it the best: the word, the manner, the movement, the idea, everything that it grasps from the grown-up—whatever seems to its own mind best. It attracts it and it builds, so to speak, a building, which is its character. It is being built all through the life.

By this we understand that when a person is absorbed in the self, that person has no time to see the other; then there is no other. But when one forgets oneself, one has the time to see here and there, and add naturally to one's character. So the character is built. One need not make an effort in building the character if only one forgets oneself. For instance, if the great actors and actresses, with great qualifications, do not forget themselves, they cannot act although they may have all capability. So musicians, when they cannot forget at the time when they are playing, they cannot perform music to satisfaction. So with the poet, the artist. Think, then: the whole work of building oneself and everything else, it all depends upon how much one is able to forget the self, which is the key to the whole life—material and spiritual life—and to success. It seems such a simple thing, and yet it is so difficult.

The wonderful thing is that during my travels, whenever I have met very great people in anything—art, science, thought, religion, philosophy, whatever be their work—I have found that they have touched that greatness with this quality, the quality of forgetting themselves. Always, everywhere it is the same.

And I have again seen people with great qualifications, but they remember themselves so much that they cannot do the best with their lives. I have known a *vina* player who tried so much, playing his instrument for six, nine hours a day. But whenever he used to go in the assembly, he became so nervous because he thought of himself. And all the impressions of the people would fall upon him. He would take his instrument and cover it and run away. He never had a chance of being great, even with all his qualifications.

Self-confidence is a great thing, but forgetting oneself is greater still.

I have seen Sarah Bernhardt. She was singing a very simple song, the national anthem of France. When she came on the stage she won every person there. At that time she was the nation; with that sentiment in the feeling and the words, she was France at that time, because of her concentration.

THE MUSIC OF LIFE

In character building it is most necessary that one learn how to face the world, the world where one meets with sorrows and troubles and pleasures and pains. It is very difficult for one to hide from the world, and at the same time the wise are not meant to show all they feel at every moment. An ordinary person, like a machine, reacts in answer to every outer influence and inner impulse, and in this way very often cannot keep to the law of the music of life.

Life, to a wise person, is music; and in that symphony one has to play a certain part. If, in one's feeling, one has dropped down so low that one's heart is sounding a lower pitch, and the demand of life at that moment is that one must voice a higher pitch, at that time one finds that one has failed that music in which one was meant to play one's part fittingly.

This is the test by which you can distinguish the old soul and the child soul. The child soul will give way to every feeling; the old soul will strike the higher note in spite of all difficulties. There are moments when laughter must be kept back, and there are times when tears must be withdrawn. And those who have arrived at the stage where they can act the part that they are meant to act in this life's drama rightly and efficiently, even have power over the expression on their face. They can even turn their tears into smiles, or smiles into tears. One may ask: "Is it not hypocrisy not to be natural?" Those who have control over their nature are more natural. They are not only natural, but they are the masters of nature. Those who lack power over nature, in spite of their naturalness, are weak.

Besides, it must be understood that real civilization means the art of life. What is that art? It is the knowing of the music of life. Once a soul has awakened to the continual music of life, the soul will consider as its responsibility, as its duty, to play its part in the outer life, even if it be contrary to its inner condition for the moment. To do this, it requires knowledge.

One must know at every moment in one's daily life, "What does life demand of me, what does it ask of me, and how shall I answer the demand of my life?" This requires one to be awakened fully to life's conditions. One must have insight into human nature, and one must be able to know one's own condition fully as well. If one says, "I am as I am; if I am sad, I am sad, if I am glad, I am glad," that will not do. Even the earth will not bear the person who will not answer life's demands. The sky will not tolerate that person, and space will not accommodate those who are not ready to give what life asks of them. If this is true, then it is best when it is wisely done and willingly done.

In the orchestra there is a conductor and there are many who play music, and the players of an instrument have to fill in their contribution in the performance. If they do not do it right, it is their fault. The conductor will not listen that they did not do it right because they were sad, or that they were too glad; the conductor is not concerned with their sadness or gladness. The conductor is concerned with the part that the particular musician must play in the whole symphony. That is the nature of our lives. The further we advance, our part in this orchestra becomes more difficult and more important; and the more conscious we become of this responsibility, the more efficient we become in performing our part in life's symphony satisfactorily.

In order to be able to have that control over oneself, what is necessary? We must have control over our inner self, because every outward manifestation is nothing but a reaction of the inner condition. Therefore, the first control that we have to get is over ourselves, our inner self, which is done by strengthening the will, and by understanding life better.

* * *

Question: *Are the beings who live on the other planets humans or angels?*

Answer: On any part of the earth human beings live. Our planet is the earth. No doubt there are differences in the evolution of the people living on different planets. Yet on all planets there are angelic people and those who are the contrary.

Question: *How do the earth and the sky and space not bear and accommodate the person who does not answer life's demands?*

Answer: Have you, perhaps, heard of a person who has been exiled from, perhaps, five different countries, and perhaps went to a sixth, and was also exiled? The earth cannot bear that person. Others would like to put that person in the water, to burn that person, because the earth does not want that person to walk upon her. It is what is called the curse. The curse manifests in many forms. A person takes that with them. That person may go from the South Pole to the North Pole; when the earth once does not want someone, it does not want that person wherever they go. Among the primitive people they will want to eat that person because the earth cannot bear that human being.

With exceptional souls there is an exceptional law. It cannot be explained with ordinary terms of expression. Great souls also go from one place to another; it is not that the earth does not bear them, but human beings.

Question: *What will be the future of those who have not fulfilled the demand of life? Shall they come back to learn the lesson again?*

Answer: We must all learn our lesson just now. They may come back or not come back—that is another question. Just now the question is before us; life's demand is just now, not after life. At every moment of our life we are asked to fulfill a certain duty, a certain work, in everything we do. With every movement we are fulfilling a certain duty, consciously or unconsciously. To become conscious of it, and do it fittingly and rightly, that is the true religion.

Question: *What do you mean by older and younger souls?*

Answer: In this particular case I only meant ripened and unripened souls. The older soul is just like an older brother or sister, the younger like a younger one.

Question: *The last sentence [of your lecture] was, ". . . also by understanding life better." What is the wisest way to understand?*

Answer: In this last sentence I meant that we understand life's demands by understanding life better. And if we do not understand life better, we cannot understand fully what life asks of us. There are some who do not answer life's demands because they do not know what life asks of them. There are others who know what life asks of them, but they have not yet advanced enough to do it. In order to know what life asks, one must understand life better.

Question: *One may ask, perhaps, "When what our outer life demands is quite different from what the inner life asks of us, which do we listen to?"*

Answer: In the Bible there is a beautiful answer to this question: "Give unto Caesar what Caesar asks, and to God what God asks."[1] What the outer life demands, those demands must be fulfilled, and what the inner life demands, we must also fulfill.

A murshid was traveling with three or four murids during that season in the East when people have their fastings for so many days—every day they fast. This murshid was visiting in a village, at a peasant's house. The peasant was so happy that the murshid had come with his pupils that there was no end of joy.

1 Matthew 20:21.

He went to the market and bought all the good things he could get and prepared a lunch, without asking the murshid or the pupils. And the lunch was brought to the table.

According to the religious law, and also the spiritual law, it is a very bad thing to break the law of fasting. It is a sacred law, a religious law. So every murid refused. This peasant could not understand why they refused. They were too modest to say that they were fasting, but at the same time they did not break their vows. When he came to the murshid, the murshid said, "Yes," and very gladly sat at the table with the family. The peasant was very pleased, and very sorry that all these young men did not eat. They thought, "Our murshid has perhaps forgotten; he is perhaps in his dreams."

After the dinner was finished, the peasant was very glad. When they went out, one of the daring pupils came to the murshid: "Murshid, I am sorry to say, perhaps you have forgotten that we are fasting." He said, "No, child, I have not forgotten; I would rather break the fast, however sacred, than to break the heart of the one who prepared that food for me." That was the idea. It is to answer life's demands. At that time life had demanded that the murshid keep his word, though inwardly.

Question: *When one may not hold tight to any original plane and gets into all sorts of unhappy circumstances, how to get out of this best?*

Answer: We do not need to waken ourselves to any particular plane. For we shall waken to every plane as we go on in life's journey. What is necessary is to be wide awake through life and see what is asked of us by our friend, by our neighbor, by our acquaintance, by a stranger who is traveling with us.

It is just becoming more and more considerate, and observing more clearly what another expects of us. Do we harm that person, or do we serve them; are we kind to that person, or are we cruel? Because all of us through life have our motive before us, and in going toward that motive we are often apt to forget whom we push away, and whom we hurt, and on whom we tread, and to whom we become unjust, and to whom we become unkind. The one who does not observe makes perhaps a hundred mistakes. It does not mean that one can be without mistakes. Still, if one can avoid nine hundred out of a thousand, it is something.

Question: *The greatest difficulty seems to me not to accord with the sad and the joyful, but to go together with those who go in another direction and who will other things. What does wisdom teach in this direction, in order not to fight with them and still to go your own direction?*

Answer: To go in your own direction is good as long as you understand your own direction and your own [willingness]. Nothing, however good it appears, is a virtue unless it is willingly done, because in the willingness in doing a sacrifice, there one experiences the breath of freedom. A virtue which is forced upon oneself or another is not a virtue; it loses its beauty. We must do what seems good to us. If we think that it is a virtue to keep to our own idea, or if we think that giving up our idea to follow the idea of another is a virtue, then it is a virtue when there is willingness. Virtue must not be forced.

SELF-CONTROL

In everyday life, what is most necessary is to have control of speech and action, for one automatically gives way to a word prompted by an inner impulse. Afterwards, one finds that one should not have said it, or perhaps one would have said it differently. It is the same thing with action. One feels "I should not have done so" after having done something, or one thinks "I should have done differently"; but once it is done, it is too late to do it otherwise.

In human nature there is an inner urge to express oneself, and that urge, so to speak, pushes a word out of oneself before one has thought it over. And this all shows the sign of a lack of control over oneself. It also is a sign of nervousness. Very often a person tries to answer somebody who has not yet finished speaking; before a sentence is completed, the answer is given. Such an answer given to an incomplete idea is often not right. What generally happens in such cases is that one takes all things in life that come from outside too much to heart and allows the outer things and influences to go into oneself deeper than they are due. In this way one becomes sensitive, and out of it rises nervousness.

In order to practice self-control in everything one does in everyday life, the best thing is to develop in one's nature a certain amount of indifference. Every word that is said to one need not be taken to be so important that it should upset one's whole being, disturb one's balance, and rob one of one's willpower.

There are things that matter, but there are many things in one's everyday life which do not matter much, and one often is apt to put an undue stress upon them.

Independence is achieved by indifference. It does not mean that one should take no heed of what another does or says. It only means to discriminate between important and unimportant things of everyday life, that every necessary and unnecessary thing must not demand so much of one's attention, thought, and feeling.

Political economy has become a subject of education, but spiritual economy is the main thing in religion. All one says and does, and all that one thinks and feels makes a certain strain upon one's spirit. It is wise to avoid every chance of losing one's equilibrium. One must stand peacefully but firmly against all influences that disturb one's life.

The natural inclination is to answer in defense every offence that comes from outside; by that, one loses one's equilibrium. Self-control, therefore, is the key to all success and happiness. Besides this, there are many who feel urged and obliged to say or do because someone asks of them, and in this way they get weaker and weaker; there are others who roughly fight against it, and in this way both are in error. Those who are able to keep their equilibrium without being annoyed, without being troubled about it, gain that mastery which is needed in the evolution of life.

No principle must be blindly followed. Spiritual economy is not always a virtue if it disturbs harmony, if it in any way keeps one back from progressing, if it puts one in a worse condition. However, it is most necessary to know the science of spiritual economy, how to guard against all influences in one's everyday life which come to disturb our tranquility, the peace of our soul.

* * *

Question: *What is the meaning of the symbol of the fish?*

Answer: The symbol of the fish is the sign of the heart. And as the fish out of water finds itself out of place and experiences discomfort, so the heart, when it is not living and moving and making its life in love, feels out of place, and all discomfort of life comes from it.

Question: *Please explain the belief that one is taught in the Church, that Christ died to save us.*[1]

Answer: Yes, apart from those who do not follow the Christian faith, there are many even who are Christian who question whether there is some truth in this. And yet it is so simple to understand that the soul of the God-conscious truly lived and moved and made his life in God. His every word, every thought, and every action was directed to the service of humanity, and he kept nothing back from sacrificing for humanity, even his life. And therefore, no appreciative heart who looked at this question in this way would ever deny the fact that Christ gave his life to save humanity. This can be the best expression of that appreciation which one can have of that self-sacrificing soul who proved, through his life, divinity.

Question: *What does the soul do at night when the body sleeps?*

Answer: Poor soul—upon the poor soul there are so many demands. When the body is awake, then it must wander with the body, wherever it will take it. When the body is asleep it must go with the mind; where the mind takes it, it goes. Of course in this connection one must think of that sentence in the Bible, "Where your treasure is, there your heart will be also."[2] It is not the heart, it is soul there where the treasure is. Is it in heaven? Then it is in heaven. Is it on earth? Then it is on earth. If the treasure is in the purse, then the soul is in the purse; if it is in music, poetry, philosophy, or thought, then the soul is with that. All one admires, values, loves in life, the soul is with it. If one loves sadness, then the soul is in sadness; if one loves to

1 Romans 5:8.
2 Matthew 6:21.

experience joy, then the soul is joyous. What one seeks after, that is where the soul goes.

Yet the soul touches all spheres from the lowest to the highest. Even the souls of the most wicked people touch all spheres, only they do not experience the benefit of it, because when they are conscious they are tasting wickedness. But when the soul is unconscious and touches the highest, what is the use? Therefore, as it is mentioned in *The Message of Spiritual Liberty*,[3] there are many paths, even ones that one could never imagine—one would be horrified if one knew the different ways—by which a person could arrive at the same goal. Still the thing is this, that the blessing of life is in the consciousness of that blessing. When one is not conscious of that blessing, it is nothing. If a kitten is privileged to sit on the royal sofa and is dwelling all the time at Buckingham Palace, it is not privileged when it is not conscious of the privilege.

Question: *Would you tell us how far it is right to take the individual temper into account in trying to build character?*

Answer: I personally, if I were to advise myself, would take extreme measures in keeping individuality pliable, not set to a certain temper. No doubt individuality is made of a certain temper, but I would not personally allow it to set to a certain temper. For another person, I would not advise an extreme measure.

I will tell you an experience of my own life. Once I began my musical work and, having that sensitiveness of an artist, if there was among my audience of five, ten, twenty people, one person lacking understanding or antagonistic to it, it would choke my breast and I would not be able to do anything. I saw it one, two, three times; but how could I do my work? The next day I said, "I shall shake it off, not take it into account. I shall sing for myself; if no one shall enjoy it, I shall still sing. If I am

3 *A Sufi Message of Spiritual Liberty,* the first book of Inayat Khan's teachings to be published in the West in 1914.

pleased, it is quite enough." Since that feeling came, that artistic temper went to pieces. It never came again. That is fighting against temper.

What is temper? It is a nature we make. What makes a nature? We have something of it; in making it, we enjoy it. By saying, "I hate it, I cannot stand, tolerate it," one does not know what one is doing. One has confined oneself to a limitation, a weakness. Why can I not tolerate? Then I cannot tolerate myself. I cannot bear it. There will come a day when one cannot bear oneself.

It is a terrible fight because the self begins to cry for nights and days. The self says, "You are my worst enemy in the world, you are so cruel, you have no pity on me," because it feels crushed. But when it is once crushed and has come under the control of willpower, then one begins to feel that the kingdom of God begins to come. Sometimes one feels that it is unjust, unfair, too cruel to oneself, and the difficulty is that the neighbors also say that you are too cruel to yourself. No one wants to encourage you in that direction.

Question: *Ascetic temperament . . . ?*

Answer: One must not go against one's happiness, but there are some ascetic temperaments who fight with themselves. There is a great gain in it, because there are not many who do it. One must not even make principles so set that one cannot bear them. There are people who are born fighters, and their fight is with themselves.

Question: *Are there people who are born fighters and their fight is with themselves?*

Answer: There is a story of spiritual pride. Once a dervish was sitting in the wilderness on a rock in a comfortable position. Akbar, the emperor of Delhi, went to pay his homage to this dervish. The dervish saw that the emperor had come and his minister was also there with him. But the dervish did not change his position. Of course Akbar did not feel uncomfortable about it. But the one who went with Akbar, he did not see from the point of view of the emperor. He felt that when he has to bow a thousand times to the king, why not this man? He asked him in a very polite way, "How long is it since you have stretched these legs?" He wanted to turn it into a kind of vow. The dervish answered, "Since I have withdrawn my hands. When the hands were the hands of greed, since I was in want, I had taken all I wanted of the world. There is nothing I want now; now my legs are stretched. If the emperor comes, it is all the same to me." That is a spiritual pride. But spiritual pride is a very delicate thing to understand. The pride that says, "I am so spiritual" has nothing spiritual about it. It is personal pride, because where there is spirituality, there is no "I am."

RELATIONSHIP

It is a most important thing in character building to become conscious of one's relation, obligation, and duty to each person in the world, and not to mix that link and connection which is established between oneself and another with a third person. One must think of everything that is entrusted to one by every person in life as one's trust, and one must know that to prove true to the confidence of every person in the world is one's sacred obligation. In this manner a harmonious connection is established with every person, and it is the harmony established with every person which tunes the soul with the infinite.

It requires a great study of human nature, together with tact, to keep on harmonious terms with every person in life. If one has admiration for someone or a grudge against someone, it is better to express it directly instead of mixing it up with many connections and relations in the world. Friendship apart, even with an acquaintance this consideration is necessary to guard carefully that thin thread that connects two souls in whatever relation or capacity. Dharma in the language of the Hindus means religion, but the literal meaning of this word is duty. It suggests that one's relation to every person in the world is one's religion, and the more conscientiously one follows it, the more keen one proves in following one's religion.

To keep the secret of our friend, our acquaintance, even of someone with whom for a time being one has been vexed, is the most sacred obligation. Once we have thus realized our religion, would we ever consider it right to tell another of any harm or hurt we have received from our friend? Never. It is in this that self-denial is learned, not always by fasting and retirement in the wilderness. Those who are conscientious of their duty, of their obligations to their friends, are more pious than someone sitting alone in solitude. Those in solitude do not serve God; they only help themselves by enjoying the pleasure of solitude. But those who prove to be trustworthy to every soul they meet and consider their relation and connection, small or great, as something sacred, certainly observe the spiritual law of that religion which is the religion of religions.

Faults—everyone has faults. Oneself, one's friend, and one's enemy, all are subject to faults. Those who wish that their own faults may not be disclosed must necessarily consider the same for the others they meet. If we only knew what the relation of friendship is between one soul and another, the tenderness of this connection, its delicacy, its beauty, and its sacredness, we could enjoy life in its fullness, for we would be living; and in this manner we must someday communicate with God. It is the same bridge which connects two souls in the world which, when once stretched, becomes the path to God. There is no greater virtue in this world than proving kind and trustworthy to one's friend, worthy of confidence.

The difference between the old soul and the young soul is to be found in this particular principle. The young souls only know themselves and what they want, absorbed in their own pleasures and displeasures and obsessed by their ever-changing moods. The old souls regard their relation to every soul; they keenly observe their obligations toward everyone they know in the world. They cover their wounds, if they happen to have them, from the sight of the others and endure all things in order to fulfill their duty as best they can toward everyone in the world.

There is a story in the *Arabian Nights* which in some way is incomprehensible, yet which explains in an exaggerated form the subject on which I have been speaking. Once a king was on a tour in the woods. Where he was camping there lived some robbers. A robber happened to go into the tent where the king was asleep and tried to get a ring from under his pillow. And when he was taking away that ring, the king got up and he looked at the thief and said, "Who are you?" He said, "I am a robber." "Why have you come here?" "To find if I can get something from you." "What did you find?" "I found your ring; here it is, shall I give it back to you?" The king said, "No, take it." The robber said, "Then do not tell anyone." "Certainly not," said the king.

* * *

Question: *Can you please tell us why there is a legend in the Talmud that says Moses died from the kiss of God?*

Answer: I should say that anyone should die of the kiss of God. In the *Gayan*[1] is said, "Sundew, why is it that every insect that kisses you dies instantly?' 'I love him so that I eat him up." The explanation is the same.

The condition of God and God's true lover is only one, and that is, either the beloved lives or the lover. Therefore, Rumi says, "The Beloved is all in all, the lover only veils the Beloved; love is all that lives, the lover a dead thing."[2]

Question: *What must we do if others do not consider our friendship and do not wish to regard our views in life? Must we always go on to see them and try to come into contact with them if we are in some way related to them?*

Answer: I would never say to anybody, "Go and consider the friend who has ill-treated you," but, "Do what you consider best." There cannot be one principle for all to follow; for each there is a particular principle. But by considering the main

1 A book of sayings of Inayat Khan, first published in 1923. See *Gayan, Vadan, Nirtan* (New Lebanon, NY: Sulūk Press, 2015), 68.

2 From the *Masnavi*, an extended poem by Jalal ad-Din Rumi, Persian Sufi saint and poet.

principles of character building, then one will be helped. It does not mean that one should follow exactly these principles which are spoken of as character building. But by knowing them, they can be a great help in choosing the best way in dealing with life. For the one who observes this principle certainly is on the saintly path, because such a principle requires a great sacrifice, renunciation, a great deal of self-denial. It wants an unselfish person who could follow this.

Question: *You spoke of covering the faults of others, but even of our own?*

Answer: Yes, this is a still higher form.

Question: *Can life be symbolized as a ladder?*

Answer: Yes.

Question: *Was it the ladder that Jacob saw?*

Answer: Yes, life's evolution is as a ladder. Every person is on a different step.

Question: *How is it to be understood that both Jesus and Buddha broke off all relations of friends and of their parents and came back from solitude as a stranger? Buddha especially says that no one can attain nirvana who still has human relations.*

Answer: Yes, but this question is a question of renunciation. The question of character building is a different question. Life is like a ladder. The principle of one step is not the principle of another. On each step there is a particular principle. At the same time those who have risen above all relations, they observe the law of relationship more than anybody else. They become so conscious of their obligation, not only to their relations, but to every little insect and germ. Their relationship is only wider and stronger.

The idea is that the claim of relationship is one thing, and the observing of relationship with all is another stage. They have passed that stage of character building; they are above it, they cannot be compared.

SUBTLETY

Subtlety of nature is the sign of the intelligent. If a person takes the right direction, that person does good with this wealth of intelligence. One who is going in a wrong direction may abuse this great faculty. When a person who is subtle by nature is compared to a personality which is void of subtlety, it is like the river and the mountain. The subtle personality is as pliable as the running water; everything that comes before that personality is reflected in it as clearly as an image in pure water. The rocklike personality, void of subtlety, is like a mountain; it reflects nothing.

Many admire plain speaking, but the reason is their lack of understanding of fine subtlety. Can all things be put into words? Is there not anything more fine, more subtle than spoken words? The person who can read between the lines makes a book out of one letter. Subtlety of perception and subtlety of expression are the signs of the wise.

Wise and foolish are distinguished by fineness on the part of the one, and rigidness on the part of the other. A person void of subtlety wants truth to be turned into a stone, and the subtle one will even turn a stone into truth. In order to acquire spiritual knowledge, in order to receive inspiration, in order to prepare one's heart for inner revelation, one must try and make one's mentality pliable like water, rather than like a rock. For the further in the path of life's mystery one will sojourn, the more subtle one will have to become in order to perceive and to express the mystery of life. God is a mystery; God's knowledge is a mystery. Life is a mystery; human nature is a mystery. In short, the depth of all knowledge is a mystery. Even in science or art, all that is more mysterious is deeper.

What all the prophets and masters have done in all ages is to express that mystery in words, in deeds, in thoughts, in feelings. But most of the mystery is expressed by them in silence, for then the mystery is in its place. To bring down the mystery to the ground is like pulling down a king on to the ground from a throne. But allowing the mystery to remain in its own place, in the silent spheres, is like giving homage to the sovereign to whom all homage is due.

Life's mysteries apart, in little things of everyday life the less words used the more profitable it is. Do you think more words explain more? No, not at all. It is only nervousness on the part of those who wish to say a hundred words to explain a thing which can quite well be explained in two words. And on the part of the listener it is a lack of intelligence when one wants a hundred words in order to understand something which can just as well be explained in one word. Many think that more words explain things better, but they do not know that most often the more words spoken, so many more veils are wrapped around the idea. In the end you go out by the same door by which you have entered.

Respect, consideration, reverence, kindness, compassion and sympathy, forgiveness, and gratefulness—all these virtues can be best adorned by subtlety of expression. One need not dance in thanksgiving; one word of thanks is quite sufficient. One need not play drums that "I have forgiven somebody." One need not cry out loud that "I sympathize with you, my dear friend." Such things are fine, subtle; they are to be felt. No noise can express them; noise only spoils their beauty and takes from their value.

In spiritual ideas and thoughts subtlety is more needed than in anything else. If spiritual people were to bring their realizations to the marketplace and dispute with everyone that came along about their beliefs and disbeliefs, where would that end?

What makes a spiritual person harmonize with all people in the world? The key to the art of reconciliation that a spiritual soul has is subtlety in both perception and expression. Is it lack of frankness? Is it hypocrisy to be subtle? Not in the least. There are many people who are outspoken, as ready to tell the truth as to hit the head of another person. They proudly support their frankness by saying, "I do not mind if it makes anybody sorry or angry. I only tell the truth." If the truth is as hard as a hammer, may truth never be spoken! May no one in the world follow such truth!

Then what is that truth which is peace-giving, which is healing, which is comforting to every heart and soul? That truth which uplifts the soul, that truth which is creative of harmony and beauty—where is that truth born? That truth is born in subtlety of intelligence, of thought, speech, and action; in fineness, which brings pleasure, comfort, beauty, harmony, and peace.

* * *

Question: *Will you explain that the heart of a human being is the heart of the universe?*

Answer: In the heart of a human being the whole universe is reflected, and as the whole universe is reflected in the heart of a human being, it may be called the heart of the universe.

Question: *What is the heart and what is the soul?*

Answer: Suppose we take a lamp, a burning lamp, as a picture of the human being. The flame is the soul, and the globe is the heart. The inner part of the globe is called the heart, the outer part is the mind, and the shade over the lamp is the body.

Question: *Will you explain the difference between a child soul and a grown-up soul?*

Answer: The difference is that of a ripe fruit and an unripened fruit. It is just like a grown-up person who has more experience compared with the child, and by that experience has learned and understood more. So is a soul who may be a young person and yet may have a greater understanding because of the soul being ripe.

Question: *How can one cultivate this subtleness; I thought one was born with it, and could not acquire it?*

Answer: If one knew how wonderful is the life of the human being, of whom God says that "I have created the human being in my own image."[1] Is there anything which is not in God? If all things are in God, then all things are in the human being, whom God has made in God's own image. No doubt, the things that we try to acquire we are able to acquire them better; the things that we neglect, we do not.

Often we see people with intelligence, with a brain, yet who are unwilling to trouble their brain very much, for they do not want to trouble; it is not that they cannot understand. If they can get it easily explained by someone, they do not want to trouble. Very often one sees that. And therefore, subtlety is a fineness. Such fineness can be acquired by the love of fineness, not only in human character, but in everything.

If artists have not the love of subtlety, their art will only be on the surface. It will become living if they have subtlety in their nature. So with poetry. If the poet only writes words, nothing behind it, that does not give life, that is only the structure. What makes a verse beautiful? Twist. A person could write five lines and make the soul dance at its fineness, its subtlety. Another person will write a hundred letters, and it means nothing: too many words, tiredness is the only result of it. The book of Rumi[2] has lived hundreds of years; the interest is always growing. Why? Because there is subtlety from the beginning to the end.

1 Genesis 1:27.

2 Another reference to the *Masnavi*, the great work of Rumi's last years.

When one does not take the trouble to cultivate fineness in nature and subtlety in perception and expression, it is just like a stubborn child who wants its food to be put in its mouth. The child does not want to take the trouble of eating itself. A subtle person is only a conscientious person, a person on guard, who has taken life as a horse, and has the rein in hand, and makes it dance when that person wants it to dance, letting it go slowly when that person wants. A dancer, a poet, a singer—in every aspect, in all one does, subtlety produces beauty. Subtlety is the curl of the beloved, a symbolical expression used by Omar Khayyam and most of the Sufi poets.[3]

Question: *How is the periodic coming and going of events, cataclysms, wars, etc., to be explained, as well as the fact of the possibility of a purely mathematical reading of all life in astrology? These things seem to speak in favor of the idea that all life is an automatically running clock, and that there is no liberty of action and thought. (Death of a babe or child.) What is the sense of a human being dying before it has reached a certain development? It seems a great waste of energy, and a great suffering in vain.*

Answer: The first question, in which it is asked if the whole universe is going on automatically and there is no free will—the answer is that, yes, a human being is born in a universe which is going on automatically, and is born helpless. Therefore, it is true that the condition is such. But what is the child born with? It is born with a desire to do as it wills. This desire is the proof of there being a free will, a free will which is put to test under all opposing conditions and influences which the soul meets with through life. And to rise above all the opposing influences and to give the fullest expression to the free will brings about that result of life which is the fulfillment of the soul's coming on earth.

3 See *The Hand of Poetry: Five Mystic Poets of Persia* (New Lebanon, NY: Omega Publications, 2012) for some of Inayat Khan's lectures on the Persian Sufi poets.

The second question concerns the reason for many things having sprung out of this automatically working universe, such as the birth of a babe who has passed soon after, and one does not see the reason behind it. But in this case we must understand that although outwardly it is automatically working, inwardly there is God. There is no mechanism without an engineer. Only the engineer does not seem to be standing by the side of the machine. And the engineer is not claiming to be the engineer. One thinks that there is a machine going on and there is no engineer. If one knew that there is an engineer, what can a little part of the machine understand about the scheme and plan which is made for the working of the whole universe? And if anybody understands, it is the awakened souls, but how much do they understand? Very little do they understand. And how do they, and what? They can only say what they can about it. That all justice or injustice, however it may seem to us on the surface, will all fit in and be perfect at the finish when there is the summing up of the working of the whole universe. There is a saying in support of this in the *Vadan*.[4]

4 See *Gayan, Vadan, Nirtan* (New Lebanon, NY: Sulūk Press, 2015), 135.

COMPLAINING AND SMILING

There are two attitudes which divide people into sections. The one attitude is an ever-complaining attitude, and the other attitude is an ever-smiling attitude. Life is the same; call it good, call it bad, call it right or call it wrong. It is what it is; it cannot be otherwise.

People complain in order to get the sympathy of others, in order to show their good points to others, and sometimes in order to show themselves more just, more intelligent, and in the right. They complain about everything, about friends and about foes, about those they love and much more so about those they hate. They complain from morning till evening, and there is never an end to their complaint. It can increase to such an extent that the weather is not good, and the air is not good, and the atmosphere is not good. They are against earth and sky both.

Everything everybody does is wrong until it develops to such a stage that they begin to dislike their own words, and it culminates when they dislike themselves. In this way one becomes against others, against conditions, and in the end against oneself.

Do not imagine that this is a character rarely to be found in the world; it is a character with whom you frequently meet. And certainly the ones who have this attitude are their own worst enemy. The person with a right attitude of mind tries to make even wrong into right, but the one with a wrong attitude of mind will turn even right into wrong.

Besides, magnetism is something which is the need of every soul. The lack of it makes life burdensome. The tendency of seeing wrong in everything robs one greatly of that magnetism which is needed very much in life. For the nature of life is such that, by nature, the life of the multitude throws out everyone and accepts only those who enter the multitude with the power of magnetism. In other words, the world is a place where you cannot enter without a pass of admission, and that pass of admission is magnetism. The one who does not possess it will be refused everywhere.

Besides, you will find many who complain always about their health. There may be a reason, and sometimes there may be a very little reason, too little indeed to speak of. And when once people have become accustomed to answer in the negative, when sympathetically asked, "How are you?" they certainly water the plant of illness in themselves by the complaining tendency.

Our life of limitation in the world and the nature of this world's comforts and pleasures, which are so changeable and unreliable, and the falsehood that one finds in everything, everywhere—if one complained about it all, a lifetime would be too short to complain about it fully. Every moment of our life would become filled with complaints. But the way out of it is to look at the cheerful side of it, the bright side of it. Especially those who seek God and truth, for them there is something else to think about. They need not think how bad the person is; when they think who is behind this person, who is in the heart of this person, then they will look at life with hope. When we see things wrong, if we only think that behind all workings there is God, who is just and perfect, then we certainly will become hopeful.

The attitude of looking at everything with a smile is the sign of the saintly soul. A smile given to a friend, a smile given even to an enemy will win the enemy over in the end, for that is the key to the human heart. As the sunshine from without lights the whole world, so the sunshine from within, if it were raised, would illuminate the whole life, in spite of all the seeming wrongs and in spite of all limitations. God is happiness, the soul is happiness, spirituality is happiness. There is no place for sadness in the kingdom of God. That which deprives one of happiness, deprives one of God and of truth.

One can begin to learn to smile by appreciating every little good thing that comes one's way through life, and by overlooking every bad thing that one does not like to see; by not troubling too much about unnecessary things in life which give nothing but displeasure, and by looking at life with a hopeful attitude of mind, with an optimistic view. It is this which will give one the power of turning wrong into right, and bringing light in the place where all is darkness. Cheerfulness is life; sulkiness is death. Life attracts; death repulses. The sunshine which comes from the soul, rises through the heart, and manifests in a person's smile is indeed the light from the heavens. In that light many flowers grow, and many fruits become ripe.

* * *

Question: *"Thou shalt not kill," and "Love thy neighbor as thyself,"*[1] *are written in the Bible. Has then the state the right to condemn someone to death?*

Answer: This was not said to the state, it was said to the individual. The law is not the same. The state is responsible for many individuals; therefore, its rights and laws are different. Suppose it had been possible in the Christian countries to obey this law, there would not have been war or any kind of killing. And suppose that the government allowed it when anybody killed a thief or robber, and the state said, "We are told not to kill." What would happen? The killing would increase; it would always increase.

1 Exodus 20:13; Mark 12:31.

Besides that, human nature is such that it comes from animal nature; every person does not live by the law of a scripture. Everyone is born selfish; everyone wants to get all they want, even at the sacrifice of the life of another. If the revolver or sword were not used at all, it would be a beautiful thing, but what would happen? Should all human beings think as a saint thinks? The law given by Christ to his disciples was given to those who were seeking God and truth. Is it everybody who is trying to find God and truth? Everybody is living for the struggle of life. Therefore, in all cases the law that is given for an individual is not applicable for all, although one cannot deny the beauty of the teaching, which will certainly help those who take the path of truth in the search of love and kindness.

But then I will tell you another thing. In one place it is said, "Thou shalt not kill." In another place Christ said to unsheathe the sword.[2] If the sword were not for any use, or were to be condemned, there would not have been that suggestion. But besides this, I ask: If the religion of Christ has existed throughout the world, can one take away credit from the sword? If it had not been for the sword, the religion of Christ would not have spread. The blood of the martyrs is the foundation of the Church, those who have exposed themselves for the cause, for the message. Without them the world would not have known the message of Christ; few would have known it, and it would have been extinguished. It was meant that it should be.

The sword has its place in bringing the message of the master, not only in the life and mission of Christ, but in the mission of the great Hindu teachers, Rama and Krishna. Moses, who was before Christ, had to take the sword. Therefore, the sword is something which today we do not need so much for religion, but it could not have been condemned at the time when it was necessary. Even today, if all the nations decided that there should be no arms, the police would have to have swords just the same. The condition of the world and human nature will not allow for

2 See Matthew 10:34.

the world to exist without a sword at the present time. We must hope that in the future humanity may evolve, that there will be no necessity for the sword. But now it cannot be practical.

Psychology must not be forgotten when discussing moral principles. Moral principles teach us that we should be kind, forgiving, we should even give our life, if it were asked, for love, truth, or kindness. But would that mean that we should go before a lion and say, "Here is my life, a prey for you; please come and eat me." For the lion will never understand the principle, the lion will only be too glad to eat you.

There are human beings worse than the lion. Even the lion will understand the moral principle, but not people; and many people are like this. What will you do with them? They will take your life and all that you have besides. The lion will leave the bones, but the human being will not. The human being will even use the skin, every bit of one. Balance is the great thing: to understand morals and to understand psychology. When there is a divergence between these two things, then religion becomes unbalanced. Religion is not only for saints. Saints do not need it. Religion must have a balance, which is sent as the message from time to time in order to give that same religion which is given before all people, to understand what is right for them and what is truly asked of them by God.

Question: *When a person with a cheerful attitude lives with a person with a sulky attitude of mind, and sees that their own cheerfulness even irritates the other, what can one do; is tact the only thing?*

Answer: You see, sulkiness is the attribute of a child soul. The sad soul is not a grown-up soul. Treat the child soul like a child. Do not take it to heart, do not take it too seriously. Even the tears of such a person, take them as flowers dropping from the plant. A child cries easily, also such a person. Only lift that person up for that time. But when you will try to sympathize, you will produce more gloom. Never sympathize at that time. Only say, "It is nothing."

There is something else: just to lift that person's consciousness. It is a kind of net in which the consciousness is caught. Lift it up. It is just like a bird, caught. Lift it out of that net. Do not let your own mind be impressed. If you allow it, then you have taken the germ of the disease; then gradually and slowly that disease will grow in you. The way of fighting against it is always to deny such a thing as sadness or depression in yourself and in another.

Question: *Why does the peasant say that one must sow the seed while the moon is growing, and not when it is waning? Has the moon really any influence, and why?*

Answer: Sufis also say, as the peasants say, "Do every new enterprise in life when there is a new moon, not in the waning moon." Because in that way you are in harmony with nature. In the new moon nature is progressive; in the waning moon, declining. The new moon is the day of nature, the waning moon is the night. Work during the day, rest during the night.

Question: *Can you give us the signification of this part of the Christ-prayer, "Lead us not into temptation"?*[3] *Does God ever lead into temptation?*

Answer: It is only a matter of interpretation. You can quite see that the words of the Lord were given three hundred years before, and then brought to Saint Paul. And then there were different versions and interpretations in different languages. All these things we must take into consideration. If I were to give an interpretation of this, I should say, "Let us not be led into temptation."

Question: *How must we explain, "Forgive us our trespasses as we forgive those who have trespassed against us"?*[4] *And if we do not forgive?*

Answer: This is a suggestion; "Forgive us our trespasses as we forgive those" only means that "we are trying to forgive others

3 Matthew 6:13.
4 Ibid.

for their trespasses, and so we expect that you will forgive us also." It does not mean that we have done it. It only means that we are trying to do it. We must remember that we cannot expect the forgiveness of God if forgiveness has not been awakened in our heart. The psychology is that the forgiveness of God is attracted by the spirit of forgiveness awakened in our heart. For instance, the relation between God and humanity apart, if those who have practiced forgiveness in their own life happen to do something wrong, you will feel ready to forgive them—because of what they have practiced you will gladly do the same to them. With another person who has not practiced this, with all your desire, you will feel a kind of difficulty, because this person does not help to make it easy for you to forgive. Does it not explain that we help God to forgive us by forgiving ourselves?

NOISELESS WORKING

The best way of working in all directions of life, at home or outside, is noiseless working—a thing of which so little is thought by many, and which is so very necessary in creating order, harmony, and peace in life. Very often a person does little and speaks much about it. In doing every little thing one makes noise, and thereby, very often, instead of finishing a thing successfully, one attracts difficulties.

The first thing that is to be remembered in character building is to understand the secret and character of human nature. We must know that all people in the world have their own object in life, their own interest, and their own point of view, and they are concerned with themselves. Their peace is disturbed when you wish to interest them in your object of interest, if you wish to force upon them your point of view. However near and dear they may be to you, they are not pleased with it. Very few consider this; they wish to pour out their own troubles and difficulties upon someone standing next to them, thinking that, "Everyone has the same interest in my subject as I myself," and that, "Everyone has the same point of view as I myself," and that, "Everyone will be glad to hear me."

There is a story told that a person began to speak to a new acquaintance about the person's ancestors. The person continued so long that the patience of the hearer was thoroughly exhausted. In the end the hearer finished the story by telling the person who had spoken, "When I do not care to know about my own ancestors, what do I care to know about your ancestors?"

There are many who are very enthusiastic to let their neighbors know about every cold and cough they had; every little gain or loss, however small, they would be glad to announce with drums and bugles. This is a childlike quality. This tendency shows a child soul. Sometimes such a tendency frightens away friends and helps foes.

With noisy working people accomplish little. Being attracted by their noise, ten more people come and interfere and spoil the work which one person could have easily finished. Noisiness comes from restlessness. And restlessness is the sign of *tamas*, the destructive rhythm. Those who have made any success in life, in whatever direction, it is by their quiet working. In business, in industry, in art, in science, in education, in politics, in all directions of life, the wise workers are the quiet workers. They tell about things when the time comes, not before. The one who talks about things before accomplishing them is like a cook who announces the dishes through the whole neighborhood before they are cooked.

There is a story told in the East of an enthusiastic servant. The master had a headache, and he told the servant to go and fetch a medicine from the chemist. The servant thought it would not be sufficient only to bring medicine from the chemist. So he also made an appointment with the doctor, and on his way home he visited the undertaker. The master asked, "Why are you so late?" The servant said, "Sir, I have arranged everything." Enthusiasm is a great thing in life. It is creative, and it is a key to success. But too much of it sometimes spoils things.

The more wise a person, the more gentle one is in everything one does. A gentleman in the English language is a quiet man. There is a fable that a donkey went to a camel and said, "Uncle, we shall be friends; we shall go grazing together." The camel said, "Child, I enjoy my walks alone." But the donkey said,

"I am most eager to walk with you." The good-natured camel consented and they both went together. Long before the camel finished grazing, the donkey had finished and was eager to express itself. He said, "Uncle, I would like to sing, if you do not mind." The camel said, "Do not do such a thing, it will be a terrible thing for you and me both. I have not yet finished my dinner." But the donkey had no patience. He could not control his joy and began to sing. The husbandman, attracted by the singing, came with a long bamboo. The donkey ran away and all the thrashing fell upon the camel. When the next morning the donkey went again to invite the camel, the camel said, "I am too ill. My way is too different from your way; from today we shall part."

There is such a great difference between the quiet person and a noisy person. One is like a restless child, the other like a grown-up person. One constructs, the other destroys. Quiet working must be practiced in every way, in everything. By making much ado about nothing, one creates commotion, disturbance in the atmosphere, and useless activity without any result. One also sees noise in the tendency of exaggeration, when one wants to make a mountain of a molehill. Modesty, humility, gentleness, meekness—all such virtues manifest in the person who works through life quietly.

* * *

Question: *Are* jalal, jamal, *and* kamal *the same as rajas,* sattva, *and* tamas?[1]

Answer: Yes, *jalal* is *rajas*, *jamal* is *sattva*, and *kamal* is *tamas*.

Question: *Have they not the slightest difference?*

Answer: Yes, there is a difference, but that is only a very little difference.

Question: *If kamal is inertia, does everything have a moment of rest, and if so, how often?*

1 *Jalal* is strength, *jamal* is beauty, and *kamal* is balance.

Answer: Rest between life and the hereafter is what is called purgatory. So there is always a gap between actions. For instance, when a person takes two steps, there is a gap between them. Also between exhaling and inhaling. Therefore, in every moment, in every breath, there is a moment of *kamal.*

In breathing, after every three quarters of an hour, there comes a short time when the breath changes, and then also there is *kamal.* So during a certain time of the day, a person feels lazy, depressed, or confused, for that is the outcome of kamal. *Kamal* has no tendency to action. Certain days come in the week when a person with all their enthusiasm does not wish to work; that is *kamal.*

In some people's lives, kamal obsesses them; they do not see the way, they feel the whole life as a stillness, everything seems so still and without movement. This is a deplorable state, and it results in a kind of insanity; a person wants to commit suicide. In other forms of insanity there is an inclination to fight another; there is hope because there is action. The cause of this insanity is disorder of breath; if these people would breathe rightly, they would be cured. They require balance in breath.

There is a good type of *kamal* also, and that is in equilibrium, which is to be seen in the sage. When the switch is closed, the electric light goes out. So when the sages bring out the *kamal,* they close the switch, that means they close the action of mind for that time. They do it by their will; they need the time of quiet. When one feels this inertia, the ordinary person must not give way, for it is like the death of the mind.

Question: *Must one not go against this inertia?*

Answer: No, it is no use to fight it. But give them some interest. The world has so many beautiful things in poetry, music, nature.

INQUISITIVENESS

There is one thing which belongs to human nature, and its origin is in curiosity, the curiosity which gives a desire for knowledge. When this tendency is abused, it develops into inquisitiveness. It is wonderful to think that at the root of all defects is a right tendency. And it is the abuse of it which turns it into a wrong tendency.

When we consider how little time we have to live on this earth, we find that every moment of our life is precious, and that it should be given to something which is really worthwhile. When this time is given to inquisitiveness, wanting to know about the affairs of another, one has wasted that time which could have been used for a much better purpose.

Life has so many responsibilities and so many duties. There is so much that one has to correct in oneself; there is so much that one has to undo in what one has done. There is so much to attend to in one's affairs and to make one's life right, that it seems as if a person were intoxicated who, leaving all responsibilities and duties, occupies the mind and engages the ears in inquisitiveness. Free will is given to attend to one's own duties, to gain one's own objects, to attend to one's own affairs. And when that free will is used in trying to find out about others, the weakness of others, the lacks of others, the faults of others, then one certainly abuses that free will.

Sometimes a person is inquisitive because of interest in the lives of others. But very often a person is inquisitive because it is an illness. That person may have no interest in the matter at all, but only wants satisfaction by hearing and knowing about others. Self-knowledge is the ideal of the philosophers, not the knowledge of the lives of others.

There are two phases in the development of the person: one phase when one looks at others, another phase when one looks at oneself. When the first phase has ceased, and the next phase begun, then one starts on a journey to the desired goal. Rumi says, "Trouble not about others, for there is much for you to think about yourself."

Besides this, it is a sign of great respect to the aged, and to those one wishes to respect, to show no tendency of knowing more than one is allowed to know. Even in such close relationships as parents and children, when they respect the privacy of one another they certainly show a great virtue. To want to know about another is very often a lack of trust. The one who trusts does not need to unveil, does not need to uncover what is covered. The one who wishes to unveil something wishes to discover it. If there is anything that should first be discovered, it is the self.

The time that one spends in discovering others, their lives, their faults, their weakness, one could have just as well spent in discovering one's soul. The desire to know is born in the soul. Only, a human being should discern what one must do and what is worth knowing. There are many things not worth troubling about. When one devotes one's time and thought to trying to know what one need not know, one loses that opportunity which life offers to discover the nature and secret of the soul, in which lies the fulfillment of the purpose of life.

* * *

Question: You told us the other day there is not such a thing as sadness. But why did Christ say "My soul is full of sadness,"[1] *and also*

1 Mark 14:34

"My father, why hast thou abandoned me!"[2] *Is this not a tragedy? And is there not a tragedy in life?*

Answer: We must know above and beyond all, the master's human side of life, his divine side apart. If the human side were not human, then why did God send a message to human beings by a human? Why should God not send it by angels? Because a human being knows human beings, because a human being knows human limitation. That is the most beautiful side of the master's life. If he did not feel sadness, how could he sympathize with others? If all were perfect, why be born on earth?

The purpose is that from limitation we grow toward perfection. If from childhood all were wise, why did we come? Beauty is in acquiring wisdom by failure, mistake. All suffering in life, all is worthwhile and all will accomplish the purpose of our coming on earth.

2 Matthew 27:46.

GOSSIP

It must be remembered that one shows the lack of nobleness in the character by a love for gossip. It is so natural, and yet it is a great fault in the character to cherish the tendency of talking about others. In the first place, it is a great weakness one shows when one passes remarks about someone behind their back. In the second place it is against what may be called frankness, and besides, it is judging another, which is wrong according to the teaching of Christ, who says "Judge ye not, lest ye be judged."[1]

When one allows this tendency to remain, one develops a love of talking about others. It is a defect which commonly exists. And when two people meet who have the same tendency, together they complete gossip. One helps the other, one encourages the other. And when something is supported by two people, it of necessity becomes a virtue, even if it were only for the time being.

How often one forgets that although one is talking about someone in their absence, it is spoken in the presence of God. God hears all things and knows all things. The Creator knows about all creatures, about their virtues and faults. God is as displeased by hearing about the fault of those creatures as an artist would be displeased on hearing bad remarks made by anyone on that artist's art. Even though the artist acknowledged the defect of the art, still one would prefer finding it oneself, not anyone else.

1 Matthew 7:1–3.

When a person speaks against others, those words may not reach those people but the feelings reach them. If one is sensitive one knows of someone having talked against one. And when one sees those who have been talking against one, one reads all that they have said in their faces, if one be sensitive and of keen sight.

This world is a house of mirrors. The reflection of one is mirrored upon another. In this world where so many things seem hidden, in reality nothing remains hidden; some time or other it rises to the surface and manifests to view. How few in this world know what effect it makes on one's own personality, talking ill of another—what influence it has on one's soul.

Not only is a person's self within like a dome where everything one says has an echo. Within the self there is an echo of all one says, but that echo is creative and productive of what has been said. Every good and bad thing in life one develops in one's nature by taking interest in it. Every fault one has, as long as it is small one does not note it, and so one develops the fault till it results in a disappointment.

Life is so precious—and it becomes more and more valuable as one becomes more prudent—and every moment of life can be used for a much greater purpose. Life is an opportunity, and the more one realizes this the more one will make the best of this opportunity which life offers.

GENEROSITY

The spirit of generosity in nature builds a path to God, for generosity is outgoing, is spontaneous. Its nature is to make its way toward a wide horizon. Generosity, therefore, may be called charity of heart. It is not necessary that the spirit of generosity must be always shown by the spending of money. In every little thing one can show it.

Generosity is an attitude which one shows in every little action that one does toward people with whom one comes in contact in everyday life. One can show generosity by a smile, by a kind glance, by a warm handshake, by patting the younger soul with a pat of encouragement, with a pat showing appreciation, with that pat which expresses affection. One can show generosity in accommodating one's fellow human being, in welcoming one's fellow human being, in bidding farewell to a friend; in thought, word, and deed, in every manner and form, one can show that generous spirit which is the sign of the *wali*, the godly.

The Bible speaks of generosity by the word charity. But if I were to give an interpretation of the word "generosity," I would call it nobility. No rank, position, or power can prove one noble. Truly noble is the one who is generous of heart. What is generosity? It is nobility, it is the expansion of the heart. As the heart expands, so the horizon becomes wide, and one finds greater and greater scope in which to build the kingdom of God.

Depression, despair, and all manner of sorrow and sadness come from the lack of generosity. Where does jealousy come from? Where does aching of the heart come from? Where does envy come from? It all comes from the lack of generosity.

One may not have one single coin to one's name, and yet one can be generous, one can be noble, if only one has a large heart, a friendly feeling. The life in the world offers every opportunity to us, whatever be our position in life, to show if we have any spirit of generosity.

The changeableness and falsehood of human nature, besides the inconsideration and thoughtlessness that come out of those one meets through life, and furthermore the selfishness and grabbing and grafting spirit that disturbs and troubles the soul—this situation itself is a test and trial through which every soul has to pass in the midst of the worldly life.

If through this test and trial one holds fast to the principle of charity and treads along toward one's destination, not allowing the influences that come from the four corners of the world to keep one back from the journey to the goal, one in the end becomes the ruler of life—even if at the end of one's destination there is not one single earthly coin left to one's name. It is not this earthly wealth that makes a person rich. Riches come by discovering that gold mine which is hidden in the human heart, out of which rises the spirit of generosity.

Someone asked the Prophet whose virtue was greater: the pious one who prays continually, the traveler who travels to make a holy pilgrimage, the one who fasts for nights and days, or the one who learns the scripture by heart. "None of them," said the Prophet, "is so great as the soul who shows through life charity of heart."

* * *

Question: *Who is the greatest saint, the person who wills everything that God wills, or the one who has the greatest sympathy with one's fellow human being?*

Answer: The latter.

Question: *Is there the same idea in the tale of the angel Iblis and the angel Lucifer?*

Answer: Yes.

Question: *Is there any symbology veiled in the expression "influences that come from the four corners of the world"? What do you mean by this?*

Answer: From all sides.

Question: *If everything has its meaning, is there any reason why the donkey's cry should be so terribly melancholy?*

Answer: It wants to show us that the sign of foolishness is noise, and the sign of wisdom is quietude.

Question: *Is there any relation in the fact that the donkey has a cross on its back?*

Answer: Yes, that is why the donkey has to take all the burden on its back; it shows its resignation by submitting its back to the will of its master.

Question: *And also with the fact that Christ rode on the back of a donkey going to Jerusalem on Good Friday?*

Answer: That is the privilege of the server. The one who serves, however humble, will have even the privilege of serving God. It is very difficult to know what makes one entitled to privileges. Sometimes it seems that the most undeserving become entitled to a privilege. There is a story of the Prophet's passing to the other world. The day when Muhammad was leaving this world he went to join the last prayers at the mosque, and after the prayers were finished he gave an address. In that address he mentioned that the call had come from above, that he had fulfilled his mission, and that he had to leave. And it produced a great panic among his devotees. There were many who were greatly devoted to him. And he said if he had ever spoken at any time in the slightest degree to the displeasure of a person, that person may return it a hundredfold. Or if he had borrowed from anyone anything, they must ask him to return it to them, as he was on the journey. And if he ever had insulted anyone, he asked them to please return it a hundredfold, and if he had in any way done any hurt or harm of any kind, that he would like it to be done to him before he left. The devotion and respect that the disciples had for the Prophet was so great that, his asking for anything like this apart, they were all choked up; they had no words to express to the Prophet their gratitude.

But there was one man, unrefined, and yet ambitious, who stood up and said, "Prophet, I remember that one day yourself touched me with a whip; and as it is your order, now I shall do it." The Prophet said, "I do not remember, but I am very glad, you may do it ten times more." And the panic was still greater in the mosque. And this man came with his whip near the Prophet, and said, "It was on my bare back." So the Prophet had to remove his shirt. Instead of whipping, he kissed the back of the Prophet, because he had believed that there was a seal of prophetship on his back. It was his belief, and in order to have that privilege, he had to make up that story. It was arrogance outwardly, but devotion inwardly. There are many privileges that one attains by methods seemingly wrong, but the devotion proves true, expressed in every form.

Question: *What is the meaning of the belief that when a glass breaks without any visible cause, it is the announcement of the death of a dear one who is far away?*

Answer: Very often it is true. Sometimes it is a thought form, sometimes it is a spirit influence, sometimes it is the influence of death itself which has its vibratory action through all things. And if the glass happens to become the subject of such vibration, if the current falls upon that glass with intensity, certainly it breaks. But that does not mean that a person must always take that warning, if a glass is broken. That would be terrible.

Question: *I thought it was good luck.*

Answer: I would at least suppose that when a glass was broken, if one thought it was very lucky, it would avoid much ill luck.

THE ART OF PERSONALITY

Contents of *The Art of Personality* are taken from a series of lectures given during the 1923 Summer School in Suresnes, France, July14–September 12. These lectures have been previously published as *Creating the Person: A Practical Guide to the Development of Self* (New Lebanon, NY: Sulūk Press 2013). The editors of *Creating the Person*, Jeanne Koré Salvato and Vakil Nancy Wilson, compiled the text on the most authentic sources as found in *The Complete Works of Pir-o-Murshid Hazrat Inayat Khan: Original Texts: Lectures on Sufism, 1923,* vol.2 (London: East-West Publications, 1988).

GRATEFULNESS

Gratefulness in the character is like a fragrance in a flower. The people, however learned and qualified in their life's work, in whom gratefulness is absent, are void of that beauty of character which makes a personality fragrant.

Gratefulness is being conscious of every little deed of kindness that anyone does to us. If we answer it with appreciation, in this way we develop that spirit in our nature. And by learning this we rise to that state when we begin to realize God's goodness toward us, God's divine compassion, for which we can never be grateful enough.

A great poet among Sufis, Sa'adi, teaches gratefulness to be the means of attracting that favor of the forgiveness and mercy of God upon ourselves in which is the salvation of our soul. There is much in life that we can be grateful for, in spite of all the difficulties and troubles of life. Sa'adi says, "The sun and moon and the rain and clouds all are busy to prepare your food for you."[1] And it is unfair indeed if you do not appreciate it in thanksgiving.

God's goodness is something that one cannot learn to know at once. It takes time to understand it. But little actions of kindness which we receive from those around us we can know, and we can be thankful if we want to be. In this way we develop gratefulness in our nature and express it in our thought, speech, and action as an exquisite form of beauty. As long as

1 From the *Gulistan* of Sa'di Shirazi.

one weighs and measures and says, "What I have done for you and what you have done for me," and "How kind I have been to you and how good you have been to me," one wastes time over something which is inexpressible in words. Besides, by this one closes that fountain of beauty which rises from the stream of gratefulness.

The first lesson in the path of thankfulness that we can learn is to forget absolutely what we do for another; remember only what the other person has done for us. Throughout the whole journey on the spiritual path, the main thing that is to be accomplished is the forgetting of our false ego. In this way, we may arrive in some way at the realization of that being whom we call God.

There is a story of a slave called Ayaz, who was brought before the king with nine others, and the king had to select one to be his personal attendant. The wise king gave into the hands of each of the ten a wine glass and commanded them to throw it down. Each one obeyed the command. Then the king asked each one of them, "Why did you do such a thing?" Each of them answered, "Because Your Majesty gave us the order," the plain truth, cut and dried. And then the tenth one, Ayaz, came near. He said, "Pardon me, King, I am sorry." He knew that the king already knew that it was his command. So by telling him, "Because you told me," there is nothing new said to the king.

This beauty of expression won the king so that he selected him to be his attendant. It was not long before he won the trust and confidence of the king, who gave him charge of his treasury in which precious jewels were kept. This made many jealous of the sudden rise of Ayaz from a slave to a treasurer of the king, a position which many envied.

No sooner did people know that Ayaz had become a favorite of the king than they began to tell numerous stories about Ayaz in order to bring him into the disfavor of the king. One of the stories was that every day Ayaz went in that room where the jewels were locked in the safe and that he was stealing them, every day, little by little. The king answered, "No, I cannot believe such a thing. You have to show me."

They brought the king as Ayaz entered this room, and made him stand in a place where there was a hole to look into the room, and the king saw what was going on there. Ayaz entered this room and opened the door of the safe. And what did he take out from it? His old ragged clothes which he had worn as a slave. He kissed them and pressed them to his eyes and put them on the table. There incense was burning—this which he was doing was something sacred to him.

He then put his clothes on himself, looked at himself in the mirror, and said to himself, as one might be saying a prayer, "Listen," he said, "O Ayaz, see what you were one day before. It is the king who has given you the charge of this treasury. So regard this duty as your most sacred trust and this honor as your privilege, and love the kindness of the king. Know that it is not your worthiness that has brought you to this position. Know that it is his greatness, his goodness, his generosity which has overlooked your faults, and which has bestowed that rank and position upon you by which you are now being honored. Never forget, therefore, your first day, the day when you came to this town. And it is the remembering of that day which will keep you in proper pitch."

He then took off the clothes and put them in the same place of safety, and came out. As he stepped out, what did he see? He saw that the king, before whom he bowed, was waiting eagerly to embrace him. The king told him, "What a lesson you have given me, Ayaz."

It is this lesson we all must learn, whatever be our position. Before that king in whose presence we all are slaves, let nothing make us forget that helplessness through which we were reared and we were raised, and that we were brought to life to do and to understand and to live a life of joy.

* * *

Question: *Will you please explain what you mean when you speak of listening to music spiritually? Can one listen to common music such as tunes played on a street organ?*

Answer: But we do not sit and meditate in the street. Besides, there is a technical stage; as a person develops in technique, in appreciating a better music, so one feels disturbed by a wrong, lower kind of music. But then there is a spiritual way which has nothing to do with technique. It is only to tune oneself with the music, and therefore the spiritual person is not concerned about its grade. No doubt, the better the music, the more helpful it is to a spiritual person; the higher the music, the better. But at the same time you must remember that there are lamas of Tibet who make their concentration or meditation by moving a kind of rattle, the sound of which is not especially melodious. But at the same time they cultivate that sense of appreciation which raises a person by the help of vibrations on the higher planes. No doubt, there is nothing better than music for the upliftment of the soul.

Question: *What is the highest perception of freedom?*

Answer: The highest perception of freedom comes when one has freed the self from the false ego, when one is no longer what one was. All manner of freedom, for the moment, gives a sensation of freedom. The true freedom is in oneself; when one's soul is free, then there is nothing in this world that binds us. Everywhere one will breathe freedom, in heaven and on earth.

Question: *Is it ungenerous to be critical in one's appreciation of things that do not agree with one's sense of beauty?*

Answer: When we are developing our sense of beauty, then naturally we shall be critical of that which does not come up to our standard of beauty. But when we have passed that stage, then the next cycle of our evolution shows us a different experience; in that the divine compassion is developed. And therefore one becomes able, so to speak, to add to all that lacks beauty, and thus to turn all into perfection, which is the contemplation of the soul.

Question: *You said once that to repeat an expression of thanks did not make it stronger. But is it not a tendency of a grateful heart to repeat?*

Answer: Certainly it is. If I said that, it was said in a sense that one may make it a kind of mechanical thing. Very often people use "thank you" so bountifully that it almost loses its meaning. But the meaning of the word *namaz* in Sufism, which means prayer, is the repeating of thankfulness. What it does is bring to one's soul one's own voice, and the voice echoes once again before God, who is within ourselves. Therefore, the saying of the prayer is more powerful than only thinking on the subject. It is like thinking of a song and singing it—there is a vast difference between [the two]. By singing there is a satisfaction of the appetite. By thinking only, there is not.

Question: *What is the difference between thinking of a melody and singing it?*

Answer: Thinking the melody has half an effect upon the soul, and singing makes it complete, its full effect. But singing with thought makes it ten times more [effective], because a person may be there but their mind is somewhere else, not thinking of the song.

Question: *The difficulty is to always sing a melody and to keep the thought?*

Answer: By singing you can retain the thought more than by not singing and just wanting to keep the thought. It helps the concentration a great deal.

Question: *Is it a distinct disadvantage for a human being to be born without a good ear?*

Answer: It is, because what is received through the ears goes deeper into the soul than by any other form. Neither by smelling or tasting or seeing does beauty enter so deeply into oneself as by hearing.

THE ART OF PERSONALITY

It is one thing to be a human being, and it is another thing to be a person. A human being becomes a person by making a personality, by completing the individuality in which is hidden the purpose of our coming on earth. Angels were made to sing the praise of the Lord; jinns to imagine, to dream, to meditate; but we are created to show humanity in our character. It is this which makes one a person.

There are many things difficult in life, but the most difficult of all things is to learn and to know and to practice the art of personality. Nature, people say, is created by God, and art by the human being. But really speaking, in the making of personality it is God who finishes the divine art. It is not what Christ taught which made his devotees love him. They dispute over those things in vain. It is what he himself was; it is that which is loved and admired by his devotees. When Jesus Christ said to the fishermen, "Come here, I will teach you to be fishers of men,"[1] what does it mean? It means: I will teach you the art of personality which will become as a net in this life's sea—for every heart, whatever be its grade of evolution, will be attracted by the beauty of the art of personality.

What is someone seeking in another person? What does one expect in one's friend? One wants the friend to be rich, of a high position, of great power, of wonderful qualifications, or wide influence; but beyond and above all, one expects from

1 Matthew 4:19.

one's friend the human qualities—that is, the art of personality. If one's friend lacks the art of personality, all the above said things are of but little use and value.

There is a question: How are we to learn the art of personality? We learn it by our love of art, by our love of beauty in all its various aspects. The artist learns art by the admiration of beauty. When a person gets an insight into beauty, then that person learns the art of arts, which is the art of personality. One may have a thousand qualifications or rank or position, one may possess all the goods of the earth, but if one lacks the art of personality one indeed is poor. It is by this art that we show that nobleness which belongs to the kingdom of God.

The art of personality is not a qualification. It is the purpose for which humanity was created, and it leads us to that purpose in the fulfillment of which is our entire satisfaction. By this art, we not only satisfy ourselves, but we please God.

This phantom play on the earth is produced for the pleasure of that king of the universe whom the Hindus have called Indra, before whom *gandharvas* sang and *apsaras* danced. The interpretation of this story is that every soul's purpose is to dance at the court of Indra. It is to learn to dance at the court of Indra perfectly, which is, really speaking, the art of personality. The one who says, "But how can I dance, I do not know how to dance," defeats one's own purpose. For no soul is created to stand aside and look on. Every soul is created to dance at the court of Indra. The soul who refuses certainly shows its ignorance of the great purpose for which this whole play is produced on the earth.

* * *

Question: *Will you please tell us if vaccination is desirable?*

Answer: Well, all things are desirable if they are properly used, and all are undesirable when they are abused. In point of fact, vaccination is the same spirit which is taught by Shiva Mahadeva, as Hatha Yoga. It is said of Mahadeva that he used to drink poison, and by drinking poison he got over the effect of poison. Mahadeva was the most venturous among the ascetics; that one can see by his wearing the serpent around his neck. Now, would you like to do it? If one can be so friendly with a serpent as to keep it around the neck, I think one can sit comfortably in the presence of someone one does not like. Hatred, prejudice, nervousness in the presence of someone we do not like will not come if one can take [on] a serpent, if one can take the bitter bowl of poison and drink it, which is against nature. When the soul has once fought its battle with all things that make it fear and tremble, shrink back and run away, that soul has conquered life, it has become the master of life, it has attained the kingdom.

Of course, the methods Mahadeva adopted are extreme methods; no one can recommend them to a pupil in this modern world where there is fear, and vaccination comes from there: it is partaking of that poison which we fear, which might come someday in some form. One might breathe it in the breath or take it in the water or from the food; those same germs might come and enter one's body.

I have heard from a friend that a man in Switzerland has worked most of his life in getting the germs of consumption, tuberculosis, in order to inject them in cases where they can be cured; and he has had a great degree of success. Of course, such new methods may meet with a great deal of opposition, but at the same time the principle behind it has a very strong reason. This brings us to a much higher realization and a greater conception of life. It causes us to think that even what we call death, if that death were put into a cup and given to us to drink, that would bring us to life.

Question: *The Vedanta speaks of fourteen* lokas. *What is a* loka *and what is* pata loka*?*

Answer: These fourteen planes of existence are a conception of metaphysics. The Sufi calls them *chauda tabaq*, and they are the experience, fourteen different experiences, which consciousness has by the help of meditation. And pata loka is the lower plane, or the lowest plane.

Question: *Are these lokas divided over the seven planes?*

Answer: Not in the angelic or in the jinn plane. But in the experience of these fourteen planes the jinn and angelic lokas also are touched.

Question: *The Greeks say that sometimes a soul, fitted for a more perfect instrument, by a mistake connected itself with an animal body instead of with a human body. Is that so?*

Answer: The mistake follows the soul everywhere, wherever it goes; it never leaves it alone. It is there, whether on the earth or on the jinn plane.

Question: *Is it not strange that God should create this whole universe in order to hear God's own praise? Is God not too great to want to hear God's own praise?*

Answer: No, it is not the praise which God wishes to hear. The praise of God is the prescription for humanity, that by this prescription we come to that sense which brings us nearer to God. In other words, by praising God we finish that art in which is the fulfillment of the soul's coming on earth.

Question: *What is the best manner for an artist to receive inspiration: by waiting, by praying, or by continual working till inspiration comes back?*

Answer: By doing all three things together. One can wait while doing the work just the same. One need not put the brushes aside and wait, but do the work at the same time. One need not go into a corner and pray for inspiration, but do it while working, all at the same time.

Question: *Whom do you mean by Indra?*

Answer: In this respect it is God himself. It is a picture. For every *manvantara* there is a bodhisattva and one *manu*. Bodhisattva is *nabi*, and *manu* is the *rasul*. These are names of people, although each of these words has a certain significance. *Manu* is the one who has touched the boundaries of human perfection. It is reaching the heights of human perfection that is *rasul* and *maitreya*; these names are very significant: *Manu* has proved in this life to be a friend to everyone who is met. The next is to prove to be a friend to God, that is *rasul*, the fulfillment, where one has proved to be a friend to every soul. It is the perfection of friendliness in which is all spiritual perfection, when the spirit of friendliness is so developed that one is a friend to all. One cannot say, "There is one person in the world I cannot bear, whom I hate." When one has passed to that stage, one's name is on the spiritual records.

Bodhisattva, the word, signifies the wise, wisdom, the boundary of wisdom, the perfection of wisdom where two opposite poles become one, where the serpent takes its tail in its mouth, which is the symbol of wisdom. It is therefore that the wise agree with all, with the wise and foolish both.

GENTLENESS

Every impulse has its influence upon the word and upon the action; and, therefore, naturally every impulse exerts its full power through words and deeds, unless it is checked. There are two types of persons: those who have acquired the power of checking their word and action when it would exert its full power and express itself with abruptness; the other kind of persons are those who mechanically allow this natural course of impulse to show itself in their word and deed, without giving any thought to it. The former, therefore, is gentle, and the latter is the human being.

Gentleness is the principal thing in the art of personality. One can see how gentleness works as the principal thing in every art: in painting, in drawing, in line and color; it is gentleness which appeals the most to the soul. The same we shall see in music. Musicians may be qualified enough to play rapidly and may know all the technique, but what produces beauty is their gentle touch.

It is gentleness, mainly, which is all refinement. But where does it come from? It comes from consideration, and it is practiced by self-control. There is a saying in the East, "The weaker the person, the more ready to be angry." The reason is that this person has no control over the nerves. It is often lack of control over oneself which is the cause of a lack of gentleness. No doubt, one learns gentleness by consideration. One must learn to think before saying or doing. Besides, while saying or doing one must not forget the idea of beauty; one must know that it is not enough to say or do, but it is necessary to say or do everything beautifully.

It is the development of the nations and races which is expressed in gentleness; also it is the advancement of the soul's evolution which expresses itself in gentleness. Nations and races, as well as individuals, will show backwardness in their evolution if they show a lack of gentleness.

At this time of the world's condition it seems that the art of personality has been much neglected. People are intoxicated with the life of avarice. And then the competitive spirit that exists, helped by the commercialism of the day, keeps people busy in acquiring the needs of their everyday life. The beauty which is the need of the soul is lost to view. Humanity's interest in all things of life—science, art, philosophy—remains unfinished in the absence of the art of personality. How rightly this distinction has been made in the English language: man and gentleman.

* * *

Question: *You spoke of Mahadeva as the chief of the ascetics; was he not a divine incarnation?*

Answer: Certainly he was.

Question: *Will you please tell us what we so admire in the beauty of the lion and tiger? They are not gentle.*

Answer: We admire them when they are in the cage. We would not admire them if they were at liberty. You must remember that very often very good reports come in the newspapers about beautiful looking Zeppelins; they looked so beautiful at night in the sky; also reports of how nicely the German army marched. They admired it. Were they only admired? So we admire the tiger and lion. But we would have admired them still more if they had been gentle.

Question: *If the angelic world is the same as what is called* buddhi *in terms of Vedanta, what is it that the Vedantist calls* atma*?*

Answer: Buddhi is quite another word. *Buddhi* is not necessarily a plane. *Buddhi* is intelligence, reason, sense. *Atma* is the soul. The essential nature of the soul is *buddhi*, the essence of reason, purest intelligence. Does the soul not pass the astral world coming from the jinn world? Just now I am not giving the terms of other expressions. I have only used these terms jinn and angel in order to simplify what I have to say about manifestation. Therefore, it would not be good to mix up these ideas which have been given to you with names of many different planes which can be afterwards explained to you.[1]

Question: *Is gentleness not the greatest power?*

Answer: Yes, gentleness is a power like the power of water. Water is powerful, and yet if there is a rock in the way the stream of water is going, it will surround the rock, it will not break it. It will make its way by the side, for the water is pliable, and so is gentleness.

Question: *But what if people will not listen to gentleness?*

Answer: Then we must talk to them in their own language. But only if it is necessary. If we can avoid it, it is still better. Gentleness, in the long run, will always prove the thing. But if we cannot manage, only in that case, we can learn that language. There is no objection in learning a language, is there?

Question: *Does Parvati stand for a quality, or was she a real woman?*

Answer: She was a real woman, Mahadeva's wife; she also stands for the property of *purusha*.

Question: *Will you tell us something about the use of asceticism in the spiritual life?*

Answer: I think that every person who is spiritually inclined, and in whom spirituality is innate, and who is to accomplish

1 For a much fuller treatment of all these terms, see volume I in the present series: *The Inner Life* (New Lebanon, NY: Sulūk Press 2016).

something worthwhile in the spiritual line, is born with more or less an ascetic inclination. There may be one person born with a greater inclination than another. But there is some inclination of asceticism in every soul born for spirituality. And now the question, what are the qualities of an ascetic? Independence, indifference, a love of solitude. The ascetic is self-sufficient, stern, egoistic, proud, celibate, contemplative, dreamy, visionary, retiring, thoughtful, and wise. And here, I have said all the ascetic's good and bad qualities.

Question: *Is egoistic among the bad qualities?*

Answer: In the end it comes right just the same.

Question: *How can one be egoistic and wise both?*

Answer: Well, there are many kinds of egoistic people. There are good points and bad points. Egoistic is selfish, and selfishness can produce cruelty, tyranny, injustice, and dishonesty. Another side to the egoistic person is pride and independence and indifference, which give a person contentment. And besides this, the real egoistic person before whom there is the ego, when that person watches that ego, which is first a statue of rock, after some time it becomes a living being. It comes to life. It becomes the very object after which one is seeking. And therefore the right egoistic person is right; it is the wrong egoistic person who is wrong.

Question: *Would you say that there is a time for everything in the spiritual life?*

Answer: Yes, a time for everything, that is so.

Question: *Someone who is egoistic is always hurting someone.*

Answer: That is the wrong side of the ego. There are different stages of the ego. In different stages different things are right. The same thing which is wrong once, is right another time.

There are certain attributes which are spoken of by a great poet and a composer, Alias, and which show the qualities of a great soul: continual contemplation; the dignity of name, and respect of the position; taking the side of those who surrender; lifting up those who are standing at the bottom of the earth; giving merit to those who are talentless; giving knowledge to those who are without; providing for those who are without supply (such as medicine for the sick); whose presence clears away depression; who gives honor to those whom no one would honor; protecting those who are without protection; being constructive by influencing everything they touch. It is such souls in whom God may be found.

THE PERSUASIVE TENDENCY

There is a tendency hidden behind human impulse which may be called the persuasive tendency; it may manifest in a crude form and it may be expressed in a fine form. In the former aspect it is a fault, and in the latter aspect it is a mistake.

When crudely expressed, one urges another to agree, or to listen, or to do as one wishes be done by fighting, by quarreling, by being disagreeable. Often such people by the strength of their willpower, or by virtue of their better position in life, get their wishes done. This encourages them to continue further in the same method until they find a disappointing outcome of their method, if they ever find it.

The other way of persuading is a gentler way: by putting pressure upon another person's kindness, goodness, and politeness, exhausting thereby their patience and testing their sympathy to the last. By this, people achieve for the moment what they wish to achieve, but in the end the effect is the annoyance of all those who are tried by this persuasive tendency.

Does it not show that to get something done is not so hard as to be considerate of the feelings of others? It is so rare that one finds a person in the world who is considerate of another person's feeling, even at the sacrifice of getting their own desires done. Everyone seeks freedom, but for themselves. If one sought the same for another, one would be a much greater person.

The persuasive tendency no doubt shows a great willpower, and it plays upon the weakness of others, who yield and give in to it owing to love, sympathy, goodness, kindness, politeness. But there is a limit to everything. There comes a time when the thread breaks. A thread is a thread, it is not a steel wire; even a wire breaks if it is pulled too hard. The delicacy of the human heart is not comprehended by everyone. Human feeling is too fine for common perception. A soul who develops the personality—what is that soul like? That soul is not like the root or the stem of the plant, nor like the branches or leaves; it is like the flower, the flower with its color, fragrance, and delicacy.

* * *

Question: *You told us on Saturday of the great refreshment derived during sleep. Many distinguished men, as Napoleon, for example, have performed a great amount of work on very little sleep. Is this because of their ability to contact the higher planes during the waking state?*

Answer: Yes, when a person is fast asleep, when the body is resting and mind still, the soul is able to freely breathe, and it absorbs in itself all the energy and vitality that is necessary for the whole being.

Question: *How is it that one recognizes, in a flash sometimes, a place or a scene that one has never visited before?*

Answer: The human body is a living wireless station. If only the senses and the mind were open to receive, we would not only receive all that comes from the world around us, but also from the world above us; in other words, within us. And so every such experience as hearing something, or seeing something, or perceiving a fragrance, a depression without reason, or laughter without a cause—all these are the phenomena proving that the human being is the living wireless.

Question: *If the matter in bodies is always changing, would someone feel anything when an accident happens to the first person?*[1]

1 The shorthand record of the question is incomplete. Another record reads, "A, who had a body and matter that had passed out of the body of another

Answer: Not really, there is no connection in the matter. There would be only a kind of little attraction, such as there is in a blood relationship, a kind of attraction. But even that does not manifest to knowledge. It is a natural attraction, one does not know it. There is a very well-known story in *Shahnamah* [2] which explains this. There was a young man of whose ancestry a great ancient king of Persia knew. And he brought up this young man with great care and made him a most qualified wrestler, and his name was Rustam. This wrestler became the champion of the country and was trying to be a world champion, and he was very promising in his youth. He was kept by the king in reserve; he was not to see people, talk with people, mix with people. There came many wrestlers, and he won, this youth.

But the custom of that time was that, among two wrestlers, the one who is defeated, must acknowledge his defeat. And if he does not acknowledge, then he must be killed. And there came a world champion, and the king wanted this young man to fight with this world champion. And they fought. In the end the world champion brought this young man under him, and he was defeated. But the young man was very proud; he would not acknowledge his defeat. And therefore this world champion had to kill him. And when the knife had pierced through his throat, while bleeding he had a little sense and he said, "Remember, you have killed me, but some day you will meet my father and certainly he will win success over you."

This world champion asked his name. He said, "Rustam." The world champion went mad when he heard his name. This young man happened to be his son. All the time they fought there was an attraction; and yet the father did not know the son and the son did not know the father. To the mind there is a silent attraction, but it is not clear, because it is matter.

---

person, B, and gone into the body of A, would that person, A, feel connection with the person, B?"

2 A classic of Persian literature by Firdausi (Abu Al-Qasem Mansur), a history of the kings of that country.

Question: *What is it that accounts for the fact that when two people meet for the first time they feel they know each other? Is it the same thing?*

Answer: Yes. The only difference between the spirit and matter is that the divine intelligence pouring out directly is the spirit, and radiated through a dense medium is matter. Therefore, either in spirit or in matter there is divine intelligence just the same.

There has been a talk about the excavation in Egypt, that people should have felt agitated and angry against this.[3] It is not so. The souls have much better occupation than to think about their body. Just as when one's nails are cut, one does not think of the nails any more. There is no link any more. If one keeps it all the time in mind, there may be a little thought. It is the thought that keeps the connection. But the possibility of the same kings who are being excavated [knowing about it] is through the minds of those who do the work; that is the medium, because they are conscious of what they are doing. It is through that medium they can know that something is being done to their body.

There are strange stories told in India about snakes guarding the place where money was buried, because in the ancient times people used to dig under their house and put money there when going to travel. They did not want to tell anybody about it. Then they died and the thought was with the person who was dead. In order to protect that, when there was no other person there, the snakes were inspired to be there and guard it. Because that guarding tendency of the one who is gone is still in the serpent and the serpent is guarding it, one thing reflected upon another.

Then there are mothers very often having left their young children with the thought of protection. There has always been that reflection of the thought of protecting the children: that

3 Howard Carter excavated the ancient Egyptian tomb of the pharoah Tutankhamun in 1922, one year before the lectures in this section were given. At the time there were rumors of a curse connected with the tomb.

either among the relatives or friends, at once, as if an intuition or an innermost desire springs up in their heart to take charge of those children. And they have proved as kind as mothers. Because the mother's love was reflecting upon the heart of someone capable of protecting, it protects them.

Question: *Is the serpent chosen to guard?*

Answer: No, there is no choice, it just happens. But in the case of the mother, there sometimes is choice.

Question: *Where does the motive come from?*

Answer: The prophetic idea rises above philosophical analysis. Because the Prophet says it is God who is merciful and compassionate; and all children are God's children, whether to their mother or to someone else they give their heart. Therefore, there is no need to distinguish the motive, because in reality all motives belong to One, and that is God. But of course that is the ideal side. On the philosophical side there is a distinction. But I should think that either guided by anybody or obsessed, an act of kindness and a service of love is always a virtue. Because after a study of metaphysics or philosophy, after reading or meditating, or after living like a saint, or after accomplishing all that a master may accomplish, in the end, one thing a person learns out of all that has been studied—and that is to serve another. There is all religion, philosophy, and mysticism in that, and if one has not learned that, one has not learned anything.

There are wealthy people with millions, and there are people of rank who are in high positions, and there are mighty magicians with great power, and yet they all will prove to be poor and useless in the end compared with those who are always ready to do what they can for their fellows. In this is the essence of the whole learning, the whole spirituality and mysticism: How can we be useful, how can we be serviceable to the person next to us?

VANITY

The whole manifestation is the expression of that spirit of the logos, which is called, in Sufi terms, *kibriya*. Through every being, this spirit manifests in the form of vanity, pride, or conceit. Had it not been for this spirit working in every being as the central theme of life, no good or bad would have existed in the world, nor would there have been great or small; all virtues and every evil is the offspring of this spirit. The art of personality is to cut the rough edges of this spirit of vanity which hurt and disturb those one meets in life. Those who talk of "I," as many times as they talk about it, so much more they disturb the mind of their listeners.

Vanity expressed in rigidity is called pride; when it is expressed nicely it is termed vanity. Often people are trained in politeness, and they are taught a polished language and manner. Yet, if there be this spirit of vanity pronounced, in spite of all good manners and beautiful language it creeps up and sounds itself in a person's thought, speech, or action, calling aloud, "I am, I am." If a person be speechless, that vanity will leap out from the expression, from the glance. It is something which is the hardest thing to suppress and to control.

The struggle in the life of adepts is not so great with passions or emotions, which sooner or later by more or less effort can be controlled, but with vanity; it is always growing. If one cuts down its stem, then one lives no more, for it is the very self, it is the "I," the ego, the soul or God within. It cannot be denied its existence, but only struggling with it beautifies it more and more and makes more tolerable that which in its crude form is intolerable.

Vanity may be likened to a magic plant. If one saw it in the garden growing as a thorny plant, and if one cut it off, it would grow in another place in the same garden as a tree of fruits. And when one cuts it away, in another place in the same garden it will spring up as a plant of fragrant roses. It exists just the same, but in a more beautiful form, and would give happiness to those who touch it. The art of personality, therefore, does not teach us to root out the seed of vanity, which cannot be rooted out as long as we live. But its crude outer garb may be destroyed, that after dying several deaths it might manifest as the plant of desire.

* * *

Question: *Is there any other way of changing the object of desire than that of satiety? I mean for someone in the world?*

Answer: Yes, which is by rising above it. For instance, that person has no virtue of fasting who is not hungry. Fasting is a virtue for that person who feels inclined to eat, and who renounces food.

Question*: Might not vanity be called self-admiration?*

Answer: Certainly.

Question: *Can vanity be rooted out?*

Answer: Vanity is life itself, and so its existence cannot be denied.

Question: *What is the Vedantic equivalent of* kibriya*?*

Answer: It is "Om."

Question: *In* Mysticism of Sound *it is said: "It is the reflection of the sun in the moon which makes the moon appear round like the sun."*[1] *Do you mean by this that the moon is round because the sun is round?*

Answer: All celestial bodies are round because they are the reflections of the sun. If the sun were square all would have been square.

Question: *Will you please tell us more about the relationship between the sun and the moon, and how they work together?*

Answer: The moon is the complement to the sun, and the contrary. One positive, one negative. One *jalal*, one *jamal*. The moon responds, the sun expresses. And so it is the power of affinity between the sun and the moon, which is a power that holds the cosmos. But the sun is again the reflection of the divine sun, a physical reflection. As the moon and planets are a reflection of the sun, so the sun is a reflection of the divine sun, which is obscure to the physical eyes.

Question: *What do you mean by reflection in that sense? Do you mean it in the same sense that they reflect the light of the sun?*

Answer: Yes, they are respondent bodies. For instance, the crystal is a body which is respondent to the light; so are the planets to the sun, and the sun to the divine manifestation. Therefore, the sun in all ages has been taken as a sign for the worship of God.

Question: *Will you tell us please the difference between the master and the murshid?*

Answer: The master or the saint is the path of those who tread the spiritual path, the high initiates. The murshid is what the Hindus call a guru, a teacher, whom the pupils accept as their

---

1 A book by Inayat Khan, published earlier in 1923. It contains lectures describing the ways in which sound is used in mystical exercises. See volume II of the present series, *The Mysticism of Sound* (Richmond, VA: Sulūk Press, 2018), 37.

guide on the spiritual path, and from whose hands they take their initiation.

Question: *One being can also be all these beings?*

Answer: Yes.

[*Question missing*]

Answer: What is the path? The path is the vacuum. When a person has removed themselves then there is a vacuum. As long as a person is stating "I am," so long one is a stone in one's own path. When one has removed oneself, then one is the path, then one is the vacuum. What everyone is seeking is the true ego, which is God. When the false ego is removed then there is no end to what one becomes.

Question: *Is the moon the eye of God?*

Answer: Yes, it is the left eye of God; the right eye is the sun.

Question: *Has the arrangement of the stars in the constellations any definite purpose, any spiritual purpose?*

Answer: Yes, they all have their part to perform in the cosmos. And the influence that each planet has upon different souls, that makes a great link between the condition of that star and the soul; and every move that particular star makes has its influence on those connected with that star. This is the key to the secret of the spiritual hierarchy, that influence of *wali*, *ghaws*, *qutub*, *nabi*, *rasul* is considered as the influence of the sun, the moon, the planets, and stars. And that every change that takes place in all the planetary system—that change has much to do with those who represent here on the earth that particular planet. That is what makes the spiritual hierarchy on the earth. And besides, as the stars and planets have their influence on the living beings, so the living beings who represent the planets—their influence is working upon the human beings just the same.

Question: *Is it wise to study astrology?*

Answer: Study is always good, but it must not be so harmful as putting one's faith in a limited condition. It is better for sensitive people never to have a horoscope taken, either for themselves or for their children, for the warnings are so retained in mind that they become true. It is wise for astrologers never to say bad things and always good things. Psychologically, it is always wrong to prognosticate bad things.

The seer sees much more than the astrologer can. For the seer, the present and past and future is written just like a letter. Every person, every person's soul, is just like an open letter, written. But if the seer would begin to say it, then the sight would become dim, more and more every day, because it is a trust from God. If the seer would disclose it, this divine power would diminish little by little. With spiritual things, they are trusted to those who can keep them secret.

Question: *Would it ever be possible for a person, for the love of power, to betray it?*

Answer: Yes, it is possible. But that brings about terrible disasters. There is a story that there was a king, and he was traveling through different places. And it happened that he came into troubles, and he had to take the profession of a baker in order to get along for some time until he again could go to his palace. When serving in the house of the baker, he made a little money so that he could go back to his kingdom. He was hiding from some difficulty. He told the baker one day, "You have been so very kind, now I will tell you that I am the king. But you must keep this as a secret." But the moment the baker heard, he said, "Ha!" And when he said "Ha," he got a kind of upset in his system; he was almost ill. He said, "Take me to the doctors, there is something wrong."

It was because he had no power to keep the secret. His wife came, his children. He said, "I am dying." He would not eat, he would not drink, not sleep, because there was no accommodation here to keep the secret. The secret was too great a secret for him to keep. The doctors could not do anything. He said, "Well, take me somewhere in the woods." They took him, and he said, "Now go away." Then he came to a tree, and he said to the tree, "I want to tell you something, listen: the person who came to my house to wash my dishes was a king." And as he said so he became better.

Then the story goes on that in that tree there was a ghost who listened to it, who could not keep the secret in its heart. He had to tell it to somebody. The ghost went to the same kingdom and obsessed someone, and the secret came out. And the king knew that nobody knew except the baker. He sent for the baker, and he came before the king. And the baker said, "I have never told any living being; I have only said it in the forest, because I was ill." But the king said, "But how did the secret come out?" Then they found that it was the ghost who told the secret.

This story tells that it is not everyone who can assimilate the drinking of the liquor of any intoxicating drink. Someone, to whom you just gave a little sip, becomes drunken; another, you can give one good glass. The one who becomes a seer, that person God trusts. The prophets and messengers have first proved themselves in their lives by keeping the secret of their friends. They have kept the trust of all those, just like a safe. People came with their mistakes and difficulties; errors, sorrows they have poured out. It all went into their heart; it was safe, no one could look at it—more safe with the spiritual beings than with themselves.

The spiritual beings told them, "Do not tell another, as you have told me." They did not trust the people with their own secrets. When that is the capacity of the heart, then in the end God begins to trust: "You have become the trust of my creatures, now I give you my trust." It is the reward of that virtue. It shows the best quality in a person when one can keep the secret.

SELF-RESPECT

The consideration of dignity, which in other words may be called self-respect, is not something which can be left out when considering the art of personality. But the question, "what is it and how may this principle be practiced?" may be answered that all manner of lightheartedness and tendency to frivolity must be rooted out from one's nature in order to hold that dignity which is precious to one. The one who does not care for it does not need to take trouble about it; it is only for the one who sees something valuable in self-respect. A person with self-respect will be respected by others, even regardless of the person's power, position, possessions, or rank. In every position or situation in life, that person will command respect.

There arises a question: Has lightheartedness then any place in life, or is it not necessary in life at all? All is necessary, but everything has its time. Dignity is not in making a long face; respect is not in making cross [eye]brows. By frowning or stiffening of the body one does not get honor.

Dignity is not in being sad or depressed. It is only dividing one's activities according to their proper times. There are times for the laughter, there are times for seriousness. For the person who is laughing all the time, laughter loses its power. The person who is always lighthearted does not command that weight in society which is necessary. Besides, lightheartedness often makes a person offend others, without meaning to do so. The one who has no respect for oneself has no respect for others.

One may think for the moment that one is without regard for conventionalities and free in one's expression and feeling, but one does not know that it makes one as light as a scrap of paper, moving hither and thither in space, taken by the wind.

Life is as a sea, and the further on the sea one travels, the heavier the ship one needs. So in this sea of life, for a wise person to make a life, there is a certain amount of weight required, which gives balance to the personality. Wisdom gives that weight; its absence is the mark of foolishness. The pitcher full of water is heavy. It is the absence of water in the pitcher which makes it light, as one without wisdom is lighthearted. The more one studies and understands the art of personality, the more one finds that it is the ennobling of the character which is going forward toward the purpose of creation. All the different virtues, beautiful manners, and beautiful qualities—they are all the outcome of the nobleness of the character. But what is nobleness of the character? It is a wide outlook.

* * *

Question: *Is dignity of position sometimes in opposition with kind impulses?*

Answer: When a person is on duty, it is better to follow the duty. For instance, when the judge is sitting upon the chair of the judge, and there is another person who is too weak to stand, the judge may be just as kind to say that a chair may be brought—not give the judge's own chair. By that the judge would not be fulfilling a judge's duty properly. When the judge is out of the court, then the judge can show kindness.

Question: *Will you please tell us how it is that sometimes when people meet for the first time there is instinctive repulsion in them, and yet afterwards they may become friends?*

Answer: It is not often so, perhaps sometimes. Because really those who are to be friends, they become friends at first sight. The first impression is, really speaking, a continual impression, and that becomes more and more. But it is quite possible that sometimes something that had a repellent influence, if one can overcome it, one can bear it more easily. Then one finds something more interesting in that person, then one becomes friends. It is only a matter of getting accustomed. One who does not withstand because one is not accustomed to those vibrations may, by tolerance and endurance, become accustomed; then that one has conquered that weakness. It is the same as becoming accustomed to poison.

Question: *"Unto the woman God said, 'I will greatly multiply thy sorrow and thy conception; in sorrow thou shalt bring forth children.'" "And unto Adam God said, 'In the sweat of thy face shalt thou eat bread.'"*[1] *But through all the ages women, except a few of the privileged ones, have had to work also in the sweat to gain their bread; so they have to bear a double burden. Is it not an injustice?*

Answer: There is not one injustice, there are numberless injustices. Only this was said long ago; now it would have been said differently. It only shows the duties of womanhood as existed before, that pertained to that idea. And the duties of man as existed before, that pertained to that. This does not belong to the present time.

Question: *Which is the quickest way to attain dignity? Dignity, by seeking to be dignified, by seeking truth which will give dignity? Or is seeking dignity and truth the same thing?*

Answer: By learning to think one develops dignity in one's nature. The more thoughtful one becomes, naturally the more dignified one becomes, because dignity springs from thoughtfulness. A person who offends is lighthearted; and the person who is lighthearted is foolish. One may seem clever and yet be lighthearted; but one goes no further than the worldly cleverness, and very often that cleverness falls at one's feet as an iron chain. As Sa'adi says, "My cleverness, thou actest so often against me."

1 Genesis 3:16–19.

Question: *Sometimes an egoistic person is very dignified.*

Answer: The true dignity is always unconscious. It is a natural outcome of thoughtfulness. It may be that a person has dignity and at the same time is egoistic. That person has not yet risen above the ego, because it is the greatest difficulty to conquer the ego. Egoism causes lack of love; love is the first and the last both, and all through.

Question: *What is love and how should one be loving?*

Answer: It is very difficult to say what is love and how one can be loving. Is it that one should be embracing or running after people or talking sweetly? What is it that one could show to be loving, because every person has a different way of expressing their love. Perhaps there is someone who has a love hidden in the heart; it does not manifest. With another it comes out in words, actions. For another, perhaps, it rises just like the vapors and charges the whole atmosphere. For another, it is like a spark in the stone: outside the stone is cold, inside there is a spark. Therefore, to judge who has love and who has not is not the power of every person. It is very difficult.

For instance, love as a fire rising from a cracker, calls out "I am love!" and burns up and then is finished. There is also a fire in the pebble which never manifests. If one holds the pebble, it is so cold; at the same time it is there, some day you can strike it, and it is there. And as many people as there are, so [love has] as many different qualities. One cannot judge the love of one person, or the other, because the manner of expressing love for every person is different.

When we ask the followers of other religions, for instance, they have a thousand things to say against the religion of their adversaries—not only about the religion, but also about the prophet. It is not only because they are of another religion that they will find fault with the very prophet who is, perhaps, the prophet of millions of people; a person can easily find fault with them, and may have quite a reason to find fault. Therefore, no one has ever been born on earth who may be called perfect in every way. Except you can say it with regard to someone who has gone already from this plane of the earth, because that person is not before you to be examined and tested again. And if the human being were perfect, then what would be the difference between the human being and God? Humanity is limited, God is perfect.

WORD OF HONOR

The noble-minded show, as something natural in their character, an esteem for their word, which is called the word of honor. For that one, one's word is one's self. And it could increase to such an extent that even one's life could be sacrificed for one's word. A person who has reached this stage is not very far from God, for it is often mentioned in the scriptures, "If you wish to see us, see us in our words." If God can be seen in God's words, the true soul can be seen in a person's words. Pleasure, displeasure, sweetness, bitterness, honesty, dishonesty, all these are to be discerned in the words a person speaks. For the word is the expression of thought, and thought is the expression of feeling. And what is a person? One is one's thought and feeling. So what is the word? The word is one's expression, the expression of one's soul.

The person upon whose words you can rely, that person is dependable. No wealth of this world can be compared with one word of honor. Those who say what they mean prove in this virtue spirituality. To a real person, to go back on one's word is worse than death, for it is going backward instead of going forward. Every soul is going onward toward its goal, and those who are really going onward show it in their word.

At the present time, when it has been necessary to have so many courts and so many lawyers, which has in turn necessitated the keeping of so many prisons which are flourishing more every day—this all shows the lack of that virtue which has been valued by the noble-minded ever since the beginning of civilization. For in this quality a person shows human virtue, a quality which neither belongs to the animals, nor is attributed to the angels.

What is religion? Religion, in the true sense of the word, is beyond explanation. It is a delicate thread, too delicate to be touched, for it is too sacred to be touched. It is the ideal which could be polluted if it were touched, and this can be found in that sensitiveness which, in other words, may be called spirituality.

Out of regard for the word, many in this world have gone through sacrifices; sufferings and pains have been inflicted on them, but it was only to put their virtue to the test. For every virtue has to prove itself by going through a test of fire. When it has passed its trial it becomes a solid virtue. This can be practiced in every little thing one does in one's daily life. A person who one moment says one thing, and another moment another thing, even that person's own heart begins to disbelieve.

The great ones who have come on the earth from time to time and who have shown many virtues, among them this virtue has been the most pronounced. Muhammad, before having come before the world as a prophet, was called Amin by his comrades, which means "trustworthy." The story of Harish Chandra is known to the Hindus down through the ages; the example that he has set is engraved upon the mind of the whole race. The story of Hatim, a Sufi among Zoroastrians, has been a great inspiration to the people of Persia. In whatever part of the world, and in whatever period, by the thoughtful and those with an ideal, the word of honor will be valued the most.

There is a man of history; it may be his name was Chava, I have forgotten. He was a Rajput, a maharaja. There was a battle between that maharaja and the Mughal emperor of Delhi, and this battle continued for a very long time. And while the emperor of Delhi made many other maharajas come to his court and bow, it was only this one maharaja who said that as long as he lived he would never bow and, therefore, he had to go through a great many sacrifices. His power was decreasing, but his mind power was increasing. But he was of a very fine nature, and a very high ideal, and he was very fond of poetry.

When this emperor became very disheartened after a long battle, he then told the brave men of his court in confidence that there would be a very big prize given to the one who would bring the head of this maharaja, for this maharaja had caused very great trouble and great expense. No one in the court seemed to take a vow readily that "I will do it," except a poet. He was a great poet of the court of the emperor. Everybody laughed at him, all the big warriors; they said they could not do it with their armies. This poet said he would do it.

This poet went to the court of the Rajput and his great talent made an impression upon the Rajput; and perhaps this was a moment of some planetary influence working, that he happened to say, "Ask, O poet, I really do not know what to give you. There seems to be nothing in my treasury that is equal to your knowledge. Ask, what do you want me to give you? What can please you?" "No, King," he said, "do not promise that." "No, once promised it is promised," said the king. The poet asked, "Will you keep it?" He said, "You do not need to ask, a promise is a promise." The poet said, "I feel very embarrassed to ask you, but it is your head that I want." He at once unsheathed his sword, put it in the hand of the poet and said, "Here it is, a very small thing you have asked; it is not greater than the word I have given."

His people, his children, his family, they were all upset. His ministers became very upset. He was not upset at all. He was in good spirits. He said, "I have promised, it must be given; here it is." The poet said, "Now as you have promised me your head, what are you to do with your body? Why not the body also? Come along with me." He said, "Yes." He walked behind the poet: the poet first, he after.

The poet brought him alive to the court of the emperor, and there was a great excitement in the whole court, thinking that for years and years they have battled, and no one could bring him; yet here the poet brought him. In order to satisfy his vanity, the emperor asked the poet to bring him into the court. He should be brought as a prisoner. He was no prisoner, still he went where the poet took him. And the emperor looked at him, at that enemy with whom there was war for so many, many years, and he said, "You have come after all. But still it does not seem that your pride has gone, for you do not even think of bowing now that you have come to the court." He said, "Who must bow, a dead person? A dead person never bows. As long as he was living he never bowed. Now this is the dead body. Let anything be done with it. It is nothing."

No doubt the iron-hearted emperor overlooked that beauty which was shown by this maharaja and said that he was to be beheaded. But the poet said, "No, emperor, if he is to be beheaded, I am the first to be killed." The emperor said, "No, this one!" "No," the poet said, "Me also, for I will never find another soul who will appreciate my merit as he has done. He has given his life." So the poet died with this Rajput. And the son of this poet, the whole family came; they were all so gifted and inspired, they were just like the salt of the soil. Every one of them said one poem and died. The whole family of the poet was sacrificed for the sake of this maharaja, in his appreciation of that merit and that great virtue that he had shown.

And though he passed through that suffering, yet there was no suffering. His ideal had gone through the test; he died that death of honor which has made the record of his merit. It is not only one case. In many cases you will find the noble souls who have proven themselves to be on the path of God and spirituality; they have shown it in their esteem of the word. Once their word was given, if the whole earth were upset, they would keep to it just the same.

* * *

Question: *Will you please tell us why in the Islamic religion, which teaches the divine unity, God speaks of himself as "us"?*

Answer: In the English language it can only be translated as "we" and "us," but it is the manner in which, in ancient times, the ruler spoke. And why? The ruler did not speak as a person, but as the nation; therefore, God speaks as the whole being, the whole creation. "Us" means all the souls that exist; all are included.

Question: *Is it better then to keep to one's word, even if one finds later that one was mistaken in giving it?*

Answer: It depends upon what it concerns. A mistake is a mistake. This question has nothing to do with the keeping of one's word. Keeping one's word is more like a promise. Besides this, one speaks without thought when one has to change. But when a person makes the habit [of saying], "Yes, I spoke by mistake," then next time that person will make another mistake. But if one will always try to speak, whatever one speaks, without making a mistake, then in time one will be able to do so without a mistake.

I mean, it is not easy always for everybody to become so thoughtful and wise that everything they say is without mistakes. Mistake is in the nature of the human being. But try to make it less and less; there must be the tendency of making fewer mistakes. But it all depends upon a person's evolution. There is a certain state of evolution when one can maintain one's word; another, where one cannot maintain one's word, one is too weak to keep it. But by having the tendency, one will get that strength as one goes on, that desire and the esteem of the word. The more one alters, the more there is a tendency to alter, and the more one keeps, the more there is a tendency to keep it.

There was a very wonderful story of a girl, a Rajput girl born in Kashmir. She was playing with the little girls, somewhere around her house. And the maharaja, the king of that place, happened to be walking about in her street disguised as an ordinary man to see the condition of his subjects. He happened to come near these girls talking to one another. They were very young. This girl was about eight or nine years old. And they were all talking about the doll's marriage. Then that conversation came to the maharaja.

One of the girls happened to say, just unconsciously, when asked, "Who are you going to marry?" She said, "Maharaja," who was standing there. He was very amused. He was like her grandfather. Only he said to the parents of the child in a joke, "Now note it down, that when the marriage of this child will take place, the dowry must be given by the state as a gift of the maharaja."

Soon after that the maharaja died. And the girl grew up, and the time came for her marriage. But whenever there came a question of marriage, her words were, "I gave my word." People said, "The maharaja has died, what do you say?" She said only, "I have given my word." That was all people heard from her, never another word. It seemed as if it was born with her, that honor of the word. The word that was given was given.

No doubt, an ideal is such a thing that one could go to an extremity; as it is said in the Sanskrit language, "The extremity of all things must always be avoided as undesirable." One might go too far in any kind of virtue. But at the same time, ordinarily, it is not so. Ordinarily, one does not consider enough. For instance, one cannot be too good, one cannot; or in being true, one cannot be too true. The way that one can practice this is in one's everyday life, in every little thing one does, if one only thought, "What I have said, I must do, even if it be a very small thing."

"First was the word, and the word was God."[1] So really, when breaking the word, one breaks God. For the one who realizes that, then in every word one speaks one can see God. When one sees God in it, then God begins to speak, because then

1 John 1:1.

God comes through the word of that person. When one begins to realize this, then what one says becomes one's religion. It too is sacred for that person.

GRACIOUSNESS

No sooner has the soul touched the inner kingdom, which is the divine kingdom, than the true nobility of the soul becomes manifest from that soul in the form of graciousness. The sovereigns and those belonging to the aristocratic families were trained in the manner of graciousness, but it is born in the human heart. This means every soul shows the aristocratic manner from the moment it touches the inner kingdom. This shows that the true aristocracy is the nobility of the soul, when the soul begins to express in every feeling, thought, word, and action that graciousness which belongs to God.

Graciousness is quite different from that wrong manner which is termed in English patronizing. The gracious ones, before expressing that noble attribute, try to hide themselves even from their own eyes. The reason why the great ones are gracious, the truly noble people, is because they are more sensitive to all the hurt or harm that comes to them from the unripe. And therefore, out of their kindness, they try to keep themselves back from doing it to another, however small in position.

There is a story of a dervish who was standing in the royal road at the moment when the procession of the king was passing. Happy in his rags as he was, he did not at all mind who was coming. He did not move an inch on the warnings of the people who were running before the procession, till they pushed him away. Yet he did not move very far; he only said, "That is why."

There came the bodyguards on horseback; they did not push him but said, "Away, away dervish, do you not see the procession coming?" The dervish did not move an inch but only answered, "That is why." Then followed the noblemen. They saw the dervish standing. They did not like to tell him to move; they moved their own horses instead. The dervish, seeing that, said, "That is why." Then arrived the chariot of the king. His eyes fell on the dervish standing in rags boldly in the middle of the road. Instead of waiting for his bow, the king bowed himself, and the dervish answered, "That is why."

There was a young man standing by his side. He could not understand the meaning of those words, "That is why," for every treatment. And when he asked the dervish to kindly explain what he meant by those words, "That is why," he said, "It explains all I mean."

There is a great truth in what Christ has said in the Sermon on the Mount, that "Blessed are the humble, for they will inherit the kingdom of the earth."[1] This will always prove true, whatever be the time and evolution of the world. Be it the time of aristocracy, be it the period of democracy, the value of that nobility of nature which is expressed in graciousness will always command its price.

It is easy to know this word, but most difficult to practice it through life, for there is no end to the thought that needs to be given to every action in life. It wants judgment and the fair sense of weighing and measuring all one does. Besides that, it needs the fine sense of art and beauty, for in making the personality finished, one attains to the highest degree of art. Verily, the making of the personality is the highest art there is. The Sufis, whose life's object is to cultivate humane attributes, in which lies the fulfillment of the purpose of life, consider this as their religion.

A young man one day showed a little impatience to his aged father, who at his age could not hear very clearly and had asked

1 Matthew 5:5.

him two or three times to tell him again. Seeing the disturbed expression on his face, the father said, "My son, do you remember that there was a day when you were a little child and asked me what the bird was? And I said to you, 'the sparrow.' You perhaps asked me fifty times, and I had the patience to repeat it to you again and again, without being hurt or troubled about it. I was only pleased to tell you all I knew. Now, when I cannot hear you clearly, you can at least have patience with me if I did not hear you once, to explain it to me twice."

It seems that in order to learn that noble manner of life, what mostly is needed is patience, sometimes in the form of endurance, sometimes in the form of consideration, and sometimes in the form of forgiveness.

ECONOMY

There is a sense and a tendency of economizing, more or less, to be found in every soul. And when this tendency works with those around one, and with those with whom one comes in contact, one develops one's personality. The desire to spare another, if one could, of exercising patience, instead of trying to test the other's patience to its utmost, is the tendency of economy, a higher understanding of economy—to try and save another, spare another, from using energy in the way of thought, speech, and action. It all saves another person's energy, and for oneself it is adding beauty to one's personality. A person ignorant of this, in time, becomes a drag upon others. One may be innocent, but can be a nuisance for having neither consideration for one's own energy nor thought for the other's.

This consideration comes to one from the moment one begins to realize the value of life. As one begins to consider this subject, one spares oneself from unnecessary thought, speech, or action, and economically uses one's own thought, speech, and action. And by valuing one's own life and action, one learns to value the same for others.

The time of human life on earth is most precious, and the more one practices economical use of that time and energy which is most precious, the more one knows how to make the best of life. Speaking apart, even hearing another speak is a continual tension. It robs one of time and energy. When one cannot understand, or at least does not try to understand, something that can be said in one word, and wants it to be put in a sentence, one certainly has no sense of economy.

Economizing with one's money is of much less importance compared to economizing with one's life and energy, and that of others. For the sake of beauty, grace, dignity, and respect, when dealing with others one must go so far and no further. One cannot drive with the same whip a friend, an acquaintance, and a stranger. There again the question of economy must be considered. Those who are sensible enough to guard their own interest in life may be called clever. But those who guard the interests of others even more than their own are wise, for in doing so they, without knowing, do things to their own advantage also. It is the same sense of economy which one uses with little things in one's everyday life at home and in business. That same sense used in a higher form of thoughtfulness and consideration makes one more capable of serving others, which is the religion of all religions.

* * *

Question: *Will you please explain where the balance is to be found in keeping your word or not? To say a promise is a promise seems to me a little rigid.*

Answer: It does not seem rigid to me; on the other hand, it seems most fine. When one gives one's word, it is one's soul, it is one's own being. And the greater importance one attaches to one's word, the greater one becomes. What is the person? One is one's ideal. As high as the ideal is, so high is the person. If one's [ideal] is something which one can move away with one's shoes, it is nothing; it is like a football. A word is something like a jewel which is mounted on the royal crown. The word is a person's beauty, the radiance of one's face. When it is lost, the radiance is gone. There are those who, when their word is lost, would not want to live any longer; life has become distasteful. There is something godly in it, something divine, because it is the divine spark which gives that sense. There is something living in it. Therefore, what we call promise in a word is not the word, it is the sense of honor. And I think that if there is anything by which you can test how high people are, how fine their greatness, their goodness, that is the best way of testing them, by their word.

Question: *And circumstances may change?*

Answer: The circumstances always change, but God never changes. Why are we, with all the beauty that is in this world—the gems, jewels, and beautiful things—why are we seeking for something constant, reliable? We are looking for something that does not change.

Question: *Speaking of the playing of a part . . . capacity for concentration . . .*

Answer: No, playing a part is the outer thing. If our inner being is unmoved, if we single-mindedly concentrate on a certain spot, then the outer part does not matter. But really speaking, what is the life of a mystic, of a God-realized human being, if it is not playing a part? The mystic's life is nothing but playing the part. Not one part, but a thousand parts: a part one has to play as a servant, as a master, as a friend, as a son or daughter of one's parents, as a parent of one's children, as a neighbor of one's neighbors. And yet in the mind, the mystic realizes that oneness of all, that love of God, that love of the whole of humanity. In all capacities the mystic is playing a part and yet keeping the link with the truth which is within. It is all playing. In this way one will have to learn to play a part.

The further one advances in the spiritual path, the more one will have to learn to play the part. When it is said that the twelve apostles, after the blessing came upon them, were able to speak all the languages, it was playing the part. From that moment they learned to answer the question of each, in each person's own language and evolution. That inspiration is the playing of the part.

And about the word of honor, there is Harish Chandra's story, very well known in India, and produced as a play. People have never learned to tire of it. And for myself, this was the first drama I saw when I was a child, and it made such an impression that I came home and produced it with the children. But they would not trouble to learn it by heart, so I had to stand behind each child and say the part. The play is very interesting in its ideal, which shows a most high plane.

Harish Chandra was known to be a king who always kept his promise, and there was a discussion going on among the rishis, the great mystics with miraculous power. They discussed this: Is there a person who really keeps a promise? They said it exists in the ideal but no such person really exists, till one said, "I know of a king." "Can you give proof?" "Yes, I will." So the rishi went to court. The king was very surprised to see a monk of such a high order at the court. As a rule they never come to the court. He said, "King, in my need I have come to you." The king said, "Ask anything of me and I will do it." The rishi said, "Do you promise, King?" And he said, "Yes." So he asked him to give his kingdom, and 3,000 pounds more. The king said, "Yes, I will do it." So the kingdom was given to this man. Of course it was a great shock to his people and his ministers and his family. He had a queen and a son. He bade farewell and left the country, and his wife and son followed him. It made a great panic. They did not want him to go, for he was a very good king, but it was his promise and this was his last trial and he would not fail to fulfill his promise. They went, and no wealth was taken from the state; and the whole kingdom belonged to this rishi.

The king and queen suffered as they went through the forest without shoes. It was a new experience to them all. And then after six months, when they had suffered, the rishi came again and said, "King, you promised 3,000 pounds more." The king said, "No, I have not forgotten. What about it?" The rishi said, "It is just a matter of the word you gave." The king said, "No,

I won't take my word back." So they went to a little town, and a rich man made a contract that he would pay 2,000 pounds if the queen and their son would serve as domestics in the rich merchant's house. And it was agreed. And the king went with the rishi further to look for 1,000 pounds.

They came to another town where at the crematorium they were looking for a tax collector for that place, and they were glad to take Harish Chandra. He did his duty there, and so at last gave the 3,000 pounds in gold coins he had promised. Not one word—there was no speaking about it, he tried to forget it. No light was thrown upon his virtue; it was forgotten.

And so Harish Chandra continued life there, while the queen and prince continued their time as servants. They heard insults from the landlady who never knew a queen was serving, doing every kind of work that came along, never saying who they were. And it so happened that the prince was bitten by a serpent. This was the last shock to the queen, for he was their only child, and he passed away.

She had no friends to call upon for the funeral; she had to carry him to another country herself. And when she came to a crematorium, she found Harish Chandra standing at the gate as the tax collector. He saw a sad woman whom he did not recognize. He said, "Woman, have you brought your tax?" She said, "No, I am too poor." He said, "My master does not allow anyone to be cremated here who does not pay the tax."

He recognized his son and the queen, and saw her grief—but he stood firm in his duty. That was his last trial. He could have had his son cremated, but he still stood firm, never speaking to his wife, who did not recognize him. This moved all the spiritual hierarchy and proved his ordeal. There appeared the same rishi, bringing good tidings that his son should be awakened and his kingdom given back. It was just a trial. All righteous souls are put to the utmost trial, and the greater the soul, the greater the trial. But when they have passed through the trial and have stood firm, the end is nothing but bliss.

Question: *But a promise may be harmful for others and for yourself.*

Answer: That is a different thing, but if that happens it is better to break it and to repent.

Question: *Some man made a promise to help some spiritual movement. After some years he found that instead of helping the cause, of helping God, that society did not help, but held the light back.*

Answer: Discovering the truth, one should not blindly follow one's promise—one has not taken it away by dishonesty, but by realizing wisely that another thing is better.

JUSTICE

After having acquired refinement of character, the merits and virtues that are needed in life, the personality can be finished by the awakening of the sense of justice. The art of personality makes a statue into a fine specimen of art, but when the sense of justice is awakened, that statue comes to life. For in the sense of justice there is the secret of the soul's unfoldment.

Everyone knows the name of justice, but rarely can there be found someone who really is just by nature, in whose heart the sense of justice has been awakened. What generally happens is that every person claims to be just, though they may be far from being so. The development of the sense of justice lies in unselfishness. One cannot be just and selfish at the same time. Those who are selfish can be just, but for themselves. They have their own law best suited to themselves, and they can change it, and their reason will help them to do so in order to suit their own requirements of life.

A spark of justice is to be found in every heart, in every person, whatever be the stage of evolution in life. But the one who loves fairness, that one, so to speak, blows on that spark, thus raising it to a flame, in the light of which life becomes more clear. There is so much talk about justice, and there is so much discussion about it, there is so much dispute over it; and in the end one will find two persons arguing upon one certain point, and differing with one another, yet both thinking that they are just. Neither one of them will admit that the other is as just as oneself.

For those who really learn to be just, their first lesson is what Christ taught, "Judge ye not lest ye be judged."[1] One may say, if one will not judge, how will one learn justice? But the one who judges one's own self can learn justice, not the one who is occupied in judging others. In this life of limitations, if one only explored oneself one would find within oneself so many faults and weaknesses, and when dealing with others, so much unfairness on the part of oneself, that the souls who really want to learn justice, for them, their own lives will prove to be a sufficient object to practice justice.

Then again comes a stage in one's life, a stage of life's culmination, a stage of the soul's fuller development, when justice and fairness rise to such a height that one arrives at the point of being blameless. One has nothing to say against anyone, and if there is anything to say, it is only against one's self. And it is from this point that one begins to see the divine justice hidden behind this manifestation. It comes in one's life as a reward bestowed from above, a reward which is as a trust given by God, to see all things appearing as just and unjust in the bright shining light of perfect justice.

* * *

Question: *Is it not very difficult to avoid judging, because in order to become just one has to come to a certain conclusion?*

Answer: Yes, but what one generally does is not only that one judges anyone in one's mind, but one is very ready to give one's judgment out. A person is not patient enough to wait and analyze the matter and think about it more. As a rule one is not only ready to judge, but without any restraint on one's part one will express one's judgment instantly. A person does not think, "Have I the right to judge that person, have I risen to that stage

1 Matthew 7:1.

of evolution?" Jesus himself refused to judge, and said, "Whoever is faultless, it is that person's place to accuse or to punish."[2] That teaches a great lesson: that even in order to learn justice it is not necessary that we should be ready to judge and ready instantly to express our judgment, our opinion. The idea of the Sufis—who see in every form the divine form, in every heart the divine shrine—for them to judge anyone, whatever be that person's position, or action, or condition, is, in the first place, against their religion, which is their respectful attitude toward everyone. And in this manner they develop that philosophy which has been learned by them as intellectuality.

Question: *Does the fact of not blaming others mean that one does not see their faults any more, that we are above seeing them?*

Answer: No. In the first place, it is a question of self-restraint or of self-control, of politeness, of kindness, of sympathy, of graciousness; of a worshipful attitude toward God, the creator of all beings, and that all are God's children, good or bad. If any person's child happened to be homely in appearance, would it be polite to say before the parents, "Your child is homely"?

Then the father and mother of all beings is there, ever present, and knows what is going on in every person's heart. When we are ready to judge and express our opinion against God's creatures, with their faults and their merits before us, it is certainly against the artist who made them, and not behind God's back, but [in God's presence]. It would not be difficult to feel the presence of God everywhere, if we only were conscious of it.

Besides this, it is not that we only judge impartially the faults and merits of people—it is always our favor and disfavor which is connected with it. Our favor is always inclined to see the merit, our disfavor to see the fault. Is there any person, however great, without a fault? Any person, however wicked, without a merit? Then if we see more faults, it means that we close

2 See John 8:7.

our heart to a favorable attitude, and we open to that attitude which is unfavorable in order to criticize that person.

Now the other question: Are we above seeing them? Yes, there comes a time, after a continual practice of this virtue, when we see the reason behind every fault that appears to us in anyone we meet in our life. We see the reason behind, and we become more tolerant, more forgiving. For instance, there are those who are ill, who are creating disturbance in their atmosphere by crying or weeping or shouting. It disturbs us, and we say, "How terrible, how bad, how annoying, what a bad nature that person has." It is not the nature, it is the illness. If we looked from a different point of view, it is the reason that makes us tolerant, which can give rise to that forgiveness, the only essence of God, which can be found in the human heart.

Question: *If death as we understand it is not necessary, what is the alternative?*

Answer: Change. Life is change. What we call death is our impression of that change. It is change just the same. And if life is a change, then death is only a change of life.

EAR TRAINING

The art of personality is like the art of music: it wants ear training and voice-culture. To a person who knows life's music, the art of personality comes naturally, and it is unmusical of a soul, not only inartistic, when it shows the lack of this art in its personality. When one looks at every soul as a note of music and learns to recognize what note it is, flat or sharp, or high or low, and what pitch it belongs to, then one becomes the knower of souls and one just knows how to deal with everybody.

In our own actions, in our own speech, we show the art. We harmonize with the rhythm of the atmosphere, with the tone of the person, with the theme of the moment. To become refined is to become musical; it is those who are musical in soul who are artistic in their personality. When a word is spoken in a different tone, the same word changes its meaning. A word spoken at the proper moment, and held back at the moment when it should not be expressed, completes the music of life.

It is a continual inclination to produce beauty which helps one to develop art in personality. It is amusing how readily human beings feel inclined to learn the outer refinement, and how slow many souls are found to be to develop that beauty of personality inwardly. It must be remembered that the outer manner is meaningless if it is not prompted by the inner impulse toward beauty.

How pleased God is with humanity can be learned from the story of Indra, the king of paradise, at whose court *gandharvas* sing and *apsaras* dance. When interpreted in plain words, this means that God is the essence of beauty. It is God's love of beauty which has caused God to express God's own beauty in manifestation. And God is pleased to see beauty in manifestation, for it is God's desire fulfilled in the objective world.

It is amusing sometimes to watch how a good manner annoys someone who is proud of their bad manner. That person will call it shallow, because pride is hurt by the sight of something which that person has not got—as the one whose hand does not reach the grapes upon the tree says at this failure that the grapes are sour. And to some it is too fine to become refined, just as many will not like good music and are quite satisfied with the popular music. And many even become tired of good music, for it seems foreign to their nature. As it is not a merit to become unmusical, so it is not wise to turn against refinement. One must only try and develop beauty, trusting that the beauty is the depth of one's soul, and its expression in whatever form is the sign of the soul's unfoldment.

* * *

Question: *What is the difference between individuality and personality?*

Answer: Individuality is the consciousness of the soul of its oneness, in spite of its various possessions with which it still identifies. And that individuality can be seen in the child who says, "No, I do not want this toy, I want another toy." The moment it says "I," it becomes conscious of an individuality in spite of having the different organs of the body and different thoughts, and in spite of knowing that this is my hand, this is my foot, this is my head. One sees one's various parts and yet has the tendency of attributing to oneself all the different parts, still realizing that "I am one." It is the realization that, in spite of being many, I am one. In plain words, I am composed of many aspects. Personality is a development, an improvement of an individuality. When an individual becomes a person, that beauty which is hidden in an individual, which is divine, develops itself; and it is the development of that beauty which is personality—what we express of ourselves as an improvement to what we are.

Question: *If a child does not show a desire for beauty, can one teach the beauty, or can beauty not be taught?*

Answer: If the child does not show an inclination toward beauty, it is only that something is closed in the child. It does not mean that the beauty is missing there; in no soul, however wicked or stupid it might seem, [is beauty missing]; the beauty is still hidden there. And it is our trust and confidence in the greatness of the soul which will help us to draw out that beauty; in some sooner and some later, but some day that which is hidden must come out.

Only the difficulty is for everyone to have patience; we have not patience enough, that is the difficulty. The lack of beauty in some people strikes us so hard that we lose our patience and become pessimistic, and try to run away from them. In doing so we encourage them to become still worse. But if we had the patience to bear it, to endure it, and trust that in every soul there is a goodness and a beauty somewhere hidden, with patience we could explore it and dig it out. Some day or other we shall succeed.

This brings one to the belief in God. If once one believes that God is the parent, then parenthood teaches us that every child has the heritage of the parent. It is not only a philosophy, it is a religion, a moral; and by trusting in the divine beauty in every person, we, at the same time, develop that beauty in ourselves automatically, because we have the belief. It will not develop when one thinks, "I have that beauty, but another person has not got it." So many people think, "I have it," instead of forgetting ourselves and thinking that it could be found one day in the other person, if only we had patience to wait. As soon as we think, "Here is someone who is lacking beauty. Away, away! That person has not got what I have," we show pride and lock the door which otherwise could have been kept open for us to toil and work. And it is a weakness to turn our backs to anyone who might seem lacking that beauty which we expect. It is the opening of the heart to every soul, whatever their state of evolution, which alone will inspire the heart with that beauty; and by opening to that beauty one will find it coming to life.

Question: *Where does the quality of conceit come from, and why is it difficult to conquer?*

Answer: It is such a difficult thing to conquer, and it is almost impossible to get rid of. The reason is that where there is a light there is a shadow; there will be darkness as a contrast. So is conceit; it is an attribute of the ego. We call it that because it is the intoxication of the ego. The soberness of the ego may be called divine vanity. The intoxication of the ego is the conceit of the human being. It is so subtle. The word vanity has been used in a very ordinary sense of the word, and there being no equivalent word, it is very difficult to express it in any other way. Just like *vairagya*, indifference and independence—*kibriya*, for the divine vanity. But if plainly explained, it is that satisfaction of God which God wanted to derive by this manifestation. But it is again not the satisfaction of the ignorant soul which makes that person conceited. Only when satisfaction is in its proper place, then it is the greatest virtue. Sin and virtue are only the changes of place. It is the inspiration which its own beauty gives which causes the peacock to dance.

Question: *Where does conceit begin?*

Answer: No doubt conceit begins wherever there is comparison. Therefore, even to a small extent, it begins in the angelic sphere, and also in the jinn sphere. It completes itself in the human sphere, where it shows itself to the utmost. But really speaking, the understanding of vanity is the most enjoyable vision of life's phenomena. What the Sufi calls "wine" is the pleasure that the Sufi derives from that phenomenon. As soon as this phenomenon is disclosed to the soul, and the Sufi sees different actions in life, nothing disappoints, but everything gives a wonderful joy and offers such amusement that it is almost like a drink. That is what Omar Khayyam calls wine. "Amuse yourself and, by seeing the phenomena of life, get above the worries and anxieties that come from self-pity." Always you will find the seers, the most evolved seers, amusing themselves with life. Therefore, they are pleasant to speak with, pleasant in their atmosphere, and pleasant in every [way]. When the self is forgotten then there is no worry. Worry comes from fear. What is fear made of? The clouds of ignorance. Life will break up the clouds. One who wishes to be happy can find a thousand things to amuse oneself with and be happy. And if one wants to sorrow over things, one will find a million things to sorrow over.

Question: *How about living worrying about others?*

Answer: By worrying about them, we do not help them.

ATTITUDE

A friendly attitude expressed in sympathetic thought, speech, and deed is the principal thing in the art of personality. There is a limitless scope to show this attitude, and however much the personality is developed in this direction it is never too much. Spontaneity, the tendency of giving, giving that which is dear to one's heart—in this one shows the friendly attitude.

Life in the world has its numberless obligations toward friend and foe, toward the acquaintance and the stranger. One can never do too much to be conscientious of one's obligations in life and do everything in one's power in fulfilling them. To do more than one's due is perhaps beyond the power of every person, but in doing what one ought to do one does accomplish one's life's purpose.

Life is an intoxication, and the effect of this intoxication is negligence. The Hindu words dharma and *adharma*, religiousness and irreligiousness, both signify one's duty in life to be dharma, and the neglect of the same is *adharma*. The one who is not conscientious of one's obligations in life toward every being one comes in contact with is indeed irreligious.

Many will say that we try to do our best, but we do not know what it is; or, we do not know what is our due or how we are to find out what is really our due and what is not. No one in this world can teach what is anyone else's due, and what is not. It is for every soul to know for itself by being conscientious of its obligations. And the more conscientious one is, the more obligations one will find to fulfill, and there will be no end to them. Nevertheless, in this continual strife which might seem a loss in the beginning, in the end is the gain. For one who is wide awake will come face-to-face with one's Lord.

Those who neglect their duty to others, absorbed in life's intoxication, their eyes certainly will become dazzled and their minds exhausted before the presence of God. It does not mean that any soul will be deprived of the divine vision. It only means that the soul who has not learned to open its eyes wide enough will have the vision of God before it while its eyes are closed. All virtues come from a wide outlook on life; all understanding comes from the keen observation of life. Nobility of soul, therefore, is signified in the broad attitude that we take in life.

* * *

Question: *How can one work on personality unconsciously?*

Answer: The best thing is to develop in one's nature love for beauty, and that can be developed by admiration of beauty. Beauty's best expression is in human nature. And if we learn to appreciate and admire the beauty of human nature, and we are impressed by all we admire, then by all with which we come into contact, that becomes our property. In that way we can make a beautiful collection of what every person has to offer. It is the critical tendency and the lack of appreciation which keeps the personality back from progress. Because the best opportunity that life offers is to get all the good from every person. That opportunity is lost by seeing the bad side and overlooking the good. But if we saw some good in every person, we could take and collect it; and in this way we develop the love of art. It is just like someone going from here to China and different countries, and finding the best pieces of art, collecting them and then making a museum, such as the Musée Guimet.[1] When in a material way a person can do this, in a higher way it can also be done.

1 A museum of Asian art in Paris. Inayat Khan occasionally lectured there.

By taking the good of a person, one does not rob that person of the good. We only appreciate it and come closer to that person, and by that become richer and richer with beauty. And beauty so collected, in the end, results in a beautiful personality. There is never an end: in the most ordinary person there is something to be found, something we can learn from every person if we only had the desire to appreciate and find good in that person, and if the good were hidden, to try and draw it out. And to draw out good from another person, what does it want? It wants currency. What is currency? Goodness in oneself. Give that currency, and it gives back that which is hidden there.

Question: *How can a soul always know its duty? May not over-scrupulousness bring confusion of thought and wrong action?*

Answer: Over-goodness or over-kindness or over-lovingness—"over" is always bad. But what generally is the case, what one always finds, is the intoxication. Soberness is very difficult. The life has its effect of intoxication upon every soul—on a saint, a sage, on everyone. That intoxication is overwhelming; it keeps a person back from a clear understanding. And therefore, however far advanced a person, even in the spiritual life, one can never be too sure of oneself, that one will not be taken up in this intoxication because one is breathing it in with everything one smells or tastes or hears, which veils everything else. Therefore, one cannot be too conscientious.

For instance, such a case may be found in the mind of a person who is unbalanced, who already has a confusion—one does not know whether one has done wrong or right. I am not talking about that person at all. That person I do not call conscientious. That person I call confused, someone who does not know what he or she is doing. A conscientious person does not discuss it, only that person is continually wide awake, and always asks, "Where should I have done something?" or "Why have I not done it?" in every situation or condition. But one does not confuse oneself. One just does what one thinks right. And if it happens that it turns out to be wrong, the next time it will be right. The person who wants to do right will do wrong once, twice, thrice, but in the end will do right, because one wants to do right.

Question: *Will you please tell us if it is possible to guard against the moments of kamal in which accidents may happen?*

Answer: No, one must not trouble about it. Because the thought of accident attracts accident. It is best not to trouble about it. But in order to avoid such accident, the best thing is to keep tranquil, because all accidents come when the tranquility of mind is disturbed. And if one keeps one's mind in a proper balance, no accident will come. An accident always follows the broken rhythm of mind. When the mind has lost its rhythm, then there is an accident. But you may say, when a person has a motorcar accident, is it their fault? Not the fault of the chauffeur? But the answer may be: maybe it is the fault of the chauffeur, or maybe it is one's own fault, in that one's mind has upset the chauffeur, or someone else's. The accident might come from another motorcar, and also be reflected by that person's mind. No one can blame the other because they do not know. An accident is not natural. It is something unnatural, and something undesirable. For instance, a false note or lack of rhythm was not meant by the composer. The composer did not mean it. And when a person plays it, it is a mistake, it is not a desire.

RECONCILIATION

Any efforts made in developing the personality or character must not be for the sake of proving oneself superior to others, but in order to become more agreeable to those around one and to those with whom one comes in contact.

Reconciliation is not only the moral of the Sufi, but is the sign of the Sufi. This virtue is not learned and practiced easily, for it needs not only good will but wisdom. The great talent of the diplomat is to bring about such results as are desirable, with agreement. Disagreement is easy; among the lower creation one sees it so often. What is difficult is agreement, for it wants a wider outlook, which is the true sign of spirituality. Narrowness of outlook makes the horizon of a person's vision small. That person cannot easily agree with another.

There is always a meeting ground for two people, however much they differ in their thought. But the meeting ground may be far off, and a person is not always willing to take the trouble of going far enough if that were required in order to make an agreement. Very often one's patience does not allow one to go far enough where one could meet with another. In an ordinary case, what happens is that everyone wants another to meet one in the same place where one is standing. There is no desire to move from the place where one stands.

I do not mean that a person, in order to become a real Sufi, must give up an idea in order to meet in agreement with another. And there is no benefit in always being lenient to every thought that comes from another; there is no benefit in always erasing our own idea from our own heart. But that is not reconciliation. Those who are able to listen to another are the ones who will make another listen to them. It is those who easily will agree with another who will have the power of making another easily agree with them. Therefore, in doing so, one gains in spite of the apparent loss which might sometimes occur. When one is able to see from one's own point of view as well as from the point of view of another, one has complete vision and clear insight. One sees, so to speak, with both eyes.

No doubt friction produces light, but light is the agreement of the atoms. For stimulus to thought, if two people have their own ideas and argue upon their different ideas, it does not matter so much. But when a person argues for the sake of argument, the argument becomes a game. That person has no satisfaction in reconciliation. Words provide the means of disagreement. Reasons become the fuel for that fire. But wisdom is when the intelligence is pliable; it understands all things, the wrong of the right and the right of the wrong.

The soul who arrives at perfect knowledge has risen above right and wrong. That soul knows them and yet knows not. One can say much, and yet, what can one say? Then it becomes easy for that soul to reconcile with each and all.

There is a story that two Sufis met after many years, having traveled along their own lines. They were glad to meet each other after many years' separation, for the reason that they were both murids of the same murshid. One said to the other, "Tell me please your life's experience." "After all this time's study and practice of Sufism, I have learned one thing: how to reconcile with another, and I can do it very well now. Will you please tell me what you have learned?" The other one said, "After all this time's study and practice of Sufism, I have learned to know how to master life, and all that there is in this world is for me, and I am the master. All that happens, happens by my will."

There came the murshid whose murids they both were. And both spoke of their experience during this journey. The murshid said, "Both of you are right. In the case of the first, it was self-denial in the right sense of the word which enabled him to reconcile with others. In the case of the other, there was no more of his will left; if there was any, it was the will of God."

MORAL CULTURE

Moral Culture consists of a series of lectures given from 1915 to 1920. First published by the Sufi Movement in 1937, *Moral Culture* was printed by Ae. E. Kluwer, Deventer, Holland.

PART I

THE LAW OF RECIPROCITY

Reciprocity

In dealing with another we ought first to consider in what relation we stand to the other person, and then to consider what manner of dealing would please us on the part of another who is related to us in the same way as we are to that person. In all favorable actions we ought to do more than we should expect another to do for us, and in unfavorable actions we ought to do less than what we should expect from the part of another.

Duty must be first borne in mind to consider in what relation we stand with regard to our relatives, neighbors, fellow citizens, the people of our nation and of our race, and with the people in the world at large. For instance, favor shown to a neighbor and disregard to a relative in the home, sympathy shown to a foreigner while we feel bitter toward our own nation—these dealings, however unselfish and broad-minded they may appear, are undesirable. It is just like trying to make a sketch of a human face before even having learned how to draw a straight or a parallel line.

"Charity begins at home." We should first begin to practice our sympathy with those who are akin to us, for we are in duty bound to look after them and their benefit. But instead of widening our sympathies, we keep within our own small circle. Therefore, we may, perhaps, never progress in life or advance to the higher standard of humanity. This is the only drawback to modern civilization, which confines itself to the thought of nationalism and advances no further. Yet this is better than the above-explained broad-mindedness, which makes one favor the outsider and neglect, and even disfavor, those akin to us.

The best way would be gradually to widen our sympathies, with a consideration of our duty and relationship to others, gradually expanding them from those who are nearest to us to those who are most remote. A sense of generosity and willingness should go hand in hand with duty; if not, instead of bliss, it becomes a curse.

Our Dealings with Our Friends

In friendship we must realize that a friend, inferior in position or poorer in life than we, must not for one moment be regarded as such. When one is a friend, in whatever condition one may be or whatever position one may occupy, the friend must be considered our equal; and the same spirit of equality should be borne in mind in dealing with a friend, however high that friend's position may be. Convention should not be more than is necessary for the friend's evolution. The sense of difference in every aspect of dealing with a friend must be avoided. There must be no secrets between true friends.

The use of friendship for a selfish motive is like mixing bitter poison with sweet rose-syrup; and it is necessary to be ready, without the least hesitation, to serve a friend attentively in every capacity of life, not expecting for one moment any thanks or return.

A friend, in the true sense of the word, is nearer and closer than our own family, relations, neighbors, nation, and race. The secret of the friend should be kept as one's own secret; the fault of the friend one should hide as one's own fault; the honor of the friend must be considered as one's own honor; an enemy of the friend should be regarded as our enemy; a friend of the friend must be considered as our friend. One must not boast of friendship but must practice it, for the claimants are so often false. In the despair of the friend, consolation must be given; in the poverty of the friend, support is necessary; in the shortcoming of the friend, overlooking is necessary; in the trouble of the friend, help should be given; with the joy of the friend, rejoicing is right.

Today friendly and tomorrow unfriendly cannot for one moment be called friendship; the value of friendship is in its constancy. Forbearance, patience, and tolerance are the only conditions which keep two individual hearts united. There is a saying in Hindustani by Summan, on friendship: "Stand by your friend in your friend's time of need, like the reed on the bank of the river." When one is sinking in the water and catches hold of it, it will save one if it is strong; and if not, it sinks also with that person.

Our Dealings with Our Enemies

Our dealings with our enemy should be more delicately considered than our dealings with a friend. This fact is generally overlooked by us, and we deal in any way with an enemy while we are considerate with a friend. Sometimes one insults one's enemy, spoiling thereby one's own habit, and making the enemy still more insulting. Sometimes, by constantly dwelling on the faults of the enemy, one impresses one's own soul with the same faults and focuses the same upon the soul of the enemy; if the enemy lacks these faults, they may, by reflection, develop and cause the enemy to become a still bitterer enemy.

It is unwise to underestimate the enemy's bitterness and power to do harm, as it is to overestimate them. In many cases one, blinded by one's own ego, fails to estimate the power of the enemy, when one says, "Oh, what can that person do? What do I fear?" giving way to an impulse when driven to it by the enemy. This is a defeat; keeping steadfast and calm under such circumstances is a victory. Complaining about the harm caused by the enemy is a weakness. Avoiding it by taking precautions, facing it with strength and checking it with power are the things worth doing. It is wise to take advantage of the criticism made by an enemy, for it can help to correct us; and it is foolish when one laughs it off, considering oneself to be too good to be like that.

In the case of revenge, an eye for an eye and a tooth for a tooth is right in such a case when one is sure that kindness and forgiveness will have no power whatever upon the hard heart of the enemy but, on the contrary, will make the enemy worse. But so long as there is a chance of meeting the enemy's revenge by kindness the above law must not be practiced. It is better to suppress the enemy before that enemy can rise against us; and it is right to throw the enemy down when that enemy has risen against us.

It is wise to be watchful of the movements of the enemy, and to safeguard oneself against them; and it is foolish to allow oneself to be watched, and to let the enemy safeguard against us. It is right to decrease the power of the enemy in every way possible, and to increase one's own power and make it much greater than the enemy's. It is right to know the secret of the enemy; and it is more than right to keep our secret from the enemy. Precaution must be taken that nobody should become our enemy; and especially care must be taken to keep a friend from turning into an enemy. It is right, by every means, to forgive the enemy and to forget the enmity if the enemy earnestly wishes it; and to take the first step in establishing friendship, instead of withdrawing from it and still holding in the mind the poison of the past, which is as bad as retaining an old disease in the system.

Distinction of Grades

We find two tendencies working through different individuals: (*a*) recognition of grades, (*b*) nonrecognition of the same. The first may be seen when a person says, "He is my chief—he is my professor—she is my mother—he is my father's maternal uncle—therefore, I have to consider him or her." And the other tendency we see when someone says, "What do I care if he is the head in my office?— I do not care if he is older in age—I do not care if she is my aunt—What do I care if he is my mother's grandfather?" We see gentleness in one and spirit in the other, and prefer them according to our nature. If we are spirited, we like the spirit of independence; and if we are gentle, we prefer gentleness.

A Sufi does not believe in one-sided tendencies. The Sufi says spirit is wanted and gentleness is needed; both are required on suitable occasions. The question arises of how are we to act: when should we show spirit, and when should we consider gentleness? Spirit should be shown when we are forced by circumstances, by a situation, to be in subordination; there spirit is needed to free oneself and be independent. But the use of spirit is not a simple matter. A match cannot stand against the air; to stand against the air you must have a torch. Therefore it is the foolish spirited ones who rebel against their life's conditions and fall through lack of enough spirit together with strength and power. For them, patience and gradual perseverance with courage and thought are necessary. But when we are morally won by someone's love and kindness—such as the care of a mother, the protection of a father, the advice of an aged friend, the sympathy of a neighbor, by the one who shows us the right path through life, by the one who may have guided humanity to light—to consider their greatness, to revere them, to respect them, to obey them can never be subordination but generosity on our part. But in this, all may not be dealt with by the same words, and all may not be treated in the same manner. The Qur'an says, "We have created among jinns and humans individuals of all grades." In this way, we must distinguish to what extent gentleness may be shown to deserving souls.

Our Dealings with God

God, to the Sufi, is not only a heavenly sovereign, or an ideal of worship, but a friend, a beloved, nearer and dearer than all others in the world; and our dealings with God must be as the dealings of an earnest lover with the beloved. When it is the time of worship, we must worship God as the soldier saluting the sovereign as the soldier's duty; but at the time of communion, we must commune with God as a lover would with the beloved.

All things we do, if they are pure, ideal, and satisfactory to others, we must attribute to God; and all things we do which are not our ideal, nor satisfactory to others, for them we must blame ourselves. Because all that comes from perfection is ideal and satisfactory, therefore its praise belongs to God who alone is praiseworthy. That which is not ideal and unsatisfactory comes from imperfection, which our imperfect self represents. Every action of kindness we do to another, we must do for God; and there will be no disappointment. For if we do it for a person whom we love or trust, who after a time may prove unworthy of our love and be undeserving of our trust, we become disappointed and discouraged in doing kindness to another or in placing trust in another.

We must give our every day's account to God, our divine ideal; lay before God our shortcomings, humbly repentant, without missing a day; and ask for help from God, who is almighty, to give us strength and courage to do better tomorrow. We should never pride ourselves on good doings, for God's goodness is greater than the greatest good we could ever do. It only produces in us false vanity, the only veil which hides God from our sight. We must begin to feel God's presence in this manner, and surely, after some time, God will become a living entity before our sight, and all will seem dead save God alone, the Living Being. When this stage is reached, then begins divine communion.

How to Take the Dealings of Others with Us

By the constant study of life, the Sufi realizes that humankind, which claims to be the most just in all creation, is found to be most unjust in the end. One is just, generally, when judging another, but is unjust when the thing concerns self, though one is not conscious of it and calls it justice too. Therefore the lesson that the Sufi learns in the law of reciprocity is to consider it a natural thing when injustice manifests from others. But Sufis try in every dealing with others to be as just as they can. They tolerate the injustice of others as much as their state of evolution permits them, but when they see that more than this is intolerable, they, by the way of explanation, by the way of temptation, even by the way of threatening, stand against it. But the tolerance with which they overlook the injustice of others, is for others only; when it comes to their own dealings with others, they do not tolerate even the slightest injustice on their own part. The sense of justice is not the same in everybody; it is according to a person's evolution and ideal.

Gracious dealings of others must be graciously received; harsh dealings of others we should take smilingly, pitying them in mind that they are not evolved enough to be gentle in their dealings. When doing a kindness to others, the first thing that must be considered is that it must be unselfish, not even for an appreciation or a return. Who does good and waits for a return, is a laborer of good. Who does good and overlooks it, is the master of good and has engraved upon the universal consciousness good; and its reecho will be no other than good.

How to Take the Dealings of Our Friends with Us

It is always confusing to the thoughtful to decide upon the right way of action when in contact with people of different temperaments and different in their evolution of life. And to the right-thinking person it becomes a puzzle when, in the bond of friendship, one has to put up with ill dealings on the part of friends. The first essential thing one must understand in friendship is to be slow in making friendship, and slower still in breaking it. Children become friends a thousand times in a day; and a thousand times they fight over little things and become unfriendly. If grown-up people do the same, it at once shows to the seer the grade of their evolution.

The consideration of others' dealings with us must not be weighed with our dealings with them, for the self is always dearer to everyone. And when weighing one's dealings with others we naturally give them more weight and do not take others' dealings with the same weight. Therefore, in order to make a balance we must always consider that a kind action, a good thought, a little help, some respect shown to us by another are more than if we did the same to our friend. But an insult, a harm done to us, a disappointment caused to us by a friend, a broken promise, deceit, or anything we do not like on the part of a friend should be taken as less blameworthy than if we did the same. Every good and kind action of a friend we ought to appreciate very much, and the same done to a friend by us we should think is not enough. We ought to blame the friends less for their dealings that are blameworthy; but for the same, we ought to accuse ourselves most. This makes the balance, and this is true reciprocity. A person who goes on making friends every day, and breaking friendship every other day, remains all through life friendless. But the one who is charitable to the friend and strict to oneself in all dealings who will prove to be the true and good friend worth having in life.

How to Take the Dealings of Our Enemies

When dealing with enemies one must bear in mind that there is a possibility of exaggerated imagination, for the least little wrong done by the enemy seems to be a mountain of wrong, as a least little right done by the friend seems to be mountains of right. It is timid to overestimate enemies above what they are; and it is stupid to estimate them at less than their real power.

Allowing the enemy to insult or harm, according to the law of reciprocity, is a fault; paying back insult for insult and harm for harm is the only thing that balances. In dealing with the enemy one must first compare the enemy with one's own self in intelligence, in power—whether it is possible to stand against the enemy and enmity or not. In the case where there is a possibility with might and courage and with intelligence, bend the enemy down before the enemy does that to us, for in enmity the first blow is to the advantage of the giver. In case we find ourselves weaker or less than enemies, the best thing would be not to show enmity until we developed to the power of standing against them. Wait with patience and trust until that time comes, till then keep peace and harmony, which is not deceit in the sense of reciprocity.

It is against wisdom to allow anybody to become our enemy if we can possibly help it. We should always refrain from this, and be cautious in all affairs of life lest we cause anybody to become our enemy; for the enemies we have in life are enough. Weakness should never be shown to enemies—always hold out the strong part before them. Never give them a chance to prepare a blow, and we should see that they get it from us before they prepare.

There must not be a moment's delay on our part to harmonize and to be friendly if the enemy desires so; nor must we lose one moment to be friends with the enemy if it is in our power. We must be always ready to become a friend to the enemy, and try our best to do it, unless by doing so we add to the vanity of the enemy.

It is most undesirable to be the pioneer in starting an enmity. It is that one who is more blameworthy, and from that one's part the effort of harmonizing should come. Sometimes by thinking bitterly of someone we produce enmity in the person's heart that may not have been there before; it only sprang from our imagination. The same rule applies to friendship. If we think strongly with love of someone, even of an enemy, our power of mind will turn the enemy into a friend.

How to Take the Dealings of Others according to Our Own Grade

The dealings of others differ in their nature according to our relation with them. For instance, a close companion has said something to tease us—we should take it as a jest; whereas the same words spoken by our servant, or by a person who is not so intimate as to joke with us, we should take as an insult, which shows that it is not the dealing that makes the effect, but the relation we are in with another that changes the effect. Dictation on the part of parents, teachers, elderly people, or a superior in office, business, wealth, position, or sense, does not become so hard as when it comes from a person younger in age, inferior in position, or devoid of sense.

It is always wise to associate with one's equals in thought, position, and power, trying always to progress and enter a still higher circle, not merely by ambition but with fitness. In every capacity of life self-respect must be preserved, and by thought, speech, and action we must guard ourselves against humiliation.

If another person treats us badly without reason or justice, we must fight against it, and prove by doing so that the dealing was improper. But if we ourselves are in fault, we should blame ourselves before resenting the bad dealing on the part of the other. If someone deals with us much better than we deserve, we should not become oblivious of the fact that we do not deserve this good treatment; we should count it as a kindness on that person's part. In case we find that we have deserved the good treatment given us by another, we should not take it as something on which to pride ourselves or to be vain about; but we must take it as a strength to have hope to become still better, that the goodness of God may manifest through us.

God's Dealings with Us

It is generally the case that people, in their pleasant experiences in life, attribute that goodness to their own worthiness; and unpleasant experiences people consider to be the wrath of God. The right way to consider it, is that every pleasant experience should be counted as God's great mercy for one's very small goodness, which cannot be compared with divine mercy—still an encouragement to increase the goodness in oneself. And every unpleasant experience must be considered as God's small wrath for our great evil, to teach us the lesson to refrain from it and to see divine mercy in both—in the former evident, in the latter hidden.

A wise person is the one who keeps the balance even between faith and fear: faith in God's mercy such that "If the whole virtuous world were drowned, I, with my faith in God's mercy, shall be saved, like Noah in his ark"; and fear such that "If the whole wicked world were saved, I may be taken to task by the wrath of God." Those who do not understand this moral are apt to go astray by seeing the wicked enjoying, and by looking at the suffering of the virtuous.

The world and its life is an illusion before the untrained eye. It deludes, puzzles, and creates all confusion before human eyes. And the first step toward the right direction is to watch the pleasure and displeasure of God by closely watching life, and constantly to endeavor to walk in the path of God's pleasure, and to refrain from taking the path of those who act to God's displeasure.

PART 2:
THE LAW OF BENEFICENCE

Our Dealings with Our Friends

Friendship, as the average person understands it, is perhaps a little more than acquaintance; but in reality it is more sacred than any other connection in the world. To a sincere person, entering into friendship is as entering the gates of heaven; and a visit to a friend is a pilgrimage to a true, loving friend.

When, in friendship, a thought comes: "I will love you as you love me," or "I will do to you as you do to me," this takes away all the virtue of friendship, because it is a commercial attitude which is prevalent everywhere in the commercial world: everything is done for a return, and measure is given for measure. Friendship must be the contrary pole to the practical side of life, for when one is tired by the selfish surroundings around one in the world, one feels inclined to take refuge under the love and kindness of a sympathetic friend. But if there is a question of selfishness in friendship, where can a soul tired and annoyed with the selfish surroundings of the world go?

Friendship is just like recreation after the toil of the day. It is to speak or to be with someone who is different from all others in life. But the difficulty comes that everyone thinks that one's friend ought to prove worthy of one's ideal, which in the end disappoints. For the law of beneficence teaches this: that goodness is worthwhile which can withstand even badness, that kindness is valuable which can withstand tyranny. Every soul is not ready to follow this ideal, and it depends to what extent one is strong enough to withstand. By having an ideal, one develops in the end, if not in the beginning, to the same ideal which one keeps before one.

A friendship to carry out one's aims and objects in life by the love and kindness of a friend is all business. The unselfish friend is the pure one, and it is such a friendship that will last; and a selfish friendship will vanish. For the selfish friend will create in the heart of a friend selfishness, and the unselfish friend will create in the heart of a friend unselfishness. One gets, sooner or later, what one gives, for the heart knows the condition of the heart. Therefore there is no better principle than wishing good to the friend, speaking good of the friend, doing good to the friend, with all kindness and love, having no thought for one moment of the friend's deserving your goodness, kindness, or love.

Our Dealings With Our Relations

Our love, kindness, service, and sympathy are due to people in the world, and especially to those around us, according to their expectation. A stranger naturally expects less than an acquaintance, an acquaintance expects less than a friend, and a friend, less than relations. Therefore these have more right to ask for our love and service, and it is our first duty to give it to them. It does not matter if they do not give us the same, or if they do not prove worthy of our ideal. It is a mistake for wise people to expect the same from them or to expect everyone to prove worthy of our ideal, when it is difficult even for ourselves to prove worthy of our own ideal. However greatly we may think of ourselves, in the end of examination we fail. Therefore the wise thing would be to do all the good we can to those who expect it from us, and especially to those who consider it their right to expect it from us, without even thinking whether they will return it or whether they deserve it.

There are some who stand by their relations with pride. Taking the part of the relation and standing by the relation with pride is right, for this is the first step toward human brotherhood and sisterhood. A person cannot jump at once to universalism. There are some who have a sort of natural hatred of their relations, and they love those who have no connection with them. But they are mistaken, for one who cannot love one's own family will never be able to consider another person as family, because one has neglected learning this lesson at home. Apart from hating relations, a wise person will not even hate an enemy. By hating relations for their unworthiness you make them more unworthy; whereas by loving them, some day you will be able to draw out the worthiness that you want in them.

Harmony at home spreads out and makes the world harmonious for us; and inharmony at home spreads out throughout the world, and builds an inharmonious world for us. For instance, a person who has quarreled at home and gone to China, and settled there to have peace, has taken the inharmony to China and can never be at peace all through that person's life.

However badly situated we may be in life, if we try our best and master the situation, it is far better and greater than wishing to change the situation, which is nothing but a weakness. Among relations it is so wonderful when there is harmony between brothers and sisters, a link of love and harmony between spouses, and especially love and devotion between parents and children. Verily, there is no greater light than love.

Our Dealings with Servants

We are so situated in life that, whatever position we may occupy in life, we are never independent, we are never self-sufficient. Therefore every individual depends upon others for help, and others depend upon that person for help—only the position of the person who is one among many who help becomes lower in the eyes of those who count themselves among the few who can help. This makes every person a master and a servant as well. And yet everyone forgets, in the intoxication of one's mastership, one's place as a servant, and looks upon the person who stands to help one as one's servant. The wise, whose feelings are awakened, think on this question deeply, and do their best to avoid every chance of even giving an idea to servants of their servantship, apart from insulting them in any way or hurting their feelings. We are all equal, and if we have helpers to serve us in life we ought to feel humble and most thankful for the privilege, instead of making the position of the servant humble.

It is wise to avoid putting one's own burden on another, however exalted we may be in our position in life. It is right to share the work with the servant, however humble it may seem; for there is nothing too humble to do of what must be done in life. If one can do a certain thing, one need not leave it to a poor person to do because one is higher in position. It is necessary to take help, but it is just to do everything that comes in life, regardless of one's riches, power, or position in life.

The moral of the ancients was that a servant was considered as a child of the family, and was never allowed to feel lower in any way than the members of the family. One cannot commit a greater sin than hurting the feeling of the one who serves us, depending upon our help. Once the Prophet heard his grandson call a servant by his name. On hearing this, he at once said to his grandson, "No, child, that is not the right way of addressing elders. You ought to call him 'uncle.' It does not matter if he serves us, we are all servants of one another, and we are equal in the sight of God." There is a verse of Mahmud Ghaznavi: "The emperor Mahmud, who had thousands of slaves to wait on his call, became the slave of his slaves when love gushed forth from his heart." Nobody appears inferior to us when our heart is kindled with kindness and our eyes are open to the vision of God.

Our Dealings with Masters

It is natural for every person to have a master, from a beggar to a sovereign. There is no soul on earth who has not another under whose control and command one is expected to act: in school, under the teacher; in the army, under the commanding officer; in the workshop, under the foreman; in a nation, under a sovereign, or a president, or an officer, or a leader. There is no aspect of life that exempts a person from this. In this situation it is wise to act toward one's own superior as one would expect consideration from one's inferior.

Faithfulness, respect, good manners, sincerity, attention—these it is always necessary to show in our dealings with our superiors in life; and those who lack these finds that the others from whom they expects also lack them. Children who are insolent to their parents will always see insolence in their own children; those who have been abrupt to their chief will always meet with abruptness in their servants. It is the law of nature. Therefore a respectful manner and goodwill to one's master in any aspect of life are always worthwhile.

Our Dealings with Acquaintances

We must always try to develop our acquaintanceship to friendship, at least with possible people; but with impossible ones we should try at least to continue acquaintance, instead of going from acquaintance to estrangement. A person always asks, "Can we make friends with everybody, for friendship is such a rare thing?" And so one perhaps waits, with one's high ideal, all through life, and does not meet one's ideal friend; and as one passes by all those with whom one becomes acquainted, one in a way avoids the chance of friendship with them, thinking they are not worth it. It is easy for every person to say about another that the person is not worth making friends with; but one does not know how much worth one is oneself.

Therefore, the wise are thankful when they see anybody with more or less friendly inclination toward them, and make the best of the opportunity in taking three benefits from it. The first, that by being friends with someone one develops in one's own self the spirit of friendliness. The second, that one adds one more to the circle of one's friends. And the third, the joy of exchanging love and kindly feelings, which is greater and better than anything in the world. There is all benefit in widening one's circle of friends, and there is all loss when one loses a friend from one's circle.

One ought to look upon acquaintanceship as the sowing of the seed of friendship, not as a situation forced upon one; for those who turn their back and look at a person with contempt do that to God. To think, "That person is perhaps of no value, that person is of no importance," is unpractical, besides being unkind. As all things have their use, both flowers and thorns, both sweet and bitter, so all human beings are of use: what position, what class, what race, what caste they belong to, makes no difference. Friendship with good and bad, with wise and foolish, with high and low is equally beneficial, whether to yourself or to the other. What does it matter if another be benefited by your friendship, since you would like to be benefited by the friendship of another? That person is wise who treats an acquaintance as a friend, and a person is foolish who treats a friend as an acquaintance. And a person is impossible who treats friends and acquaintances as strangers; you cannot help such a person.

Our Dealings with Our Neighbors

The word *neighbor* is used in tradition for those who are around us at home, or at the office, or in the workshop. Tulsidas, the Hindu poet, says that the essence of religion is kindness. Those who are inclined to do kindness in life must not discriminate among the people around them—those to whom they must be kind, and those to whom they must not be kind. However kind and good one may be to the one whom one likes, to those one wishes to be kind to, that person cannot be called kind by nature. Real kindness is that which gushes out from the heart to the worthy and to the unworthy.

There are some people who are kind by nature and yet do not know the way of its expression; and therefore, with all their kindness, they prove in life to be unkind. There are different ways of expressing kindness. Among them are the following few: to be harmless, to be undisturbing, and to be considerate to those around us. These three are the first principles of kindness.

By harmlessness is meant that though human beings do not seem to harm other humans as the animals of the forest harm one another, yet by keen study one sees that human beings can harm another human more than the wild animals harm one another. For humanity is the outcome of the development of the whole creation; therefore the ego, which makes one selfish, is developed in humans more than in any other creature. Selfishness keeps one blind through life, and one scarcely knows when one has caused another harm.

By not disturbing is meant that even a little crudeness of thought, speech, or action can disturb another, which a person easily does in life without considering. And the sense of a human being has the delicacy of God. It disturbs another very much when we do not even notice crudeness on our part.

By consideration is meant that one's life in the world is a life of poverty—poverty in some way or other even if one lives in a palace. In the Qur'an it is said, "God alone is rich, and everyone on earth is poor." Humans are poor with their myriad needs, their life's demands, the wants of their natures; and when one keenly observes life, it seems that the whole world is poverty-stricken, everyone struggling for the self. In this struggle of life, if one can be considerate enough to keep one's eyes open to all around one, whom circumstances have placed about one in life, and sees in what way one could be of help to them, one becomes rich and inherits the kingdom of God.

Our Dealings with Our Fellow Human Beings

To be just and fair to our fellow human beings is not only a virtue, but a benefit to ourselves, even from the practical point of view. Sometimes a person thinks, "I have got the better of another, and thereby I have profited; so at the loss of virtue, I have been benefited." The secret is that our benefit in life depends upon the benefit of others. We are dependent upon each other. The inner scheme of working is such that it gives among all, the share of the mutual loss and benefit, though outwardly it does not seem to do this. Human beings are deluded and kept from realizing this fact, because they see one is in pain while another has pleasure, when they see that one is benefited by the loss of the other. It is true that it is so in the outer plane, but it is not so in the inner workings. The robber, after having robbed, is as restless during the night as the one who is robbed. Christ's teaching to be kind and charitable, and the teaching of all other teachers who showed humanity the right path, though it seems different from what one could see from the practical point of view which is perhaps called common sense, is yet, according to uncommon sense, in other words, super-sense, perfectly practical. If you wish to be charitable, think of the comfort of another; if you wish to be happy, think of the happiness of your fellow human beings; if you wish to be treated well, treat others well; if you wish that people should be just and fair to you, come out first to set an example yourself.

Our Dealings with Wrongdoers

People are always ready to accuse another of having done something which they themselves would not mind doing. There are others who would perhaps not commit the same fault of which they accuse another, but they have committed it in the past. There are those who accuse another of doing something wrong, which, owing to circumstances, they themselves are incapable of doing. The picture of this Hafiz has made in his poetry. He says, "O pious one, I would listen to you if you were young, and if it were spring, and there were a garden and a fair one offering you a bowl of wine, and you refused it at that time." It is easy to blame others for their wrongdoings, as it is easy to examine and difficult when one is examined. The words of the Bible refer to this, "He that is without sin among you, let him cast the first stone."[1]

---

1 John 8:7.

Many times one gives such importance to a wrong action done by another which is made wrong by the standard of one's own understanding, whereas the right and wrong of every person is according to that person's stage of evolution and according to that person's understanding. Many times one accuses another of having committed some fault without considering what has prompted that person to commit that fault, what is the real condition of that person's life, whether that person did it willingly or unwillingly, whether that person was compelled to do it by the person's own self, or by someone else, or by some unforeseen circumstance. There is another way, that is when one accuses another person without having even seen the wrongdoing but because one has been told of it by someone else, which is a still greater mistake; it is not even a fact known at first hand.

When we see through the brain, we see so many faults in others. And when we see through feeling, we can do nothing else than reason out how we can justify their having done as they did, or at least tolerate their having done so through weakness or by mistake, which is natural to every human being since Adam, the father of humanity, was liable to faults. The more feeling is developed in the a person's heart, the more forgiving that person becomes. For to such a person the world's inhabitants appear as little children, as they appear small to the one who flies in the aeroplane. And as one is ready to forget the faults of children, so the wise become ready to forgive the faults of human beings.

Our Dealings with Enemies

The difference between the law of reciprocity and the law of beneficence is that in the former a person is justified in giving measure for measure, and in the latter one is supposed to tolerate and to forgive and to show kindness, so that the enemy may grow to be a friend. There are cases where one cannot show kindness; but yet one can be tolerant. There are cases where one cannot forgive; and yet revenge, for a humane person, is an unnatural thing. One can overlook the faults of another, and by that one will give less occasion for disagreement and still less occasion for enmity.

Then a person thinks, "By being kind to our enemies we encourage them in their tyranny." But so long as we have kindness in our heart, instead of hardening the nature of the enemy, it will soften it, since we receive all that we give out. A kind word in return for a harsh word, a kind action in return for a cruel one, a kind thought in return for an evil thought make a much greater effect than measure for measure. The iron which cannot be broken by hammers can be melted by fire. Love is fire, kindness is its chief expression. And if one has sufficiently developed this in one's heart, one can, sooner or later, change an enemy into a friend. It is unkindness, mostly on one's own part, that generally causes enmity all around; and one blames the enemies and becomes horrified at their number, then blames the world and its nature and its life. And when the creation has been proved blameworthy in a person's mind, then how can the Creator be kept free from blame? Then one alone feels blameless, and all else is blameworthy; and life becomes a torture. One thinks it is not worth living and becomes self-righteous, and everybody seems to be against such a person.

It is always wise to avoid every chance of causing enmity, and to make every effort to turn every enemy—even a person in the least degree offended, even a person who has slightly misunderstood you or perhaps has felt vexed with you—into a friend again, not for the sake of your own happiness or even of that person's, but for the sake of the good principle, for material benefit. For however small an enemy may be, that enemy can cause you very great pain or suffering. And however little friendship you have with a person, that person may become most useful some day. And apart from all material benefits, this benefit is in itself so great: to feel "that person is pleased with me, is well-disposed toward me, is no longer my enemy."

Our Dealings with God

God is the ideal that raises humankind to the utmost reach of perfection. As one considers and judges in one's conscience one's dealings with human beings, so the real worshipers of God consider their dealings with God. If they have helped anybody, if they have been kind to anybody, if they have made sacrifices for anybody, they do not look for appreciation or return for their doing so to the people to whom they have done any good; for they consider that they have done it for God, and therefore their account is with God, not with those with whom they have dealt. They do not care even if, instead of being praised, they are blamed; for in any case, they have done it for God, who is the best judge and the knower of all things.

There is no ideal higher than the God ideal, that can raise the moral standard high, although love is the root of all and God is the fruit of this. Love's expansion, and love's culmination, and love's progress all depend upon the God ideal. How much people fear their friend, their neighbor, when they do something that might offend the one whom they love, whom they respect. And yet how narrow is their goodness when it is for one person or when it is for certain people. Imagine, if they had the same consideration for God, then they would be considerate in all places and in dealing with all people. There is a verse of a Sufi who says, "Everywhere I go, I find Thy sacred dwelling place; and whichever side I look, I see Thy beautiful face, my Beloved."

Love for God is the expansion of the heart, and all actions that come from the lover of God are virtues; they cannot be otherwise. It is a different outlook on life when the love of God has filled one's heart. The lovers of God will not hate any one, for they know that by doing so they will hate the Creator by hating the divine creation. They cannot be insincere, they cannot be unfaithful, for they will think that to be faithful and sincere to humanity is as being faithful and sincere to God.

You can always trust the lovers of God, however unpractical or however lacking in cleverness they may appear to be, for only holding strongly in mind the thought of God purifies the soul from all bitterness, and gives human beings a virtue that they could attain from nowhere else and by no other means.

PART 3:
THE LAW OF RENUNCIATION

Life in God

"In God we live, and move, and have our being."[1] This teaching of the Bible tells about the nature of God: that God is the ocean, the waves of which are all its activities, small or great. The Qur'an says in support of this that not a single atom moves, groups, or scatters without the command of God. Rumi explains it still more plainly, "Air, earth, water and fire are God's servants; to us they seem lifeless, but to God living."[2] In those who are conscious of this knowledge, to the extent of their realization of this truth, arises a spirit of renunciation, which may be called a spirit of God.

The one who wants anything, becomes smaller than the thing wanted; the one who gives away anything, is greater than the thing given. Therefore, to a mystic each act of renunciation becomes a step toward perfection. Forced renunciation, whether forced by moral, religion, law, convention, or formality is not necessarily renunciation. The real spirit of renunciation is willingness, and willing renunciation comes when one has risen above the thing one renounces. The value of each thing in life—wealth, power, position, possession—is according to the evolution of a human being. There is a time in one's life when toys are one's treasures, and there is a time when one puts

1 Acts 17:28.

2 Edward Henry Winfield, trans. *Teachings of Rumi: The Masnavi of Maulána Jalálu'd-Dín Muhammad i Rúmí* (1898), book 1, story 4.

them aside. There is a time in one's life when copper coins are everything to one, and there is another time when one can give away gold coins. There is a time in one's life when one values a cottage, and there is a time when one gives up a palace. Things have no value; their value is as a person makes it, and at every step in evolution that person changes their value. Certainly there is no gain in leaving home, friends, and all affairs of life, and going to the forest and living the life of an ascetic. And yet who has the right to blame those who do so? How can the worldly person judge and understand the point of view of the one who renounces? Perhaps that which seems to the worldly person of most value, to the one who has renounced is nothing. The Sufi makes no restrictions and principles for renunciation, nor does the Sufi teach renunciation. The Sufi thinks that to sacrifice anything in life which one does not wish to sacrifice is of no use, but renunciation is a natural thing, and it grows in one with one's evolution. A child who cries for its toy at one stage of its childhood, comes to an age when it is quite willing to give away the toy it cried for once.

There are three stages of moral. The first stage of moral is the moral of reciprocity. This moral is natural to the one who sees the difference between oneself and another, who recognizes every person as such and such. The second law of moral is the law of beneficence, where one, recognizing oneself as an entity separate from others and recognizing others as distinct entities themselves, yet sees a cord of connection running through oneself and all, and finds oneself as a dome in which rises a reecho of good and evil. And in order to have a good reecho one gives good for good, and good for evil. But the third stage of moral is the moral of renunciation, where the difference of "mine" and "thine," and the distinction of "I" and "you" fade away in the realization of the One Life that is within and without, beneath and beyond. And that is the meaning of the verse in the Bible, "In Him we live, move, and have our being."[3]

3 Acts 17:28.

Renunciation 1

Those who in the East have renounced pleasure, comfort, riches, possessions, with a mystical view, have not renounced because they were too weak to hold them or because they did not desire them, but only because they wished that before a thing they possessed passed from their hands, they could renounce it. All things one possesses in life one has attracted to oneself. And when one loses them, it shows that power of attraction is lost and that if, before that power of attraction is lost, one can renounce them, one rises above them. All things that are in one's hold are not really one's own, although for the moment one thinks so. When one loses them one realizes that they were not one's own. Therefore the only possible way of everlasting happiness would be to think that all one possesses is not one's own, and to renounce it in time, before all that one possesses renounces one. The law of renunciation is great, and it is the only way of happiness there is.

Renunciation 2

When one sees deeply into life, one sees that there is no gain which is not a loss, and that there is no loss which is not a gain. Whatever people have gained, they have also lost something with it that sometimes they do not know. And sometimes, when they know it, they call it the cost, when they know it is a lesser loss. But when they do not know, the loss is great; for every gain is, after all, a mortal gain, and the time that is spent in its acquisition is a loss, and a greater loss in comparison to the gain. The loss of every mortal thing is a gain in the immortal spheres, for it wakens the heart, which is asleep both in the pursuit and the pleasures of the gain. When one closely watches one's own life and affairs, one finds that there has been no loss that would be regretted, that under the mantle of every loss a greater gain was covered. And one also notices that with every gain there has been a loss, and when this gain was compared with the loss it proved to be a greater loss.

In the eyes of the world people who renounce their pleasures, comforts, and happiness seem to be foolish; but there is nothing that a person has renounced without receiving a greater gain. And yet renunciation for gain can be called nothing but greed; renunciation for the pleasure of renunciation is the only renunciation that is worthwhile.

Greed and Generosity

When a person has in view an object to attain, the person is smaller than the object; but when a person has attained the object, that person is greater than the object. But as one holds the object which one has attained, so one diminishes one's strength, and the value of the object becomes augmented. But when a person renounces the object once attained, that person rises above the object, takes a new step in life, and a higher step. As at every step taken in climbing a mountain, one goes higher and higher, so one progresses in attainment of any kind in life, be it spiritual or material. For instance, when a person has a desire to have a hundred pounds, that person is smaller than the hundred pounds; when a person has earned them, that person is greater than the sum earned. But when one holds them, the value of a hundred pounds in one's eyes increases more and more, and may increase to that of a million pounds in one's sight; and in one's own estimation one becomes smaller and smaller, as if one would never be able to earn those hundred pounds again. But when a person has earned a hundred pounds and has spent them, that person has risen above them; that person's next ideal will be a thousand pounds.

So it is in any aspect of life. The moral must be remembered that what we value we must attain, but once attained, instead of being crushed under it, we must freely rise above it and take a further step in life. Those who have made progress in life, have made it with this view. And those who come to a standstill in life are the ones who hold fast to that which they have attained, never inclined to renounce it; and in that way they have met with failure. Therefore greed, however profitable it may seem, in the end is weakening; and generosity may seem at times unprofitable, but is strengthening.

The Necessity of Renunciation in Life

The saying, "There is no gain without pain," when rightly interpreted, would mean that everything costs something as its price. And it is this law of nature that teaches one that for every kind of attainment in life, from the highest to the lowest, renunciation is necessary. It may be in the form of patience, in the form of service, in the form of modesty; it may be in the form of sacrifice. In whatever form it happens to be, it has to be for some purpose. When attaining something in life, one always risks or meets with some loss. It does not appear loss in the presence of an immediate gain, but before things that take time to gain and conditions that want patience for their attainment, an immediate and seeming loss means a bitter renunciation.

Therefore, it is justifiable if a person shows a tendency to find a reason before renunciation of any kind. But the difficulty is that one will not be able to attain things that are abstract and things beyond ordinary comprehension, for one will not risk renouncing anything for such gains. And those who renounce without reason, lose also, for they renounce and yet may not gain anything. Therefore the success of the renunciation lies in the renunciation itself, to be pleased with renunciation, not for the gain. That renunciation alone is the renunciation which may be called virtue.

There are four desires that a human being could pursue: pleasures, wealth, duty, and God. And every one of these attainments costs something, and nobody should deem it possible to attain any one of these without renunciation. Therefore, though renunciation is the last lesson, one must begin to learn it from the beginning.

The Relativity of Gain

Life consists of a continual struggle for gain, of whatever kind it may be. Gain seems to be the purpose of life, and it is accomplished by mastery. Therefore, naturally, this proves that one must try to gain whatever seems to be good and attainable in life, or whatever one needs in life. And when one is able to attain, it shows mastery; and when one is unable, it shows the lack of it. But by a still deeper view of the subject, one sees that every gain that one has in view limits one to a certain extent to that gain, and directs one's activities in a certain channel, and forms the line of one's fate. But at the same time it deprives one of a still greater or a better gain, and of the freedom of activity which may perhaps accomplish something still better. It is, therefore, that renunciation is practiced by the Sufis; for with every willing renunciation, a person proceeds a step forward toward a higher goal. No renunciation is ever fruitless. The one who is looking for a gain, is smaller than the gain; the one who has renounced a thing, has risen above it. Every step toward progress and rise is a step of renunciation. The poverty of the one who has renounced is the real riches compared with the riches of the one who holds them fast. One could be rich in wealth, and poverty-stricken in reality; and one can be penniless, and yet richer than the rich of the world.

Renunciation and Loss

There are two different renunciations: one is renunciation, the other is loss. Renunciation is that renunciation that a person makes who has risen above something that once was valued; or whose hunger and thirst for the thing are satisfied, and it is no more so valuable as it once was; or who, perhaps, has evolved and sees life differently, no longer as that person saw it before. And renunciation in all these cases is a step forward to perfection. But the other renunciation, which one is compelled to make when circumstances deny the achievement of what one wishes for, or what one has lost helplessly; or when one is placed in a position where one cannot reach the object that one wishes to have, by weakness of mind or body or by lack of position, power, or wealth—that renunciation is loss; and instead of leading toward perfection, it drags a person down toward imperfection. The wise, therefore, renounce willingly what they feel like renouncing; but what they feel like gaining, of that they are constantly in pursuit. One failure, or two failures, will not discourage them. After a hundred failures they will rise with the same hope, and will gain the thing desired in the end.

But there is another weakness, and that is holding what has been gained and indulging in what has been attained. That limits people to their gain, deprives them of a greater gain, and even prevents them, in the course of time, from holding the gain they already have. This philosophy was lived in life by the ascetics who traveled from place to place. All happiness, comfort, and good friends they made in one place, they enjoyed all that for one moment and left it, lest it might bind them for ever. It does not mean that it is necessary that this life should be made an example for a wise person, but our journey through life's experience is also a continual journey. And the good and bad, and the right and wrong, and the rise and fall of yesterday one must leave behind, and turn one's back on them and go on forward with new hope, new courage, and enthusiasm, trusting to the almighty power of the Creator in one's spirit.

The Learning of Renunciation

People think that renunciation is learned by unselfishness. It is the looker-on who sees renunciation in the form of unselfishness, as perhaps a dog would see renunciation when a someone throws away a bone: the dog does not know that the bone is valuable to it, not to the person. Every object has its peculiar value to every individual; and as a person evolves through life, so the value of things becomes different. And as one rises above things, so one renounces them in life; and the one who has not risen above them, when looking at a person's renunciation, calls it either foolish or unselfish.

One need not learn renunciation, life itself teaches it. And, to the small extent that one has to learn a lesson in the path of renunciation, it is this: that in the case where in order to gain silver coins one has to lose the copper ones, one must learn to lose them. That is the only unselfishness that one must learn: that one cannot have both the copper and the silver.

There is a saying in Hindi, "The seeker after honor dies for a name, the seeker after money will die for a coin." To the one to whom the coin is precious, the name is nothing; to the one who considers a name precious, money is nothing. So one person cannot understand the attitude of another unless a person puts on another's cloak and sees life from another's point of view. There is nothing valuable except what we value in life; and those are fully justified in renouncing all that they have or that may be offered to them for the sake of that which they value, even if it be that they value it for this moment. For there will never be a thing which they will value always in the same way.

> Ah, make the most of what you yet may spend,
> Before we too into the dust descend,
> Dust into dust, and under dust to lie,
> Sans wine, sans song, sans singer, and sans end.
>
> Omar Khayyam[4]

The Nature of Renunciation

From a practical point of view, life is like a journey starting from the unmanifested state of being and going to the manifested state, and from manifestation returning again to the unmanifested, or perfect, state of being. As human being, life has the fullest privilege of knowing about the journey, and directing, to a certain extent, the affairs on the journey, and making this

4 Omar Khayyam, *The Rubaiyat of Omar Khayyam,* trans. Edmund Fitzgerald (1889), verse 24.

journey comfortable, and arriving at the destination at the desired time. The mystic tries to make use of this privilege, and the whole spiritual wisdom teaches the manner in which this journey should be made.

As human beings come from the unmanifested, it is evident that we come alone—no one with us, and with nothing. After coming here we begin to own objects, possessions, properties, even living beings. And the very fact that we came alone, without anything, necessitates our being alone, in the end, to enter the destination. And once one has owned things of the earth, one does not wish to part with them, and wishes to carry the weight of all one possesses on this journey, which weighs one down and naturally makes the journey uncomfortable. As really nothing and no one else belongs to one, it must all fall in time; and one is made lonely against one's desire. And it is only willing renunciation which can save a person from this burden on the path.

It is not necessary that this renunciation should be practiced by indifference to one's friends. No—one can love one's friends and serve them, and yet be detached. It is this lesson which Christ taught when he said, "Give unto Caesar the things that are Caesar's, and unto God the things that are God's."[5] They have renounced who get the things of the world, but give them to the world; but those who do not know renunciation get the things of the world and hold them for themselves. Love is a blessing, but it turns to a curse in attachment. Admiration is a blessing, but it turns to a curse when one tries to hold the beauty to oneself. Then the way of those who renounce is to know all things, to admire all things, to get all things, but to give all things, and to think that nothing belongs to them and nothing they own. And it is this spirit which will liberate human beings from the earthly bondages which keep the generality of humankind in captivity throughout the whole life.

5 Matthew 22:21.

The Final Victory

The final victory in the battle of life for every soul is when a person has abandoned, which means when that person has risen above what once was valued most. For the value of everything exists for a person so long as that person does not understand it. When one has fully understood, the value is lost, be it the lowest thing or the highest thing. It is like looking at the scenery on the stage and taking it for a palace. Such is the case with all things of the world: they seem important or precious when we need them or when we do not understand them; as soon as the veil which keeps us from understanding is lifted, then it is nothing.

Do not, therefore, be surprised at the renunciation of sages. Perhaps every person in the spiritual path must go through renunciation. It is not really throwing things away, or disconnecting ourselves with friends that is renunciation; it is not taking things to heart so seriously as one naturally takes them by the lack of understanding. No praise, no blame is valuable; no pain or pleasure is of any importance. Rise and fall are natural consequences, so are love and hatred. What does it matter if it be this or that? It matters so long as we do not understand. Renunciation is a bowl of poison no doubt, and the brave one will drink it; but in the end, this alone proves to be nectar, and this bravery brings one the final victory.

CONSCIOUSNESS AND PERSONALITY

The contents of "Consciousness and Personality" have been compiled from the previously unpublished "Supplemental Papers" with two additional chapters. The chapter "Beauty" is from *The Complete Works of Pir-o-Murshid Hazrat Inayat Khan: Original Texts, Lectures on Sufism 1922,* vol. 1, 51–53. "Are We Masters of Our Destiny?" is from *The Complete Works of Pir-o-Murshid Hazrat Inayat Khan: Original Texts, Lectures on Sufism 1925,* vol. 1, 37–42.

CONSCIOUSNESS AND PERSONALITY

When we look at the world we see that everything makes a circle. The plant grows from the seed to its developed state and returns to dust. Human beings grow from childhood to youth, to maturity, then to old age. This, it is said, is an argument for our passing through many lives. But it is not the circle that journeys, but the point which, journeying, forms the circle and returns to the place from which it started. It is the consciousness that performs the journey at all times, and not the individual soul.

The drops of water in a fountain go up, some higher, some lower, some go a very little way, some rise very high. When each drop falls down it sinks into the stream, flowing away with it, and does not rise again, although the water of the same stream rises again and falls again in drops—which proves to us the fact that the water has a continual rise and fall, not the drop, yet apparently it rises and falls as drops though the portion of water in every drop is different.

The wheel of evolution is such that the consciousness gradually evolves through rock, tree, animal, to humanity. When it reaches humanity it cannot manifest further toward the surface, because through this journey all its force is spent. Human beings are the most active beings, they have to do with most things. A rock has very little activity; it lasts long. A tree has a little more activity, and its life is not so long as that of the rock. There are many animals which live much longer than human beings. Humanity has the most activity, and in humanity consciousness reaches the highest point of manifestation.

IMAGINATION

It will be asked where the imagination is. It is in the mind. And then the question comes: Where is the mind? Whether it is in the body, or out of the body; whether, as some scientists and naturalists have said, it is the brain that produces mind and that is all. But if that is so, the mind exists as long as the brain exists; and when the brain is destroyed, the mind is finished. If this were so, all a writer's work of three or four months, so many pages and books, and all an artist's work of ten years, a studio full of pictures, would be in the brain. And where, in the little brain, would there be room for all this?

It will be said that when a person thinks, the eyes show the thoughts. When a person is sad, the eyes and eyebrows and forehead change; and when a person is glad, the eyes and the forehead smile. We may keep back our smile, but the forehead smiles. If we think very much, our brain becomes tired. Sometimes a feeling of depression comes, and a heaviness, especially in the chest and in the left side. If a joy comes, a feeling of lightness is felt in the heart. This is because, as thought has its organ, the brain, so the heart is the organ of feeling. With the blood, it sends its vibrations to every pore and every atom of the body.

The mind is thought of as something small, because we say: "My mind, in my mind," and that which is called "my" always seems small, like "my purse," or "my grip"—smaller than the material body, something that can be carried about in a grip.

Really the mind is much bigger than the material body. The shadow of the body is much larger than is generally known. By the practices of mysticism you may learn how very far it reaches, and the mind is much larger than the shadow.

I may be sitting here, and I may send my thought to Paris. But then, it may be asked: "If I am here, and my thought is in Paris, am I separated from my mind? Can I go out, and leave my mind in the house, and come back and find it again?" No, the mind has wings that stretch from here, not only to Paris, but to New York, or to Russia, to Japan, to the North Pole, the South Pole, and much further still. If from here I send my thought to friends in India, if I send it without letting anything interfere with my thought, they will feel it in their lives; something good will happen to them on account of this good thought.

There is a couplet by my murshid:[1]

> I, the poor, have such a strength,
> That if the eyes had eyes,
> They could not see the rapidity of my steps,
> If the eyes had their utmost power,
> they could not see the rapidity of my paces.
> This is the strength of the strong.

If a person reads this, who does not know the hidden meaning, that person will not understand. The step means the "step of thought." We are so contracted in this material body because it is the nature of matter to contract. But even here, in this material body, we can expand a little. We can move our hands and arms, and though we are so little, we can walk many miles. This shows the expanding tendency within us.

1 The author's murshid was Shaykh al-Mashaykh Sayyid Muhammad Abu Hashim Madani.

THOUGHT AND FEELING

We often speak of thought and feeling as being much the same as the other, but they are as different as fire and air, or as earth and water. It is sometimes said: "My mind is my thought, and my thought is my brain."

Some scientists have said that the brain is a substance that produces thought, but the brain could never be large enough to contain the whole of thought. The brain receives the vibrations from the mind invisible, and the heart receives the vibrations from the mind invisible. If we think very much, we hold our head, the head becomes heavy. Scientists do not give the heart any importance as an organ of feeling. They say that it is simply an organ that helps in the circulation of the blood. Really the physical heart receives the impressions from the heart invisible. A feeling of joy or pleasure is not felt in the brain. It is felt in the chest, and especially in the left side, where the heart is. A feeling of fear is not felt in the brain, but in the place of the heart. A feeling of depression or sadness causes a heaviness in the chest.

A dull person will understand less of what is said than an intelligent person. If two people are sitting next to each other, and someone is speaking to them, one may understand much less than the other. The vibrations come to both in the same way, but one brain is better able to receive them than the other.

The brain and heart also change. We find a person moved, touched, and shedding tears at the smallest thing that has to do with love or truth; and five years later that person may not show any sign of being moved by the greatest joy or sorrow. So also we may find a person very indifferent and cold, and then, three or four years later, the same person may show a tender and melting state of heart. This depends upon the physical condition of the brain and heart, and this has to do with the subject of physical culture. The brain and heart may be developed. This is why the *zikr* and *fikr* and the various practices of the Sufi are done in connection with the heart. The Sufis give great importance to the cultivation of the heart.

Thought comes from feeling. In the next inversion, thought may create feeling. The thought of an enemy may produce a feeling of sadness and revengefulness. One may be feeling very joyous, and a picture of a friend not seen for a long time may produce a feeling of sadness. Still, it is feeling that has creative power, and thought is responsive. A person may be sitting in a room full of people, and may be laughing. Though that person may hide the laughter and it may not be seen, the tendency to laugh will arise in others. A person who is sad or gloomy may come into our presence and, though the person may say nothing, the tendency toward sadness arises in us.

If you look at the sky and watch closely, you will have solved a great problem. You will see that there is a small, white cloud somewhere. It is joined by another cloud, and its form is changed. Then another cloud meets them, and its form is again changed. Then one part is taken away, and two parts only remain. Then it grows to ten times its size, and then nine parts are taken away. So it is with thought. It changes constantly like the clouds. The mind is the sky. It is the sun that disperses the clouds, and the soul that disperses thought. In India and other countries where the sun is very strong, the clouds are quickly dispersed. When the soul's power is great, the clouds of our thoughts will be scattered.

People often say: "Hold the root of the thought, hold the feeling which creates it." If a person has the feeling, "I want money," the feeling will grow and grow. That person will watch every cent and collect, and may become a millionaire. If a person has a spark of anger against an enemy, it will grow in thought and feeling until the person feels bad not only toward the enemy, but, in time, we shall feel full of enmity toward the friend also. Thought is much greater than all the material objects that it has made. The thought of Shakespeare is alive today; his body has disappeared. The thought of Beethoven lives on the paper, though there may not be an atom of his body remaining. The thoughts of Jalal ad-Din Rumi, at the time when his soul was longing for its liberation, move the heart of the one who reads them.

People often say: "I said it, but I did not mean it." That is never true. If you said it, you thought it, and if you thought it, you felt it. You may be in a hurry, and say "cat," for instance, instead of "hat," or you may not know the language very well, but to say a thing you have not thought, is not possible.

If a thought comes that, "I want some roses," and the thought repeats itself in my mind over and over again, one of two things will happen: either my thought will make me go out and buy some roses, or else it may make someone else bring them to me. If you think that you want fish for dinner, and the thought makes its circles in your mind, the cook will bring fish. It is not that the cook wished to bring fish, but your thoughts make the cook bring it.

It is by the power of thought that the black magicians can kill a person, or make a person go mad. I have known some so great that they make boxes in a house catch fire and burn without anyone going into the house. And yet they cannot be called saints or sages, because they do what they do without renunciation—not by the power of the soul, but by the power of the thought.

If this power can be used for a better purpose, that is more desirable, but practice it in your own affairs first. If it can be used for others, with renunciation, with love, that is most desirable.

From morning till night we think how to make our house more comfortable, how to have a nice dress, a nice motor car, and we do not think of the one who lives in the house, of the personality. We want incense in the house, we do not want a bad smell. Of what use is it if the motor car runs well, if the motor car of the mind does not run smoothly? First take care of the one who lives in the house.

If we can say to our soul: "You are my real self. Shine in my mind. To you all this that surrounds me is a show, whether I like it, or whether I do not like it. To you it is an experience. See it, even if it be sad or unpleasant, but you are not moved or affected by any of these things. You are much too great for them to leave any stain upon you. You are always the same, always unaltered. And you are also the soul of all else. You are the light of God."

This is what is meant by "Seek ye first the kingdom of God."[1] The kingdom of God is the soul. It is the light of God. If we can say this, whatever our circumstances may be, our depression and sadness will be dispersed like the clouds before the sun, and we shall be in the light and peace of our soul.

* * *

Question: *If all knowledge is in the consciousness, what need is there of thought? And if thought is drawn from the external world, how could the universe be created without thought?*

Answer: The consciousness contains all knowledge. Thought is the activity of the consciousness impressed by the external world. Thought is needed to control the activity of the consciousness.

1 Matthew 6:33.

BEAUTY

Beauty is the significance of God. One cannot explain God nor can one can explain beauty; at the same time one tries to explain God and beauty. The sura of the Qur'an, therefore, which says God is beautiful and loves beauty[1] supposes this idea. One can admire a form, a color, or beauty in any visible or invisible form, but what is it that is beautiful in it one cannot explain. This shows that everything that makes up a form of beauty suggests beauty, but beauty in reality is that missing point in it which shows and does not show at the same time. In the beauty of poetry, music, personality, one will try perhaps to point out this particular phrase, that particular manner is beautiful, and yet one cannot really point out the central point of beauty. Therefore if one wishes to explain what is beauty, one can only say that the cause of every form and its result, when summed up, makes beauty.

If beauty is explained a little more briefly, it can be said that beauty is harmony, beauty is the result of harmony. When lines stand in harmony, when colors are formed in harmony, when words are formed in harmony, and when notes are formed in harmony, when movements express harmony, beauty manifests.

The narrower the vision, the more one finds a lack of beauty. The wider the vision, the greater the beauty, for the very reason that beauty is the total sum of many different things.

1 Hadith.

The idea of beauty for each person is different. It differs according to the evolution of individuals. Again, every person's world of beauty is different. One person sees in a certain thing a world of beauty; the same world to another person is nothing but darkness. Therefore it is absurd when beauty is discussed by two argumentative persons, and in the same way it is absurd when two people discuss their idea of the deity. Beauty is a region which one can penetrate by growing toward some evolution. Beauty is perceived by the senses of saints. The more the sense which distinguishes beauty is developed, the more capable it becomes of enjoying beauty. By opening the doors of this sense one can progress toward beauty; by closing the doors, one distances oneself from beauty.

The external five senses—sight, smell, hearing, touch, taste—are but the vehicles of that inner sense which senses beauty and experiences the different worlds of beauty. If the sense is accustomed to see beauty through the eyes, it can sense that world of beauty; it may either appreciate the beauty of lines or of colors. If the sense is in a habit to experience beauty by hearing, it can enjoy the harmony of tones and of rhythm. If the sense that perceives beauty takes the head as its center, it enjoys intellectual beauty. If the same sense takes the heart as its vehicle it enjoys the sentiment and the beauty of feeling. Amir, the great Indian poet, says: "Oh, searching soul, if thou only could see the beloved is manifested in so many different forms of beauty, wherever thou would cast thine eyes thou could see it."

Why do we seek for beauty? Because the source of our being is the center of beauty. All distress in life is caused by missing that vision of beauty, and all that makes us happy is beauty in its different forms. The searching of every soul is for beauty although the direction of every soul is different, for there are different worlds of beauty, which different souls seek for. The more one observes beauty, the more one reflects beauty. A soul becomes beautiful by the contemplation of beauty, just like that insect that turns green in the spring when the trees are growing green.

Beauty is the key to happiness. The one who searches for beauty no doubt opens the doors for the beauty in the heart. The one who constantly contemplates beauty, one day arrives to a state in which the whole of manifestation becomes one single vision of divine beauty.

THE DESTRUCTION OF IDEALS

Those who have never had an ideal may hope to find one; they are in a better case than those who allow the circumstances of life to break their ideal. To fall beneath one's ideal is to lose one's track of life. Then confusion rises in the mind, and that light, which one should hold high, becomes covered and obscured so that it cannot shine out to clear one's path. The fall of Napoleon may be dated from the day that he abandoned Josephine. With the breaking of the ideal, the whole life cracks and dissolves. As soon as one begins to think, "I have done wrong to such and such a person, or such and such a principle," one ceases to be a king within, and cannot be a king without. This does not mean that the good succeed in life, and that the evil fail, but rather that a person progresses alone through sincerity to that person's ideals, for the good of each is indeed peculiar to oneself.

Religion is the school that has developed humanity; and the ideals that religion presents form a path that leads upward to perfection, that innate and yearning desire of every soul. The difficulty arises when a person sees principles as the goal and not simply as a means to the goal; for when one begins to worship one's own principles one becomes a simple idolater, and destroys the essence and the life of one's ideal.

Can anyone point to a date in history when humanity first gained wisdom? Wisdom is the property of humanity. The expressions of this wisdom differ at different times, to suit different peoples; and it is the differences that have always been noticed and not the similarity. We are apt to insist on the external forms: "My religion, my scripture, my custom is different," we say. And thus, in endeavoring to enforce our ideal, we depart from the very spirit which produced that ideal and act upon some primitive impulse which we despise ourselves, whenever we recognize it. We may say, "I wish to reform and to reach," when we are simply driven by a blind and animal impulse to inflict pain perhaps, or to tyrannize, or perhaps to assert our personal power. This element of falseness and treachery in human motives proves, to many truthful observers, that there is nothing in life worthy of devotion, and no cause worthy of allegiance.

But the wise of all ages have taught that it is the knowledge of the Divine Being that is life and the only reality. Although a human activity consists of a number of complicated motives—some of which are base and gross—it is the aspiration toward divinity, the desire toward beauty, which is its soul, its life, its reality. And it is in proportion to the degree of the strength or weakness of our aspiration toward beauty that our ideal is great or small, and our religion great or small.

THE DREAM

The dream is the most wonderful subject of study in life. It has its different aspects.

In one aspect the dream is the exact picture of reality, which one may sooner or later experience in one's so-called real life. This again teaches the fact that the incidents which we experience unexpectedly in life were preordained for us. It also teaches us that here in the physical plane, though we appear to be one separate from the other, in the plane of the dream, upon the surface of the individual's mind, the whole world exists. One single being in the physical plane, inverts into the whole world in the plane of the dream, although one still holds fast one's individuality even there where one is alone.

The second aspect of the dream has the opposite nature of manifestation, as everything in it appears to be the reverse to what may be going to happen. For instance, a person seen dead in a dream will have a long life, and the sickness of a friend seen in a dream would, on the contrary, bring the friend good health. It is because of its negative nature everything, either the printer's block, the photographic plate, the humorous glass[1] and all things of a negative character will show opposite before they manifest aright.

The third aspect of the dream is of little importance, as is the case with the dreams produced before the view of a person either caused by the unbalanced activity of mind or by the disorder

1 A wavy or curved glass that distorts images, like a fun-house mirror.

of the health. Such dreams have, as a rule, no importance; and they are surely a waste, although they create before that person a moving picture.

The first aspect of dreams is generally manifest to the spiritual person; seldom are they also noticed by the average person.

The next aspect of the dream generally manifests before the view of those who possess the attribute of humanity, who first think of the world and its responsibilities, together with the thought of God.

The third aspect of the dream is vouchsafed to each person in one's everyday life, caused by the activity of one's mind.

A dream is an inspiration, according to the point of view of the Sufi. There are four kinds of dreams.

The soul dream is the actual vision of something that has passed, or that is going to happen, or that will happen.

In the heart dream there is a feeling more dominant than when one sees. The feeling itself is expressive of what has happened or will happen.

The symbolical dream, the mind dream comes to a person of artistic mind or mystical spirit, when, in the language of dreams, so to speak, that person knows the past, present, and future.

In the dream of the mind, whatever the mind is impressed with during the day, the mind goes on repeating it, and the dream is the same kind of impression.

PERSONALITY AS A BUBBLE IN THE WATER

Our personality is just like a bubble in the water. As little probability as there is of a bubble once merged in the sea coming out again composed of the same portion of water, so little probability is there for the soul once merged in the ocean of consciousness to come out again formed of the selfsame portion of consciousness. The bubble may come back in the same place with the same portion of water, or it may be another portion of water. There may be half of the first drop of water in the second bubble, there may be a small part, or there may be some portion of water added to it.

If one bubble comes, and we call that bubble Mr. John, then we call the other Mr. Tom, and another Mr. Henry; yet they are all the same water. And if we call the water Mr. John, they are all the same Mr. John. All is the same spirit, the same life, involving itself in all the forms and names. According to this point of view there is no I, no you, no he, no she, no it, in the light of reality; all are but the differences of a moment. Every bubble loses either reflections or any properties it possessed during its existence as soon as it merges in the water, and, if once in a thousand chances it came formed of the selfsame portion of water, it does not retain its previous property.

In the same way, supposing as a groundless assumption that the selfsame portion of consciousness, which in the first place is not so solid and stable as water, could possibly appear again on the surface without any addition or deduction, still it is utterly impossible that it should possess its past qualities and impressions, for it has been absolutely purified by sinking into the consciousness. And if even a drop of ink loses its ink property in the sea, why should not the ocean of consciousness purify its own element from all elements foreign to itself? If Hinduism teaches the belief that bathing once in the Sangam at the uniting of the two rivers[1] can purify people from all life's sins, how can it deny that this bath of the soul, sinking into the consciousness even once, purifies the soul from all the properties it has gathered during its previous life? In the first place, the nature of absorption of itself in the spirit is purification from the material state of being, and the very nature of manifestation is for the soul to come new and fresh.

1 The Sangam is at the conjunction of the Ganges and Yumna Rivers where the invisible Saraswati River descends from above in blessing.

THE MYSTERY OF SHADOW

In speaking on this subject I recall a poem of Shams-i Tabriz. He says:

> When the sun-faced One had arisen,
> Each atom of the two worlds arose.
> When the light of God's face sent its shadow,
> By this shadow various names became.
> The things, what were they?
> The pictures of the names.
> The atoms, what were they?
> God, in reality.
> The waves, what were they?
> They were in reality the sea.

He explains clearly in this the mystery of shadow. What an astonishing thing it is that a thousand years ago someone should have explained this clearly, not as a belief or as a religion, but as a science. Much earlier still in the Vedanta this science has been explained fully; the Purusha Shastra, it is called.

Let us now consider the sparkling things lying on the carpet. Is the light contained in them? No. There is no light in them, but they reflect the light from the gaslight. The wood of the mantelpiece reflects the light. Its purity makes it able to reflect. If there were some other dark substances here, they could not reflect the radiance. If I take this brass cup and hold it against the light, its shadow will be very thick and dark. If I hold my handkerchief against the light, its shadow is not so dense. The substance of the handkerchief allows the light to pass through it. If I were to hold a glass against the light, its shadow would be very light. This shows us that the more the particles of any object group and collect together, the less it allows the light to pass through it. From this we see that it is not God's fault if one is wise, another foolish, one is virtuous, another a sinner. The light of God is always shining there, but according as we allow it to pass, we reflect its brightness less or more.

As I am sitting here, each one of you holds my reflection in your eye, and each has a different reflection according to the position in which you are sitting. This shows us how everything in the world is formed by the reflections and shadows falling according to the situation. In the East they have a great many superstitions connected with the shadow. They do not allow a child to look at the shadow, nor to see its reflection in a looking glass. In Malabar, Brahmins going to the bath will never allow the shadow of another person to fall upon them. If someone is walking on the same side of the road as they, they will cross to the other side, rather than allow that person's shadow to fall upon them. Now they have given up these customs very much. They say, "We have lost the true meaning, and we are ridiculed." But there is a great meaning behind this.

According to our situation, our shadow is long or short, narrow or broad, it falls to the right or to the left, and all these things have a significance for the work upon which we are engaged. If we can compare the shadows of different people, we shall see that they differ from each other. Some are darker, some are lighter. It is very difficult to note the degree of depth of shadow, just as it is difficult to distinguish which of several shades of a dark stuff is the darkest. But if there were some machine which could register the depth of the shadows, we should be aware that they differ.

All the historians of Muhammad's time agree in saying that his shadow was never seen. This is found in Bukhari Sharif, and no contemporary historian contradicts him. In the strong sunlight of Arabia, the Prophet's shadow could not be seen. This was the living miracle of his existence. *Nur*, the light of God, was already shining in him. The light was there, the Prophet was not there. How should not the light of the sun shine through him?

The reflection in the looking glass, the shadow upon the earth, the reflection in the water, are different from one another. The shadow upon the earth is dark, because the earth has no light and is dark. These are the external shadows. There are also the shadows and reflections within. What is called clairvoyance is to allow the light within to pass through one so that these reflections are seen within. The shadow falls upon the earth; it falls also upon the space, and there it is much clearer. In the space the colors of the elements are reflected. It is very difficult to see this reflection in the space, because our eyes are so much accustomed to look at the things of the earth that they have become material, and they do not see that which is finer. The mystics, the Sufis, have ways of developing the eyes. They show you ways of looking into the space that make the eyes capable of seeing what is reflected there. From these reflections the past, present, and future can be told, and all that surrounds a person.

Then there are the internal shadows, the shadows that fall upon the mind, all the shadows of the earth. These make our joy, our sorrow, our happiness, our misery, all that we are, according as they fall upon us. What is spoken of as inspiration, revelation, is to make oneself open to the light, to allow the light to pass through one. Then everything becomes known to the soul. The soul sees everything. It is the *nafs*, the self, that darkens us and makes us unable to see. The more we group the atoms composing our self, the more solid we make it, the less the light is able to shine through us. The light is always there, but we do not give it a way through. The more our self is dissolved, the more the light of Allah will shine within us.

CONDITIONS OF THE MIND

The mind has three conditions: *jalal*, *jamal*, and *kamal*.

Jalal is that state when one thinks of what one will do, when one is planning what to do, when one thinks, "I should start a soap-factory," or "I should learn this thing." Then the mind is in its full force, and there is the strength of the thought.

Jamal is when one thinks of what one has done. One thinks, "I went to the British Museum and I saw so many beautiful jewels and books and beautiful statues."

Kamal has two conditions. Either there is no thought at all in the mind—this is for the mystic only, because the mystic practices it—or no thought is intentionally formed, and we take the first thought that comes into the mind and do that.

If we could always do this we should need no other guidance, we should not need to learn very much, we should know all things directly, because this knowledge comes direct from the universal consciousness. Do you not think that God, who has the experience of all things and all ages, can know more than any of us can learn in our short life?

THE WILL

The activity directed by the intelligence is the will. When there is no intelligence guiding the activity, there is blind impulse. Where there is no activity there is no will. The will can be strengthened by practicing it; by exerting it to overcome obstacles without and within; by acting contrary to our inclination; by holding impulses in check, not allowing them to go to the full length of their swing; by refraining from any action or expression to which we may be inclined; by not allowing ourselves to be overcome by a fit of anger, of laughter, of tears, by extreme joy or sorrow, or whatever mood; and either changing the emotion to its opposite—anger to mildness, laughter to sorrow, tears to joy—by checking the emotion and effacing it, or by letting it have its course and yet holding it in our control.

To know when to persist in our own will, when to allow the will of others, is often difficult; and sometimes we think it most difficult to know what is the will of God and what is our own will. Sometimes, six months afterwards, sometimes a year afterwards, or years afterwards, we see clearly what we should have done in a certain case, what course we should have taken, which at the time we could not discern although we tried to. If at the moment of difficulty we were as calm, as free from these thoughts of the pleasure, the happiness, the discomfort or the loss that will result to ourselves, we should see as clearly in that moment and perceive plainly the will of God.

INFLUENCE AND INNOCENCE

Influence

Perhaps you have read the story of Daniel in the lion's den,[1] therefore you can understand that there is no greater sign of spiritual advancement than one's personal influence. This is an example of advancement in spiritual life. People want to know whether they are progressing or going back. One need not see how much one has read or learned to find out if one has advanced. The principal thing is if one attracts people or if one repels them, if one is harmonious or inharmonious. This can tell us how far we have advanced. No doubt one day is not the same as the other. One day one may, perhaps, have more influence than the other. Life is like water, and it will have its waves rising or falling. Sometimes there are conditions or influences which are contrary. By keen observation we can find out if we are advancing.

Another sign of advancement is that we must become modest, kind, and respectful to others. Another sign is that we must have wisdom and power; if one has both these things one will create beauty in life.

Now a question is: "How are we to attain this advancement?" Practices and exercises are the main things. We must have faith and trust in the practices we do. According to our faith we will succeed. Mind and body must be kept in a proper tune. For instance, one moment of excitement takes away the advancement

1 Daniel 6.

of six months. It is like a person who is making a necklace of pearls; if the thread breaks, the person must do it all over again. If we get excited, and our mind and body are out of tune, we spoil the practices of six months' time. For those who walk in the spiritual path it is of great value to keep themselves tuned to the pitch which is necessary. The difficulty is to endure all the time many things which upset one, conditions which excite and exhaust one's patience. We must have the power of endurance in spite of all. Life is a continual battle to fight; and in order to keep fit, one must keep one's power reserved and preserved. This is done by keeping tranquil and equable in mind. Practices, concentrations, meditations, and prayer will win the battle of your life.

Innocence

The way of attaining spiritual knowledge is quite opposite to the way by which one attains worldly knowledge. As the sky is in the opposite direction to the earth, so the source of knowledge of spiritual things is opposite to the knowledge of the world. As one becomes intellectual, one knows things of the world; but this does not mean that one becomes spiritual; on the contrary, one goes further from spirituality by this thought: "I understand worldly things." What is the best way of attaining spiritual knowledge? First, one must develop in one's nature that little spark which is divine and which was shining in one's infancy, showing something pure, of heaven.

What attracts us most is innocence. It is innocence which gives an impression of purity, but we must not understand this wrongly. Knowledge of the world is necessary—more than necessary. It is necessary to live in the world, to make the best of one's life, to serve God and humanity. It is not necessary to attain spiritual knowledge—innocence is necessary for that. One sees among friends, relatives, something which attracts one most; perhaps this is the side of the nature which is innocence. People forgive those who are dear to them, they tolerate their faults. They say: "This one is wrong, but innocent." There is a purity which is divine, and which attracts everyone. Innocence is like a spring of water, purifying all that is foreign to heart and soul.

How can one attain innocence? Innocence is not foreign to our nature, we have all been innocent. By being conscious of this nature, we develop it; in admiring that nature, appreciating it, we also develop it. All things which we admire become impressions. Those who have a bad nature but who have collected good impressions will, in time, turn their nature.

During my traveling in India, the purpose of which was to pay homage to the sages of that land, the thing which appealed most to me was that the greater the soul was, the greater was the innocence. One sees in them innocence, not simplicity. The one who is simple does not understand; we see this in everyday life: the simple ones close their eyes. Innocence is to understand and rise above. Everyone sees another through one's own glasses; prejudice stands often between. For insight, unity is necessary. When that attribute is developed one has attained spirituality. People become wise when, after having been intellectual, they rise above the intellect; they see cause behind cause and understand the way of an enemy. Would it be practical to live altogether according to this principle? A principle is to be used, not to guide our life. When people make of principle a chain, it becomes captivity. Life is freedom. One cannot force oneself to innocence. Can there be any sign of piety or spirituality? There is no better sign than innocence with all understanding.

VAIRAGYA

The word *vairagya* comes from the Sanskrit and means "indifference." Indifference is called by the Sufis *fana'*, and is shown in the cross, the symbol of the Christian religion.

This indifference comes to every being and it is the first step to its annihilation, because not one atom can have its evolution without annihilation. The lower beings, the mineral, vegetable, and animal, evolve toward the higher; and because humanity is the highest creation, there is nothing for humanity to evolve to. But this indifference, when it comes, opens a way to God, from whom humanity came.

It comes to the child when it realizes that its dolly is not so interesting as it thought, and that it would be more interesting to play with other children who, at least, are alive. Then the dolly is thrown away. But before that the child takes the dolly, and loves it, and carries it about. And if the dolly's hand is hurt, the child wants some remedy, and a bed is needed to put the dolly in, and a carriage is needed to take the dolly out. But when the nature of the dolly is understood, the dolly is thrown away and the child realizes that to play with children of its age is better than those dollies who never speak.

Such is the case with us, the children in the world. Our likes and infatuations have a certain limit; when that is expired the period of indifference commences. When that water of indifference is drunk, then there is no more wish for anything in the world. The nature of the water that we drink in this world is that the thirst is quenched for so long, and then it comes again. When this water of divine knowledge is drunk, then the thirst never comes again. It comes when the nature of the world is understood. It is the higher knowledge. Then is understood that all these objects to which we attach so much importance, that we strive to attain, to achieve, are not important.

Before that a person attaches too much importance to joys and to sorrows. If a person is sad, the whole world is full of sadness. If a person is a little joyful, the whole world is full of joy, as if the sun rises and sets by one's joy and sadness. But indifference must be reached after interest has taken its course. Before that it is a fault. One becomes exclusive, one becomes disagreeable, without interest in life. It must come after all experience. Interest must end in indifference. One must not take the endless path of interest; the taste of everything in the world becomes flat. Then one realizes that all that we seek in all the objects we run after, all beauty and strength is in oneself; and one is content to feel all in one's own self. This may be called the kiss of the cross. Then one's only principle is love.

Vairagya means satisfaction, the feeling that there is no desire more to be satisfied, that there is nothing on earth that is desired. This is a great moment, and after that comes that which is the kingdom of God. Why is God satisfied with the world when even human beings, when they reach a certain grade of intelligence, are not satisfied? Or is God not satisfied?

There are two sorts of dissatisfaction. The first is when a person has so given in to the external self that the world cannot give that person satisfaction. The other is when the desire for more experience, for more enjoyment ceases. This is called in the Hindi language *vairagya*. This is indifference. Such a person is not unhappy. That person is happier than others and has lost only that intense interest in the world.

There is a story told of a comedian who every day disguised himself and fooled the king, the Badishah, at whose court he was. But the king recognized him in all his disguises. Then the comedian thought that he should disguise himself as an ascetic. He went to a cave in the mountains, and there he lived with two disciples, also comedians. He fasted very much, thinking that he should disguise himself well.

After forty days people, seeing his disciples, began to speak of the sage living in the cave of the mountains. They brought him presents, a hundred, two hundred dirhams. But he refused all, saying, "Take it away. The sage does not want money or presents."

His fame spread more and more, and the king heard of him and became anxious to see him. He went to the cave, but for a long time, the disciples would not let him enter. At last he was allowed to come into the presence of the sage. He said, "I have been kept waiting very long, before I could see you." The sage said, "The dogs of the world are not allowed to enter the house." The king was very much insulted. He thought that this must be a very great person.

He gave him a piece of paper, saying, "This is a *parvana* for the support of your disciples." A *parvana* means a grant of land. The sage said, "If it is a *parvana*, its place is in the fire," and he put it into the fire, which was burning before him. *Parvana* has two meanings, it also means "a moth."

The king went away, and the comedian got up, thinking, "Now I must tell the king how well I have fooled him." Then a voice came, saying, "Your feigned indifference has brought the king before you. If it had been real indifference, We ourselves would have come before you."

ARE WE MASTERS OF OUR DESTINY?

Often a person wonders if we were meant to be the master of our destiny, for life's experience has taught us to say, "Man proposes, God disposes."[1] But I will still say that we are the masters of our destiny for the very reason that we may be resigned to destiny, but we cannot be happy with that destiny which we do not wish to have. If we were meant to be the slaves to our destiny, then we would have been content with it, we would have been happy in it. For the very reason that we do not wish to be contented, for the very reason that we cannot be contented with our destiny shows that we are seeking for mastery; and it is in order to get the key to this mastery that we strive through a right way or a wrong way. By going the wrong way we have the same motive, but we do not accomplish it because then, in that way, we go through an illusion. We think that we are striving in order to master our destiny, but we go the wrong way. The one who goes the right way finds that key to that mastery, the mastery over our destiny.

Well, now is the question of how far we are granted that power of mastering our destiny and how far we stand in this life helpless? And the answer is that it differs with every person. Every person has a certain degree of that power. But this must be seen in this way: that a soul is born on earth helpless, and out of this helplessness it grows and then learns to help itself. A soul grows from infancy to youth, from helplessness it becomes

1 Thomas à Kempis.

able to help itself. So is the soul. As we evolve, so we develop to help ourselves.

Do you not hear sometimes a relation or a friend say about a friend, "That person is a child"? That person is a child means that person is still helpless. And this shows that in us there are both things: there is part of our being which is helpless, and there is a part of our being which has mastery. The external part is the part which represents our helplessness; it is our inner part which represents the mastery.

And since everyone is conscious of one's external being, and rarely is one is conscious of one's inner being, so rarely is one a master, but everyone experiences helplessness through life. And after all, it is the consciousness of a thing which makes the person possess it, and if the person is not conscious of it, it may belong to that person and yet that person does not possess it. For instance, there may be a large sum of money put in the name of a child in the bank The child still does not possess it, is not conscious of it, cannot utilize it. It belongs to that child, not to the others. To the child it is nothing, it does not belong to that child.

And now you will ask me what explanation have I to give about that belief which has always existed and believed by the wise and foolish, that there exists some such a thing which is called predestination. And I will explain it. There was an artist, and he planned in his mind and wanted to produce it on a canvas. And no sooner he took the colors and brush in his hand and began to paint his picture, every line made and every color he put suggested something; and that altered altogether his plan. The very plan with which he began then became an obscurity to his mind, and what was produced before him was quite a different thing than he had thought before. What does it show? This shows the three stages of the picture. The first stage of the picture is that plan which, before bringing on the canvas, the artist had designed, the artist had planned. And the other aspect is that action of producing that picture which went as changes—right and wrong, and right and wrong, and so on it went. And the third aspect is the completion of that plan, the completion of that picture which stood quite different from the plan first conceived. Therefore, what may be called predestination is that plan which is made beforehand. And what may be called karma, as they say in the Hindustani tongues, is that process through which the picture is made; and the completion of that picture is what may be called mastery.

It does not always happen that the picture is altogether different from what is planned, and yet it often happens. And however much different the picture may be from the plan, yet the foundation remains there as first planned. And therefore, how much different the life may be from that mark of predestination which was before, and yet the life is built, the life is erected upon the same plan which has been first made.

No doubt, the astrologers and the fortune-tellers, the future-tellers, the prophets, will not always say the thing that is really coming. They may mistake, and yet the predestination is there. The mistake is in their reading, not in the predestination.

And still that saying of the old that the feet of the infant tell what it is going to be will always prove true. It is the lack of seeing, that others cannot see; but the one who can see, can see from infancy what the child is going to be. And that old saying that the fate of the child is written on its forehead is the same. In reality, every part and particle of the infant is expressive of what it is going to be. The one who can read the eyes and the ears and the features and the form as letters, can read an infant, a human being, as a letter. This person need not consult with planets and mathematics, need not know other sciences. That intuitive sense can see what the soul is going to be like. And the eyes which are open to see this are also open to see the process, that middle part of life's journey, how the person is developing, how the person is going through changes. They can see in the failure of a person a success; there can be in the success of a person, a failure. And the one who is capable of doing this also can see, when this picture will be complete, what sort of picture it will be. What the picture is going to be, this person can see it beforehand.

And in order to support the argument of the fatalist we do not need to go far to find examples. Everyone has examples nearby. There are those most qualified and who yet fail; there are people most clever, and yet who always lose.

In order to support the argument of the one who thinks free will is something, there are reasons too, because it is the active, it is the persevering, it is the courageous who attain to success, and those who lack it can sit and wait, and wait forever. And this teaches us that it is a great mistake to divide destiny from free will, because behind destiny there is a free will, and behind a free will there is destiny. What we call destiny is a kind of cover upon the free will; it is the free will working in the form of free will, and yet the spirit of destiny is working.

I am now coming to a question: How does a mystic look upon this question? The mystic thinks that in the human being there are two aspects: one aspect is like a machine, the other aspect of being is like an engineer. The machine part is dependent upon climatic changes, upon what is given to it, what is put into it, upon what it depends on in order to keep in working condition. And there is another machine of fine mechanism, which works as the inner part of this machine, that is finer than its outer part. And that fine part feels atmosphere, feels vibrations, feels pleasures and displeasures, enjoys comforts and rejects discomforts; every kind of feeling exists there. Then the mystic looks on life in this manner: that this machine is made for the use of the other part of one's being, which is the engineer. But as long as that engineer is asleep, and that engineer is unaware of this machine, the engineer does not run it; it is just left to conditions and environment, they run it. And so it means illness, with depressions, with fears, with failures, with helplessness when this engineer part of one's being is asleep and the outer part of one's being is subject to conditions. On the day when this engineer part of us begins to waken, that day we begin to feel mastery over this machine. We begin to know on that day this machine was made for us to work it to the best advantage.

I am coming to a still deeper side of metaphysics. We shall find that God, from God's own experience, manifests and experiences life through all its aspects, and especially through humanity. For what is this whole manifestation? This is nothing but the sublime vision of divine being. And with all the beauty that one sees in manifestation, the greatest and the most important thing is the fulfillment of this whole creation, and that is to be found in humanity. And this object is only fulfilled when we have wakened to this part of our being which represents the master—in other words, God's divine self. But as long as we are interested in borrowing all that is necessary for this mechanism, which we call our mind and body, from the external world, we depend upon it and we live in it. And since this becomes our occupation, and this becomes our nourishment, this outer world, then we become mortal. In other words the immortal being becomes mortal by borrowing all that we need from the mortal world. The more we depend upon the external life, the more we forget the inner life. And there comes a time when we entirely forget that there can exist a life which is above, which is beyond this external life. We do not need to go very far to see the example of this when we see just now the condition of the world. We see that, with all this progress, there is materialism every day on the increase and all the suffering that humanity has gone through, and just now humanity is going through, has been caused by this ever-increasing materialism.

What human beings believe in is in all that is external, that which we can touch, which we can see, which we can possess externally. In connection with this it may be said, quite contrary to what is said in the Bible: that we live and move and make our lives with what is in the material world.[2] And when

2 See Acts 17:28.

we will live like this, our eyes will keep closed to that part of mastery which needs to be blown upon; and by that blowing it can be risen to a blaze which can lighten, which can illuminate the path of our life.

Therefore, the object of the Sufi Movement just now in this world and its work, is only to waken in humanity the importance of that side of life which is much more important than the earth side of life. The Sufi message, therefore, is not a message of a particular creed; it is the message of understanding life better. And the question of how can one attain to it, is to be answered that it is not one day's work, or two day's work. It is the work of a whole life, as every art and science is the same: if one says that, "In ten years I will accomplish learning music," that person does not know what music means. If a person says, "In ten years I will be a great poet," that person does not know what poetry means. A whole lifetime is not sufficient. If these things are so difficult to attain, one cannot suppose to attain in one day the knowledge of the deeper side of life; and there are some enthusiastic persons who will talk enthusiasm one day and another day will run away, because they did not see something wonderful.

When one takes the spiritual path, one must understand first that one has taken a path for eternity. If eternity one does not know, one should not take the first step, because one is not entitled to take the first step in the spiritual path. And the one who wants to seek that truth must not seek it superficially, for truth is not sought, it is discovered. For truth is not something that is to be attained or to be possessed. Truth is the self of one's own being, and it is oneself that is to develop into truth, and what is to be found in this whole strife is [truth].

Very often people think that sorrow or pain is the sign of spirituality. One must not mistake spirituality for sorrow or pain. Yes, in many cases sorrow or pain becomes a source or a process of attaining spirituality quickly, but for that one must not ascribe to oneself a sorrow or pain, for life has enough of sorrow or pain.

Why does a human being seek for happiness? Because in reality one's real self is happiness. One has lost that self and therefore is unhappy. The greatest tragedy in life is helplessness, limitedness; and the idea is to rise above this limitation in every way possible. And this rising is climbing toward spiritual ideals from materialism. It is the summit of this spiritual ideal which must be climbed, and in the climbing then is the fulfillment of life's promise.

ART AND THE ARTIST

The contents of "Art and the Artist" have been compiled from the previously unpublished "Supplemental Papers," with the addition of "The Divinity of Art," which is from *The Complete Works of Pir-o-Murshid Hazrat Inayat Khan: Original Texts, Lectures on Sufism 1922*, vol. 1, 19–24. "The Divinity of Art" comes from a lecture at the Musée Guimet, Paris, January 7, 1922, and the transcribed text has been preserved in French language notes. Cannon Labrie has provided an English translation of this text.

ART

Life is like the movement of lines. The beauty of lines is the wisdom and the beauty of life. Who understands lines understands God's plan. Color is a later creation than the line. Color is the fulfillment of the line. The line is God's power (mind); color is God's softness (mercy, wisdom); light is God's ever-enduring life. Symbology means to understand every form, every color, every light. To understand this in its ever-creating action is to understand the language of symbology.

The artist needs three faculties: observation, concentration, expression.

Observation in itself is a concentration when it is keen and well-focused. The keenness of observation comes from the clearness of mind and from the appreciation of beauty. The mind becomes clear when it is stilled, as the reflection is clear in water which is still. When the water is disturbed, the reflection becomes blurred. For appreciation of beauty, love for beauty is necessary, which is inborn in the artist but is developed by a continual tendency to admire all that is beautiful.

Concentration is divided into three aspects: designing, filling, finishing.

In designing, whatever one is concentrating upon one must first be able to form the outline of. This faculty can be developed by observing and taking in the outline of the object.

Filling has its two aspects: (*a*) filling with the parts and items that compose the object, however minute; (*b*) grasping the right sense of the color. The former comes from the analytical observation and exactness in taking up the object into one's mind. The latter comes by the development of the sense of color, which is a natural faculty in human beings.

Finishing is again going over the object one has in mind with an examining attitude, and noticing every little detail separately and collectively, and comparing it with the object that the eyes have seen. This requires not only an analytical tendency, but also exactness and development of memory.

Every atom of the body, the eyes which see and the hand which holds the brush, are obedient servants of the mind. When an artist produces a picture on the canvas at a time when the artist's body is not in perfect submission to the mind, and the mind not completely disciplined by the spirit, that artist cannot produce the picture to the artist's own satisfaction. The artist's mind must be respondent to the guiding voice of the soul, and the hand must be led aright by the power of the mind. It is necessary that the hand of the painter be well practiced in order to act rightly according to the suggestion of the mind. If the hand is not trained enough, the mind is not satisfied. It is necessary that the material, in the way of brush and color and canvas, is all up to the choice of the painter to the best of the artist's own satisfaction. It is necessary that the surroundings of the artist are congenial and at least harmonious if not inspiring. But artistic environments, harmonious atmosphere, and beautiful surroundings are helpful.

The mind of the artist must be free from the worries and anxieties of life. No thought of ugliness and badness of anybody's nature, nor bitterness or spite must take hold of the mind of the artist. For the mind must be perfectly free for receiving beauty in order to produce beauty. The artist must reject all badness of the artist's own nature. It is the sweetness of one's nature which will express itself in the beauty of one's art. The artist must not be irritable by nature, must not be impatient, and must not have bitterness against anybody, for these are the things in life which hinder beauty.

Artists must love beauty of manner and express it in their own actions, and must refrain from all that is lacking beauty in thought, feeling, word, and deed. The purer the hearts of the artists, the greater their art; the greater their love in their art, the more beauty they will produce.

NATURE AND ART

Nature is the perfection of whatever choice human beings can make, and this itself is the proof that it is a creation of a creator who has not created blindly, but with intention and choice, proving thereby the creator's perfect wisdom and skill. Nature, therefore, is the art of an artist who has made it to come up to the artist's choice. Mineral, vegetable, animal, even human creation are from God, but in the human creation God changes God's own choice by experiencing life through a human mind and body.

As the perfect spirit, God creates in nature all God wishes to come into being, and does not find anything lacking, for God has the capability of creating what is not there. But when the ray of the same Spirit works through the human garb, in the first place it is incapable of seeing nature as a whole and enjoying the perfection of its beauty. And yet, being the ray of the perfect Spirit, and as by nature it seeks perfection, it wants to create what it does not find there, and it is this which brings about the necessity for action.

Nature, therefore, is an action of God, and art the reaction of humanity. Art is divided into two classes: imitation (copying), and production (improving and improvising). The first wave of the artistic impulse is to imitate what one admires, and in this there are two tendencies that the artist shows: to copy and to improve. There is one artist who is more capable of copying, another of improvising. The skill in both aspects is equally great. To copy nature fully is beyond human capacity, and the greater artists are in their art, the better they can copy nature. To copy nature, not only a keen observation but a deeper insight into the object before one is necessary.

The improvising faculty may show in certain ways greater, for the artist tries to make the copy of nature better than it is. In reality nature cannot be bettered, considering it as a whole; but when nature is observed in its parts it most often requires to be made better. And the ray of the Creator's spirit, which is the soul of the artist, tries to perfect that piece of nature which is imperfect when taken as apart from nature, proving thereby the action of God and the reaction of the human being.

COPYING 1

In copying nature there are two essential things: single-mindedness and fixed observation. Single-mindedness comes from concentration. The artist must realize that it is the hand that can keep still which is capable of holding the brush, and so it is only the mind that can stand still which has the power to copy. By fixed observation is meant the capability of holding the gaze in focus, and by the latter is meant the penetrating glance. It depends a great deal upon the object that the artist paints. If its beauty is catching the eyes and the mind of the artist, and if it can hold the interest of the artist, it helps the artist to paint. There is always one thing that works against the artist: that is an ever-changing temperament. It may work so actively that it may take away the fixed glance toward something more glaring, and thereby one may not have the patience to persevere in observing the one object before one.

Though the changeableness of the artist, in a way, shows the liquidity of the mind which is natural to the artist, still, control over that changeableness brings efforts in art to a successful issue. Concentration therefore helps the artist most in work. Keen insight into beauty does not only help in art, but it leads the artist to spiritual perfection. There is a very thin veil between the artist and God, and it is insight into beauty, with constant practice, which can sometimes lift the veil so that all the beauty of nature will become to the artist one single vision of the sublime immanence of God.

COPYING 2

Copying is the pupil's tendency, and the great master is the one who is a great pupil. The one who copies must by nature be a respondent lover of nature and a follower of nature. There is a verse of a Hindustani poet, "I will undo your curls, O blowing wind, if you disturb the curls of my beloved." The copiers are the lovers of the beauty they see, and they do not wish to alter it. Their whole effort is to keep its originality, and that is the nature of the lovers of God. The copiers in their constant efforts draw closer and closer to beauty, thereby producing in their own nature beauty; and holding the beauty in themselves, they develop harmony in their nature and arrive at oneness with nature.

The copiers develop the faculty of thinking deeply. Patience is naturally developed by copying. Also the copiers will always keep balance, since nature, when seen as a whole, is nothing but balance. Balance is life, and the lack of it is death. The copiers develop moderation in their nature, for they gently follow nature; and so they are always protected by nature, which has every support and protection of the Almighty Being, itself the very manifestation of God.

THE ART OF COPYING NATURE

The art of copying nature is suggestive of the perpendicular line, which represents all between heaven and earth. Also the perpendicular line denotes concentration and observation, the higher point of the line showing heaven, the lower part the earth. It is the straightness of glance in copying and the steadiness of the impression of nature which the artist gets that are both symbolized as the straight line. Therefore the ancient mystics have called the straight line *alif*, which means "first," the origin and source of all things. The word *alpha* comes from the same root.

IMPROVING 1

The tendency to improve upon nature is a wave of activity of the mind which rises higher than the tendency of copying nature, the former being productive, the latter more impressive. However, the virtue of both tendencies is peculiar in every case. The former tends toward the Creator, whereas the latter toward creation. Success in the first aspect of art is slow but sure; but in the second aspect, of improving, it may turn the right or the wrong way. The rhythm of the former is smooth, slow, and mobile; of the latter active, emphatic, and balancing. The art of copying is less intelligible to many than the art of improving.

To appreciate the art of the one who copies, a deep insight is needed, even so deep an insight as that of the artist who dived deep into the ocean of beauty and from the bottom brought forth pearls in form and color. There is a tendency which often seems to increase in an imaginative artist, whereby the interest in the artist's own art may go far from nature. Very often even this may prove successful; but at the end of a close examination it must prove to have turned fatal, for the safety of art rests only in keeping hand in hand with nature.

IMPROVING 2

The artist who improves indeed develops creative faculty, and this is rooted in that spirit which is the spirit of the Creator. To improve upon nature is to add to nature that which human nature has produced by a certain angle of vision. Improving is the perfection of nature. The path of the improvers is risky. They sometimes have to produce what the human eye has never seen. Therefore their art, instead of appealing to the sense of beauty, often appeals to the sense of curiosity; and instead of bringing satisfaction, which must come through beauty, it may create a feeling of marvel. The artist must have a wonderful grace of form in order to improve to satisfaction.

There are many artists who develop an art which produces confusion in the spectator, and these are called illusionists. They sometimes answer to the symbolical fancies of humankind; sometimes they appeal to the spiritualistic point of view; sometimes they produce a vision in their art, a feeling of something in a mist. This kind of art becomes of course a means of expressing the mystical ideas, but in the hands of the incompetent it is nothing but a meaningless art. And in the hands of the pretentious who wish to mystify people with their skill, it is nothing but a means of entertainment. The best way of improving upon nature is by keeping close to nature and yet amplifying the beauty of nature in painting, which is no doubt the true art.

THE ART OF IMPROVEMENT

The art of improvement is, in a sense, opposed to the natural form, for it is not the same. And therefore, this attitude of the artist toward nature is symbolized by the horizontal line, which supposedly means to say that you, the original nature, must not remain as you are: "I will make you different and better." It is this attitude that can be pictured as a horizontal line against the straight line, which forms the symbol of the cross. Since the cross is the way to perfection, the spirit which is in the artist brings about a perfection in the matter which is in nature. When looking from this point of view, no one can say anymore that it is premature on the part of a human being to interfere with the skill of God, as soon as one has realized that God created nature as God but perfected divine creation as the artist.

THE ONE WHO IMPROVES

The improvers have two tendencies. One tendency is to respect the form they improve by refraining from demolishing the originality of the form. They walk gently after nature as followers of nature, which no doubt assures the success of their art. They improve, but do not go very far from nature. They touch the original form and yet do not touch it; they gently work out their destiny of perfecting the original nature. This they do by patience and by thoughtfulness. They are, so to speak, diffident before the Creator.

The other tendency is the tendency of exaggeration. In this there are two kinds. One is to give one's own form to the color of nature, or giving one's choice color to the form of nature. Another is a slightly pronounced tendency of exaggeration, which is to improve a form even to the extent of deforming it, so that the artist may make the length of the leaf, which originally is a palm, the size of an elephant's ear, make round what is oval, make an oval into a round form, make even into uneven, and turn a natural into an odd form. Undoubtedly, in doing so the artist, if a really gifted one, will produce what very few artists will be able to do, and surely will get successful results as a prize for the artist's courageous ventures.

But since this tendency of an artist is adventure, it has every chance of failure. Very few artists are able to succeed in exaggeration in their artistic executions, and those who are incapable of doing this, when attempting to exaggerate their art, prove themselves to be nothing but premature. In the art of improvement, no doubt the creative faculty of the artists has as vast a scope as they may require, but no artist has ever been able to produce, nor will any artist ever be able to produce, the form that does not exist. There is no form nor color that does not exist in nature, and there are many forms and colors which remain, and will remain, unknown and unexplored by science or art. And this shows that a human being, however great an artist, is but a copier of nature; and by this one comes to the realization that after all, human is human, and God is God.

OBSERVATION

To have the real knowledge of color and form is not easy for every artist. The sensibility for the minute shades of different colors and for the variety of shades in one color is a natural gift, which no study or practice can teach unless the artist is inspired by the artist's own genius. It is difficult to have the feeling of the slight differences of thinness and thickness of the structure, and it is still more difficult for the average person to distinguish between the slight changes of color and form unless a person is gifted by artistic insight. No doubt there is only one way of development, and if that way comes by itself, so much the better.

Keenness of observation is both cause and effect of patience, love, and perseverance. A keen observation in reality is a concentration with open eyes; and when the gaze is fixed on an object of beauty and the mind, stilled by its effect, reflects the same effect from within, it becomes a complete concentration, a heaven in itself, if viewed mystically. This brings one to the realization of the philosophy that beauty in every form is perfection, and this perfection can be brought about by the harmony of two opposed things.

When the eyes are looking at a certain object and the mind is thinking of something else, this must naturally create a collision; for two activities going on at the same time in different directions, having no touch of harmony, must of themselves fail to prove successful since conflict is a breach of the law of perfection. No one can concentrate better than a real artist, and no one can become great in art without developing concentration of mind. Both mind and body act and react upon each other, so as art helps concentration, so concentration helps art.

ILLUSION IN ART

Illusion is produced in art by two kinds of artists: those who have great intelligence with the fine sense of art, and the others whose minds are not clear and who express in their art their own confusion. Therefore the former are the real illusionists; the latter may be taken for what they are not.

One kind of illusion in art is to show at first sight something quite different from what a second sight would suggest. This no doubt requires great skill, besides a gifted talent in art, in that side of art. In this particular side of art one can see many forms in one form. By looking from different sides, and sometimes from each side, quite a different picture is seen, each proving the skill of the artist. In this form of art, no doubt, skill is more pronounced than beauty.

An example of this may be seen in the Lion Gate of Mycenae. This represents "seek all power at the feet of God." The column represents the foot of God. The lions represent power. It also represents that God is all power, that all the powerful of the world receive their power from God. This means, God is all powerful, God is the source of all power, in God is centered all power. The four round marks at the head of the column signify the four directions, which means that the reign of God is everywhere. The two altars show that the power manifests in two aspects, although they are of one and the same God, one aspect being might, and the other being beauty.

The whole figure also shows a human head, the column being the nose, the altar the mouth, and the two lion heads being the eyes. This represents that the all-powerful God is found in the human being, the true temple and altar of God.

There is another kind of illusion. It is to produce before the concentrated gaze a picture that appears as real, and this is a proof of the best gift in art.

There is a third kind of illusion, a suggestive art in which a suggestion is made of a certain idea or action, so that only the mind developed enough to comprehend it may know it, although to all others it stands as a picture. This no doubt requires an awakening mind with creative power, and in this the artist has an opportunity in the realm of art to convey a thought to others. The artists of ancient times were generally mystics, and they always expressed their thoughts concerning the law of life and nature, their imagination of heaven, in art.

There is a fourth kind of illusion, which is more mystical than a simple suggestive illusion. It is to picture thought or feeling, a character or a quality which is of the abstract. It is like putting into form and color what is much beyond it. However, this art cannot be a common language. It is a language which no one understands better than its inventor, and yet it is beyond the capacity of the ordinary mind to picture the abstract. In this way there are many who try to picture music or thought-forms or emotions. No doubt this kind of art may easily lead an artist to mystify people with meaningless forms and colors of the artist's own fantasy, though in every case it must prove to be an advanced adventure on the part of the artist.

The most important aspect of illusion in art is symbology. Symbology is a language of art. It does not mean something to the artist only, but it is known to all who are supposed to know its meaning. Symbology means "recognized illusion." The origin of symbology is in the inspiration of the artist, for to the artist, wisdom is revealed in dreams of art; and though an inspired artist certainly gives a message in the form of art, it is not necessary that every artist should be equipped in symbology, for talent in this direction is inborn in certain artists. An artist in the mystical path may develop this, but there must already be a spark of it in the heart of the artist. To understand symbology means to understand the language of nature, for behind the recognized symbols are numberless symbols, represented by every form that exists on earth and in heaven.

Lion Gate
Mycenae, Greece
c.1250 BCE

SYMBOLOGY

Symbolic art lies between the art of copying and the art of improving. In symbolic art, the art of copying and improvising unite; and therefore, in symbolism both principal aspects of art become perfected. A person inspired by the symbolic expression of nature sees in all things of nature a symbol representing something, at the same time revealing some mystery of life and nature. This knowledge is a key to the whole creation. To those possessing this knowledge everything in the world seems a closed box, the key of which they possess. As soon as they give their attention to anything they see, they immediately find at hand a symbolic expression which, used as a key, opens the door to every hidden treasure.

There are two aspects of symbolic knowledge. One aspect is *nazul*, when everything in nature begins to give its key to the artist in the form of a symbol. And by using the key, the artist becomes able to find out the mystery that every form represents. The other aspect is *'uruj*, in which a wave arises from the heart of the artist, bringing before the artist's view a design which can best express the artist's thought symbolically. The artist produces this wave that rises in the heart by pain, satisfying thereby the demand of the spirit for perfection. In *nazul*, therefore, the artist receives the message; in *'uruj* the artist gives it to the world, thereby fulfilling the spiritual act to which the inspired artist is destined.

According to the temperament of the artist, one is either more inclined to *nazul* or to *'uruj*. The temperament of the one who is inclined to *nazul* has the *jamal* temperament, and the one who is inclined to *'uruj* has the *jalal* temperament. However, *'uruj* and *nazul* both act and react upon each other. Without *'uruj*, *nazul* is impossible; without *nazul*, *'uruj* cannot be. They act and react upon each other; and so perfection lies in receiving both, at times *nazul* and at times *'uruj* as one divides the time of one's life during day and night into action and repose.

ART AND RELIGION

A time has come when life seems so divided that people feel afraid to connect in any way or in any form, art and religion. In reality art has always done the greatest service to religion. In all ages and to most of the world religions, no doubt, there has always come a reaction in the great service that art has done to religion; then that reaction has swept away art from religion. But no thoughtful person will ever deny the fact that when the art is taken away from religion, it is just like taking away breath out of body. And if we go still further we shall find that art in itself is a religion, for art fulfills that purpose toward which religion works.

If I were to give a definition of art in words, I would say that art is a harmonious expression of the soul. And what is religion? Religion is the way by which one arrives at that harmonious response. Yes, there are souls who look upon art as something made by human beings, and then they say, "But art is art, nature is nature." They are right, but it would not be untrue also if I said that art is nature and nature is art. What is produced in the art is a reflection of nature, and besides this, if you will take a philosophic point of view, you will also see that art is an improvement upon nature. It will not be an exaggeration to say that what was not produced in nature was made by the Creator through the pen of the artist.

It is primitive to divide works of human beings from the works of God. If God is the light of the heavens and of the earth, then God's creation is that which we call nature, and God's creation again is that which we call art. As long as the artists are unaware of this truth, their art is only art; but no sooner are they acquainted with this truth, their art becomes religion.

Imagine to what extent the sculptor, the painter, the poet, the musician have inspired humanity. Suppose there was no music, there was no poetry, no sculpture or painting to inspire humankind—how far would we have been inspired only by what we call religion? Art has taken a central action, the central activity in each religion. Art has an influence, a power to suggest an idea, an idea which cannot be very well spoken in words. And a person who only can understand an idea through words has not yet arrived at that delicacy to understand an idea without words, for real inspiration comes by communicating with life. When one can communicate with a piece of art, with a picture, with a poetry, with music which can convey to one's soul some idea, some feeling, then really one begins inspiration in one's life.

When we trace the sense behind the whole creation, we find that the whole creation is working toward one object, and that object is to arrive at a perfect harmony. And it is that harmony which may be called beauty; there is no other explanation of beauty. For everyone sees in an object a beauty, but if you ask, "What is beautiful, what is in this object which makes you think it is beautiful?" a person cannot say it because it is abstract; it is the feeling of harmony which is produced by that object which makes one feel this is beautiful.

There are several notes of music, there are numberless words in different languages, there are numerous colors which have their peculiarities; but what we call beautiful is the harmonious combination, harmonious arrangement, harmonious grouping in all different things.

Therefore the mission of art is to produce harmony, to combine lines or colors or notes or words in a harmonious group, and this is the art. Therefore, if I were asked to explain that which is beautiful in this picture, I would say the music that this picture conveys. Also in poetry, what gives the sense of beauty is the music of that poetry, the music of its sense, the harmony of its words, rhymes, of the idea.

And what does religion teach us? Religion teaches us also the ways of harmony. The mission of religion is to teach us how to live in the room, outside, with friends, with neighbors, how to be, how to harmonize with one's soul, with one's mind. Therefore, in the ancient Arabic language there is a name which they give to the deity, and that name is "the artist."

There is a story, a story which is symbolical but expressive of the mission of art for the artist. There was an artist, a young lady who gave her whole life, her thought, to the piece of art, to the little marble piece that she was working on. This was the one piece of art which interested her more than anything else she had ever met in her life. She was such a devotee of art that her studio was her temple; that was the place for her soul's rest. Nowhere else did she feel at home; it is there that she was working with her art. Her friends, her comrades, all found her quite devoted in one thing and engrossed. She did not mix with others. Though she was in the midst of life, she was quite retired, quite devoted to her art; nothing else would interest her. They used to tease her and they used to dislike her tendency of giving her whole soul to her work; they could not understand her.

Very often at home and outside, a psychological influence came out of that piece of work that she was accomplishing. As more it became finished, the more that piece of art had an influence upon her. She began to see more life in it; she began to see a beauty which was wakening in it. She could no longer consider it a statue. She began to see in this statue life. She said, "I have sought you my friend, my beautiful one. In you I see the beauty that all else in this world is unreliable. I do not feel attracted to it. You have come as the expression of my being; you are my soul, you are my life, nothing else in the world interests me. It is in you that I see there is any real beauty in life." So it is in art. A voice arose in the ears of her heart, "Yes, I am living and I will live. And I can speak, and I will speak only on one condition: that you will take a bowl of poison out of my hand. For the condition of my being alive, my coming to life is only one, and that is that you die and that I live." And she said, "Nothing can please me but to see you live—you, the expression of my soul—for in you I see the beauty that is in that soul of my spirit. And I will most gladly take the cup of poison in order to see you alive." And what happened? She took the bowl of poison, and as she was dying this statue became alive, lifted her, and then restored her. This is the picture of all those who have really made the art, those who have found the real benefit from their art.

The musicians such as Beethoven, whose whole life was devoted to their work, to their music, they themselves were nothing. To them, self-vanished, art becomes living; they are dead. The art still lives, and the art kept them alive also. And so it is with the dead poets in the history of the world. Those who have produced a piece of art in their poetry, a work of their poetry which is living till now, they have been dead and yet they are alive. The beauty that they have created—when they were creating that beauty they forgot themselves, and after their death they are still alive in the arms of their art.

And this shows what devotion can do. The artists' devotion to their art is just like the devotion of worshipers to their deity. But if they also know the secret of the art, then it is no longer art to them; it is the expression of the deity in the form of beauty.

And now we come to realize that there are many different aspects of art, but art is one and the same. What painting cannot express, poetry expresses; what poetry cannot explain, music expresses. But greatest of all arts is the art of personality. No doubt, devotees of art, without knowing, develop art in their personalities. But it is possible also that one may be a good artist and yet may miss that something which should be developed in one's own personality. And in that case one has not yet perfected one's art, or one's personality would have been developed.

The Mughal emperors used to have some artists in their court. And very often the courtiers were very annoyed with that idea, but at the same time they said, "There is something living in the association of the arts." But one might ask that "Everybody is not born with the gift of the artist, and if they were all artists, then how could the world go on? And therefore what could we do with the art?" In order to learn art, in order to practice art in life, we need not be painters, we need not be sculptors. Whatever be our condition of life and whatever be our occupation, we have sufficient scope in our everyday life to develop that artistic faculty that is in us. The best expression of artistic faculty can be given by an artistic personality. That agreeable manner, that politeness, that fineness which proves a person to be harmonious, of beautiful personality—that is the best art that one can ever learn. Those who lack this faculty show that lack in everything they do: writing, reading, walking or sitting; in every action they show that what they lack is that artistic faculty. Those who are awkward in manner, are awkward in what they say, awkward in what they do—awkward because awkwardness represents lack of harmony. Fineness, beauty, can be expressed in every form. Those who love beauty, those who worship beauty, those who devote themselves to beauty, express beauty in everything they do.

To arrive at that aim for which every soul is born is not in being perhaps so earthly, or so spiritual as an angel. For on this plane of the earth souls were not created in order to be angels. They were created to be perfect human beings, and this perfection is not only gained by thinking deep, by realizing deep, by attaining to that harmony in which is the fulfillment of the whole life. One who cannot get along with those one lives with, one who cannot live in harmony among those with whom one is put, one who cannot agree with those one comes in contact with, that person has not yet wakened to that harmony which makes personality.

For it is just like painting a picture which nobody admires, nobody likes. It is like a violin so inharmoniously played that everybody would go out of the room. The greatest art is the art of personality. When one can draw others toward one by goodness, by kindness, by fineness, by forgiveness, by understanding, one knows the greatest art there is. It is the spiritual personalities who not only attracted people, but they attracted beasts and birds. Today that power can be developed which is spoken of in the Bible: that for Daniel, in the cave in the mountains, in the lions' den, the cruel animals in a moment's time were quiet. The great ones had such charm that they impressed the world with it, and for thousands of years, millions of people have read their scriptures, remembered their names as the holy ones. And what had they? They had the art of personality. When Christ said to the fishermen, "Come hither, I will make you fishers of men,"[1] what was he going to teach them? It was the art of personality.

Today the time has come when humanity should be wakened to the higher ideal, and there cannot be a better means of elevating the human ideal than the idea of harmony, of love, and of beauty.

1 Matthew 4:19.

THE DIVINE ART

People belonging to different faiths very often make the mistake of considering art as something outside of religion. The fact is that the whole creation is the art of the Creator, and one sees the perfection of the Creator's art in divine humanity. This shows that the source of the whole creation has the spirit of art at the back of it. In all ages human beings have developed their artistic faculty, and they have tried to progress in art. But, in the end, where do they arrive? They remain far from touching either the beauty of nature or the art of creation. Human art always fails to equal the art of God.

This shows that the source of every soul is the spirit of art, and art is spirit; that everything which has come out from that spirit has manifested in the form of art. If we look more at nature—at the heavens; the beauty of the stars and planets; of the clouds and the sun, its rising and setting, and when the sun is at its zenith; the waxing and waning of the moon; the different shades of color which we can see in the sky—the more would we always marvel at the art at work behind it all.

When one is alone with nature, near the sea, on the riverbank, among the mountains, in the forest, in the wilderness, a feeling comes over one which is never felt among a crowd, not even if one were in the crowd for years. In one moment a feeling becomes born, as soon as one is face to face with the true art of God. It then seems as if the soul had seen something which it has always admired and worshiped. The soul now begins to recognize One whom it has always silently worshiped, and now the presence of that mighty Creator, that Artist, is realized through seeing God's art. Many experience this, but few will express it. None can come back from such an experience without a deep impression, without something having been awakened to consciousness through having seen the divine art.

This shows that this creation, this manifestation which is before us, has not been made mechanically, has not been created blindly or unconsciously. As a great poet of Persia, Sa'adi, says, "The more one looks at nature, the more one begins to feel that there is a perfection of wisdom, a perfect skill, behind it, which has made it; and it will take numberless years for humankind to imitate that art. In fact humankind will never be able to attain it perfectly."

Whoever studies the kingdom of flowers, of vegetables, of minerals, the birds, the insects, the germs, and the worms, the animals and their forms and colors, and the beauty which each form suggests, will surely recognize, as did the prophets of old, that the world is created by the Spirit—that divine Spirit who has created it with eyes wide open, and showing perfect wisdom behind it, and perfect skill in it, and a sense of beauty so perfect that human beings must always be incapable of achieving it. But now the question comes, "What is a human being?" A human being is the miniature of God, and human beings have inherited as their divine inheritance the tendency to art.

Therefore, anyone with intelligence and with tender feeling, which goes to make a person a normal human being, must admit the beauty of art. One is born with that tendency. A child is born with the love of art, as is proved by the infant being attracted to toys and beautiful colors. Lines attract it. And the first thing which the infant begins to like or desire is color and movement. This is the time of its life during which the infant is impressed by artistic things. When a person loses the sense of art, it is just as when the heart has become blind. It cannot see the art anymore because of the clouds of all manner of ugliness and undesirableness, and all that one does not like to look upon. All such things and impressions cover the heart and the soul, and make a person, so to speak, blind to beauty, blind to art. But this is not the normal condition. The normal state of a sound mind in a sound body with tender feeling is love of beauty, is to admire art.

No doubt, very often people do not live a natural life. That is, their business or profession or responsibility holds them. Some work or some thought for the needs of the body, for bread and butter or any other everyday need holds them and absorbs the whole of their thoughts, so that they become useless for the discovery of the beauty and joy and happiness of life. Hence, as we see around us today, life is becoming so difficult and so full of anxiety and trouble and responsibility. From morning till evening people are just loaded with their responsibilities and toil day and night. They have never a moment to think of the beauty of art. Since art is the first step which leads to the cause of art, how can a person who has never admired or understood the beauty of art hope to admire or understand the Artist?

So God remains unrecognized, and not through the fault of God, but through the fault of human beings. The Creator, in the role of an artist, has created beautiful art which is not far from human eyes. But human beings are so engrossed in thoughts and occupations which have nothing to do with that art. All their time and thought and effort are devoted to occupations which never allow them one moment to think of art and admire it and understand and appreciate it. Naturally, then, they remain as if their eyes were covered over from the vision of the Artist.

The real purpose of human life was not that humans be born to toil for bread and butter; the real purpose of human life was not that humans should be avaricious and compete with their fellow human beings and hate them and view another with prejudice and use the whole of their time in a kind of spirit of rivalry and competition, in which there can be no harmony or joy or peace. With the necessarily ever-increasing avariciousness there is an absence of that beauty for which the soul so constantly longs.

It would be no exaggeration to say that all these disagreeable things which go on in this world—wars, diseases, and the like—all come from the lack of artistic attitude in life, the lack of a sense of beauty, and the lack of that vision which unites the whole humanity in one center; and this center is God. When one closes one's eyes to beauty, one will never think of looking for the beautiful, although beauty is constantly beside one. Behind the beauty, as the Qur'an says, "God is beautiful and loves beauty."[1]

The natural tendency to love and admire beauty is a divine inheritance; it is the spiritual thing which leads to spirituality. Through this tendency one accomplishes one's spiritual duty in life. When that tendency has gone and religion is left without art, then the religion may be perhaps useful for an inartistic society but it turns into a sort of formality. One does one thing, one does another. As one does weekday work, so one also does Sunday duty.

People very often separate nature from art. They consider nature different from art; they consider the one superior and the other inferior. But in reality art is that which, by divinely inherited tendency, plays its role through humanity. God working in nature with God's own hidden hands has created nature, and God shows divine art in that nature. In the other aspect of art which we call art, God produces beauty through the human hand and the human mind, and so finishes that which has been left over to be finished and has not yet been finished in nature. Therefore, in one respect art is a step forward to nature, although compared with nature art is so limited. Nature is unlimited. But at the same time, art is an improvement of nature.

Seen metaphysically, the artistic spirit of God is satisfied by fulfilling its artistic tendency through the art of the human be-

1 Hadith.

ing. Therefore, those who consider art from a higher point of view recognize the artistic impulse not only as a human impulse, not only as brain work, but as a true artistic impulse, as an inspiration in itself. But in order to prepare the mind for the artistic impulse, what is necessary? Does one need some kind of learning, or some kind of study? Is there some preliminary study to be made first? No. It requires a tuning, a bringing of ourselves to an object to whose beauty the human heart can respond, to a beauty which the heart can appreciate. When the heart can concentrate upon beauty, then it works itself up to a certain pitch, for inspiration is not a thing which one can pull upon to obtain as by pulling a rope. Inspiration is a thing which comes only when the heart is tuned to that object, when it is in a position to receive it. Therefore inspired artists have been divinely gifted, and the spirit of art is one, though the arts are so many. When the heart is tuned to the proper pitch, it is not only capable of producing or appreciating one kind of art and beauty, but all kinds.

Thus there can be an art in architecture. Gifted architects can produce a great deal of beauty in their work. So too with drawing, with embroidery, with the work of dyeing, of sewing. In fact there is nothing which people do which cannot have art in it if they know how to attune themselves to that pitch which enables the art to be expressed. Poetry is an art in the same way. Unless one is tuned to the proper pitch, one may write poetry all one's life, and yet it will not please either that person or anyone else. So with a painter, or a musician (violin, piano, any instrument): one will not please oneself or anyone else during one's whole life unless one has become tuned to that pitch.

This shows that the question as to what grade of evolution a person has attained comes in every walk of life. Whether a person be a painter, or sculptor, or architect, or designer, or singer, or dancer, whatever walk a person may follow, there is no better source of inspiration in nature, whence to draw inspiration from above, than by means of art. The more cultivated the sense of art is, the more able one is to respond to the beauty of art, and the more able one is to produce or create something beautiful in oneself. The more one comes into touch with that Spirit who is constantly helping every soul toward beauty, the more one can produce. Everything that helps a person to approach the beauty of God is sacred. Therefore art can become religion. It would not be an exaggeration to say that there is no better religion than art itself.

When one has reached to that degree of understanding, when one has reached that knowledge of art by which one can become profited, when the heart is once tuned to that pitch by which one can understand and appreciate art, and when one has changed one's outlook upon life so as to see in the beauty of art the beauty of the Divine Being, then one can progress in the true art.

From this we learn, consciously or unconsciously, that which our soul is really seeking is art; and yet at the same time one very frequently avoids this very thing that one is really seeking. The right way and the wrong way are so near to one another. The only difference is that a person is journeying along the right way when at every step that person can say, "I see the signs that support and help me to go on further and promise that the goal is before me." When one is journeying along the wrong way, every step tells one, "I am not in the right way, I must go back; I am not on the road on which I ought to be."

Consciously or unconsciously, every soul seeks for beauty. And at each step of our lives if we think that beauty is receiving us as we go, that beauty meets us at every step on our path, then the soul is satisfied, is full of hope, knowing that the road we are on is our proper road and that someday or other we will arrive at our goal. The person who thinks at every step of the journey, "I am not on a right road, I do not like this; I am not pleased with that," is making no progress. The beauty the person is looking for, is ever being left behind. The person is travelling in quite another way from that which that person is expecting.

So we see that whether our road is right or wrong depends on our appreciation of the artistic side of life or on our lack of it. But by saying this, one does not wish it to be understood that everyone must necessarily practice to become an artist or learn some branch of art. It is only to say that there is a spark of artistic faculty in every soul. There is not a single soul who has not got this spark. Some have more, some have less. Yet that spark does not have to be used by everybody to that extent which is called artist. No. But we must exhibit and utilize that faculty in our everyday life. One with the artistic faculty is sure to show it in everything one does, even in dusting a room or keeping it tidy, or in keeping a machine in order. In all these directions can a person show art. One does not require a palace before one can begin to manifest art. If one really has the love for beauty, one can show the artistic faculty in quite small things.

Besides this, there is the fact that the soul manifests outwardly that which it holds inwardly, so that it is the beauty which one has within oneself which one expresses without. One shows the artistic faculty in one's manner toward a friend and toward one's surroundings. A person who has no sense of art is called "rude," "inconsiderate," "thoughtless," "foolish," "simple-minded," "crude," "coarse."

A person does not need to have much money in order to be able to express art. One can express it in various circumstances. One may be the poorest person in the world and yet one can express the beauty of one's soul in whatever state one may be placed. Beauty will not be hidden. One shows one's art in one's words.

When one is in business, or in the family, or among friends, one does not know how many times during the day one hurts the feeling of others; one does not even notice them. Even though one were very learned or experienced, the lack of art would still manifest. Even a loving, kind, and good person will never be able to express the goodness which is hidden in that person's heart if art is lacking.

When Jesus Christ taught in the Sermon on the Mount, "Blessed are they who are gentle, who are meek, humble, poor in spirit,"[2] what lesson does it teach us? It is this lesson of art. The lesson is: produce in one's personality. Even so-called artists, musicians, poets, painters, if they have not fostered art, if art is not impressed on the soul, and if the soul has not expressed the beauty of art, they do not know art. They are profane, they claim to be something they are not.

Having thought much upon this subject, and being especially interested in art, I have come in contact with artists of different countries both in the East and West. It has always proved that those who have really attained some greatness in their art were those who showed glimpses of art in their personality. It showed in the words they spoke, in the way they received me, and in the manner in which they spoke with me: their tenderness of heart, their friendliness, their interest in my affairs. Every sign of art could be seen in such personalities. Even if not an artist literally—-a painter, a singer, a poet—whatever the real occupation, it does not matter as long as one has realized beauty in that occupation, and has perceived beauty around one, and has collected around one all that one finds beautiful. All this must be expressed in return, and it is that which is true art.

In the Hindu language there are two attitudes mentioned by the philosophers, namely, *hamsadi* and *sukradi*. The former attitude is that of a bird of paradise, a mythical bird of the Hindus called Hamsa. If you put milk mixed with water before Hamsa, it will drink the milk and leave the water behind. The *sukradi* attitude is that of the people. It is the tendency of looking to find where there is any dirty spot and then wanting to sit in it. Such is the tendency of human beings. One person is always looking for what may be wrong in people, and is delighted to hear something wrong about them, and is very interested in discussing their faults and hearing of their being disgraced

2 See Matthew 5:7.

or insulted in some way. Such persons are always wanting to see the evil around them, in whatever form it may be.

This pleasure grows until the whole life becomes a burden, for the presence of evil produces its bad impression. And bad thoughts collect around that person, for they are reproduced just as a gramophone record produces sounds. Such a person becomes the gramophone record for the evil that person collects; the person utters it, retains the bad feelings within and spreads them abroad wheresoever that person goes. Nobody likes that person, nor does the person like anyone either. The time will come when that person cannot even like that person's own self. Another kind of character is the one who overlooks all that does not seem to be harmonious; this one looks only for good in every person, and finds some good even in the worst person in the world. This one seeks for good, wishes to see it wherever this one can find it, and in this way constantly gathers good impressions. And what is good? Good is beauty. What is Beauty? Beauty is God.

What is virtue? Virtue is beauty. What is beauty is also virtue. One does not have to learn in a book or a scripture or from some other person what is good and what is bad. We can learn from our own sense of art. The greater our sense of art, the more it will show what is right and what is wrong, what is good and what is bad. As soon as the senses begin to develop and understand what it is that takes away beauty and what it is that imparts beauty, then such a one gathers beauty as one gathers flowers. Such persons welcome others with beauty, they express beauty, they impart it to others. Others love them. They love others. They live and move and have their being in love, just as it is said in the Bible, "They live and move and have their being in God."[3] So those who live and move and have their being in love will certainly also live and move and have their being in God.

---

3 See Acts 17:28.

This may be called the divine art, for which a person may study and strive. But besides this there is the art which every person must look for and develop in one's own nature. The message of Sufism to the Western world has this as its chief object: to awaken the spirit of the world from this thought of antagonism and mutual hatred, and to bring about the feeling of human sisterhood and brotherhood, so that all humanity may meet with one another, whatever be their nation, race, or religion, in one place, in one center, namely, the thought of God. And in order to rise to this ideal, and in order to tune our soul to this pitch, so necessary from beginning to end, it is necessary to seek the path of beauty, and to recognize in beauty the Being of God.

THE DIVINITY OF ART

What is divinity? Without a doubt, it is a subject of very great importance to be able to distinguish between God and divinity.

God can be recognized in two ways: as the seed or germ of creation, and as the fruit of creation. The seed of creation is God, and the fruit of creation is divinity. In order to express this divinity, God was obliged to manifest in the human being. And it is this doctrine that gives us the secret of what was the soul of Christ. In fact, in every human being there is a divine spark, because the human being is the fruit of the tree of which God is the seed.

The word *divine* has its origin in Sanskrit in the word *doa*, which means "bright" or "light." And the word *deva*, which means "divine," comes from the same root. The plural of *deva* is *devan*, which is almost the same as *divine*. And this shows us where the divine spark is found in a person: it is in the intelligence. And when this light is veiled, it is like the "lamp under a bushel" that is mentioned in Holy Scripture.[1] The Bible says, "Raise your light,"[2] that is, raise your intelligence by delivering it from earthly things. The Qur'an, speaking of the divinity, says: "God is the light of heaven and earth."[3] This shows that no prophet has ignored the fact that human intelligence contains a divine spark.

---

1 Matthew 5:15.

2 See Isaiah 60:1.

3 Qur'an 24:35.

There is another aspect to this question. Intelligence is not only conceiving and perceiving; it is beauty itself. If you see a clever animal—for example, a dog, horse, or bird—it is more beautiful than the others; its behavior and movements manifest beauty, and this is the sign of its intelligence. And the human, as the most perfect of beings in creation, must manifest intelligence to the highest degree. This intelligence has manifested itself in all creation, and when it manifests in the human being, it reaches its highest note, and it is this note that we call art.

Often the one who does not know the divinity of art has considered art to be a secondary thing, but we can say that if nature is the theme composed by God, art is God's improvisation. What God, the great Creator, has done, is finished by human hands, that is to say, in art. That is why in the oldest languages the name that was given to the divinity meant artist.[4] No doubt the abuse of anything brings about its degeneration; this is true for art, and for religion too. In order to know the value of things, it is necessary for us to use them appropriately and seek to understand them. There is a spirit behind all things, and this spirit must be recognized as the divine spirit. When one ignores this truth, everything one does lacks life.

Doubtless, art is an improvement on nature, but when it gets too far away from nature, it breaks the link that binds it to creation. At all times in the history of the world, when art has distanced itself from nature, it has produced works that are unintelligible. Nature and art complete each other, they must go hand-in-hand. And the wider the gap between them, the more difficult the art is to understand.

Let's now consider the psychology of art. What creates art? The creator is the soul, the inspiration is nature. If the soul is almost entirely absorbed in its worries and earthly joys, it cannot reach very high. It is by uniting with divinity that the soul finds its life, by uniting with the creative power of God. And

4 One of the ninety-nine Beautiful Names of God is *mussawir*, the artist.

this link can be maintained when we consider God as the seed of creation, of which humanity is the fruit. A Persian poet says: "From you, the nightingale learned its melodious song, from you, the rose found the delicate colors of its petals," which indicates that divinity is reflected in all things, that beauty is reflected in all things for those whose eyes are open. When artists become conscious of this truth, anything, then, can inspire them, because they find in all things a reflection of divinity.

It is not only beauty that gives ecstasy to the seer, but behind this beauty, the seer sees the source of all love. A Hindu poet has said: "If there was no hand to offer me the cup, what does it matter if the house is full of wine?" The pursuit of art would not be of much interest if, behind all of these things, there was no divinity.

In our everyday life, we are sometimes inclined to hum an air, as if some beauty were trying to express itself. This is due to the divine impulse that seeks to express itself in beauty. The little child, who is not stopped by conventions, gets up and dances. Obsessed by the worries of life, we ignore this impulse; but it is this impulse that is the origin of all art. Whenever art has manifested itself in the history of the world, it is because of those pure and simple souls who have felt this impulse and followed it. The great musicians, the great poets, who preserved the purity of their souls and followed this impulse—they were the dancers of the court of God.

This proves that it is not great musicians who made beautiful music, nor great painters who made beautiful paintings, but rather that they came to complete creation. The more we think about the essence of art, the more we understand that this impulse must be allowed to express itself abroad. There is art in all things. In architecture, in literature, in science, in the many occupations of our life there is art, if we follow the divine impulse that is in the depths of our soul. Those who follow this impulse, whatever they do, will express art; scholar, philosopher, religious person, or worker, all will express that feeling that is at the bottom of the heart. There is no doubt that in music, in poetry, in painting, art can express itself best of all. In painting, poetry, music, or any art, every true manifestation of art is a true manifestation of beauty. Beauty takes hold of the means at hand. The heart inflamed by the spirit of art reveals the spirit of beauty in all. It is those who are inartistic that are clumsy, or disagreeable to their neighbors. When art lacks sincerity, it lacks beauty; for example, people can be polite and cultivated without ever expressing their own essence.

Art must have life; if it does not have life, it is not art. The poet can write verses in which something is missing. The painter can make paintings in which something is missing. The musician can write music in which something is missing, and what that something is, is difficult to explain. In all of these cases, life is what is missing, for life is indispensable to art. There are some poets, painters, and musicians whose works never get old, whose works the centuries do not erase, and this is because a little divine life is infused in them. Just as God, having no form, is invisible to our eyes, so is this something invisible and intangible.

Today, it seems that the world has gone from bad to worse when it comes to art and divinity. One sees advances in certain things, but still, something is missing in many others. Art is tarnished with a kind of rust, which comes from materialism and from commercialism. There are two kinds of products: the first is divine, the second is earthly. But the product of heaven is hindered in its expression because it is beyond the understanding. When beauty is sold for money, when it has to wait at the door, when it is analyzed and dismembered, then its beauty is lost. There was a time when much consideration was given to this subject. In ancient times in India, beauty was considered divine, and all the arts—especially history, poetry, and music—were thought of everywhere as divine arts, and treated as sacred things. And in the period when these ideas prevailed we saw the greatest manifestation of art. At that time, art had great influence on the community.

Very often, too much uniformity in life has a bad effect on the development of art. It is the development of art that gives it its freedom, whereas uniformity causes it to be hindered and stifled; this is destructive for art.

Is art solely for the purpose of providing pleasure in life or does it have a greater purpose? The first aim of art is to express divine beauty outwardly. The second aim is to help people ascend from this outer beauty to the source of all beauty. All the religious traditions of humanity, whether of Krishna, of Buddha, of Moses, of Muhammad, or of Jesus, have always been given in a poetic form. True wisdom always expresses itself in a beautiful form, because wisdom is beautiful.

There is a very great sense of symbolic beauty in the image of the goddess of beauty holding a vina and sitting on a lotus. And in China, in Japan, the statues of Buddha are always very beautiful and placed in beautiful places. The message of God is always given in beautiful words, thus verifying these words of the Qur'an, "God is beautiful, and loves beauty."[5] When the meaning of this is lost in a religion, then it dries up; whatever be the religion, when it renounces beauty, it renounces life.

The races, the peoples, through different religions, are against each other. After this terrible war,[6] it does not seem that there really is peace. This shows us the lack of art in the human spirit. Something must be reborn. Are the churches, and different ethnic groups responsible? No, it's each of us who is responsible. We can create new conditions, not make them worse. We are the world, we must know the value of our soul, our responsibilities. The Sufi purpose is to awaken the consciousness of these things in humanity. Our spirit can make us recognize what we are, and what the work of this life should be. Each of us can understand our individual responsibilities; we must

5 Hadith.

6 World War I.

understand that we are part of a whole. If each of us gave five minutes a day to meditate on ways to do good in the world, we could do a lot. If everyone fell asleep, what would happen? Instead of working for the world, let's recreate beauty, harmony, and peace.

THE ART OF MUSIC

The contents of "The Art of Music" have been compiled from the previously unpublished "Supplemental Papers," with the addition of "Composition," "Music, Astrology, and Alchemy," and "The Religion of Harmony," which are from *The Complete Works of Pir-o-Murshid Hazrat Inayat Khan: Original Texts, Lectures on Sufism 1922,* vol. 1, 314, 361, 386–87; and "Indian Music 1," which is from *The Complete Works of Pir-o-Murshid Hazrat Inayat Khan: Original Texts, Lectures on Sufism 1922,* vol. 2, 197–201.

INDIAN MUSIC 1

In Indian music, when several instruments are played together the effect is not produced by the chord or by harmony but by melody. Each instrument has the melody. When music is played before a thousand or ten thousand people, then of course many instruments are needed. In the West, the music is made brilliant, impressive, and lively by the chords. We make it so by the melody alone. When music is played before a few hearers only, then three or four instruments are needed, or only one. When it is used for concentration, then one instrument, one voice is quite enough. If ten instruments each play a note, then there can be no concentration, the mind is drawn to the ten notes.

The mystics, especially the Sufis, have used music in their prayers, in their meditations. It was a part of their devotions. Khwaja Mu'in ad-Din Chishti and Khwaja Banda Nawaz made great use of music. I have practiced and experienced myself the use of music in meditation, and I have understood that it is the best means of meditation, the quickest means of freeing the consciousness.

Sound has been called God, Nada Brahma, in the Vedanta. In the Gospel of Saint John it is called the Word,[1] from which all things have come. When the poets imagine a lake and a mountain, they have the forms, the lake and the mountain, before the eyes of their mind. When musicians think of a

1 See John 1:1.

melody, they have no form, no name before them. They are on a plane higher than the poets. First there was the sound. God was sound; and from the sound, by the sound, all this world was manifested.

The story tells that when the human being was created, first the soul was unwilling to enter the body, saying, "This is a prison, it is dark, and I have always been free." Then God commanded the angels to sing. When they sang, the soul was in such an ecstasy that it entered the body, not knowing where it was going. By music, also, it can be freed from the physical consciousness. The mother's voice, when she says, "Sleep, sleep," puts the child to sleep, and her voice awakens it again.

In ancient times music was the sacred art. The great musicians were great mystics. Such were Tansen—whose miracles are known all over India—Narada, and Tumbara.

Music produces so great an ecstasy. Even among those musicians who were not mystics, such as Beethoven or Paderewski, you may see that their ecstasy is so great that they have no attention left even to arrange their hair. To brush their coat becomes a very difficult matter for them. In the West and in the East also it is so. In the East you may see a musician going out to play and leaving the sitar at home; the musician's abstraction is so great that even the instrument is forgotten.

By music the highest state of samadhi can be produced much more quickly than by any other means. There are many different practices, but music is the best mystical practice.

At the present time in the East, music has sunk very low. It has been regarded as an amusement, as a diversion. It was regarded as a national possession, as a source of pride to the ego, to the *nafs*. The heritage of the ancestors, which had been built up with so great an effort, with so much care, is now being lost by carelessness, by negligence. In the West also, music is being brought down. The musicians who advertise themselves very much are great artists; the one who does not advertise is nothing. All is done for money: it is commercialized and degraded. That which should be valued highest is brought down to the lowest circles.

Our work is not only to speak before you, to lecture before you, to bring you the Sufi message in books and lectures, but to bring it to you also in music, to play before you, to sing before you, to bring the truth before you in music. In ancient times it was very difficult to speak openly of the truth. The governments were so strict, the religions were so narrow in their interpretations, in their understanding. Especially it was difficult for the Sufis. Many of them have been beheaded for speaking the truth. The mystics therefore invented a way of speaking the truth in music, in words that apparently had no meaning, such as *tum*, *dim*, *tarana*, *la*, so as to be understood by the initiates, while to the uninitiated it seemed merely a meaningless song. At the present time, even in the East, there are many who do not know that such words have any meaning. They know that the song is called *tarana*; they do not know what it means.

INDIAN MUSIC 2

The science of Indian music is founded on a most natural basis. Sound is graduated into tones, semitones, and microtones. Time is divided into six finer divisions, besides the usual six. Each note has its color, a planet, and an element, according to the mysticism of sound. Our music is based upon the principle of ragas, scales. Mystically they are subject to time and season, and each raga has an effect upon the spheres. Poetically ragas have their images; they are also idealized as ragas (men), *raginis* (women), *putras* (sons), and *bharjas* (daughters). Mathematically, they have increased from one to innumerable ragas. Artistically, they are taken from the natural music of diverse people. And scientifically they have five divisions: ragas of seven notes, six notes, five notes, even notes, and odd notes.

The art of Indian music is remarkable for its vocal culture, and it requires years of study to attain proficiency in it. Our instrumental music is considered next to the vocal in importance. The vina is the oldest instrument in the world's history, and it is also the only instrument for the correct production of Indian music. Indian dancing follows on the same principles as vocal and instrumental music. The Indian musician is recognized chiefly for the inspirational beauty expressed by the musician's improvisation. Therefore, our composers are much less known, because their compositions are performed by each artist differently; only the foundation and poetry remain the same. The artist is supposed to be a composer before being able to become an artist. Even if the artist sings one song it will be different each time. Therefore notation did not become universal in India until of late, when Maula Bakhsh, the great composer, invented a system of notation for beginners and founded a school on modern principles in the state of Maharaja Gaekwar of Baroda.[1]

1 Maharaja Sayaji Rao Gaekwar.

COMPOSITION

Composition is an art rather than a mechanical arrangement of notes. Composers of music perform their small part in the scheme of nature, as creators. Music being the most exalted of all arts, composers of music—their work is no smaller than the work of a saint. It is not only the knowledge of technicality, the knowledge of harmony, the knowledge of theory that is sufficient. Composers need tenderness of heart, opened eyes to all beauty, the conception of the beautiful, the true perception of sound, and rhythm, and its expression in human nature. By composing music, composers must create their own world in sound and rhythm. Therefore, their work is not a labor, it is a joy, the joy of the highest order.

If composers write music because they must write something, that is not the thing to do. Composers must write music when their hearts feel like writing, when their hearts are singing, when their souls are dancing, when their whole being is vibrating harmony. That is the time that they must write music. Composers must not make an effort of writing. What they must try is to make themselves a perfect channel, to let it flow freely out of themselves, what comes from within, and express that sentiment coming in the form of inspiration, in the realm of music.

MUSIC, ASTROLOGY, AND ALCHEMY

The mystics have found a relation between notes and planets. And as astrology is a science which indicates the law of the working of nature, this part of musical science is the astrological side of music. Every time has a certain influence, and at that time certain ragas are beneficial for the bodily health, state of mind and condition of soul.

As modern science has analyzed matter in its different elements, so the mystics of the ancient time have analyzed the elements of vibrations, which each have their color: earth, yellow; water, green; fire, red; air, blue; and ether, gray. And they have analyzed the different effects of notes: warm, cool, wet, or dry. Undoubtedly, those who knew the alchemy of vibrations, have worked wonders by the power of music.

IMPROVISATION

The characteristic of Indian music is that it depends upon the creative talent of the musician in improvisation. An outline is given by the composer, and the musicians fill it in as they please. Very little is given by the composer, the outline only, and the rest is the expression by the singer of the singer's feeling at the time of singing. Music in India has always been used not as an amusement but as a means of mystical development. Therefore the sound of the instruments is faint, and even when several instruments are played together the effect is not produced by the chord, by harmony, but by melody. Each instrument has the melody.

There is very little written music in the East. There are many reasons for this. There is a system in the Sanskrit manuscripts, but there are very few who read it. The system must needs be a very complicated one, yet, that is not the hindrance. Notation would hamper the musicians, and not leave them free to sing and play what the soul speaks. In India singers, when they begin to sing, sing first the keynote. Then they repeat it over and over again so as to put themselves so much in union with the instrument that the voice and the tone of the instrument may be one. Then they go a little further and return to the keynote. Then they go a little further still, but always return to the keynote.

The musicians may take one raga and play that for hours, or they may go from one raga to another. But the more they play one raga, the more they indulge in that, the more they impress their souls with it, the more they will find in that. The ragas have sometimes been understood as scales. They are not scales but patterns of notes within the octave. There are four different sorts of ragas: ragas of six notes, ragas of seven notes, ragas of odd notes, and ragas of even notes, ascending and descending.

Different ragas have always been played at different times of day. The inner reason for this is that every time of day has its atmosphere, its influence on us. The material reason is that, as evening dress is wanted at a banquet because for so long the eyes have been accustomed to see it, so our ears have been accustomed for very long to hear these ragas at night, in the evening, or at midday. Several ragas are usually sung before dawn. In India before dawn, everyone goes to work or to devotions, and there one finds oneself very much helped by the stillness of the hour, by the finer vibrations. At midday the noise from all around is much greater and stronger notes are needed. The ragas for midday are made all with natural notes. The ragas of the night are with odd notes. The ragas of the early morning are made with flat notes.

I have seen myself that, in playing the vina and singing the *raga jogiya* in the early morning when people were going to the temple and to the mosque, sometimes they would stop to listen and be rapt in the music. At other times with the same raga I did not even impress myself, according to what the mood was. In the old legends we find that in ancient times music had an effect not upon people or upon animals only, but upon things, upon objects, upon the elements. The flames of fire burst out or the waters stopped running when music was sung or played. In the poem of Tansen, which you may have heard read and recited here many times, you will have heard that this was so. A person may ask, "Is this an exaggeration, or is music different now from then, or have we lost this art?" I will say that such singers as I have heard sing in India when I was a boy, I never heard since in the next generation.

The singers of the ancient times sang the same raga, the same song, hundreds of times, thousands of times, a million times. It is by repetition of one thing, by association that we can produce in ourselves the creative power. To have acquired a great store of knowledge, so many songs, so many ragas is nothing. It is the power of producing from within oneself, of creating, that is great. Indian music gained very much by its contact with Persian music. It learned grace and the expression of Persian music. And it gained much from the beauty of the Arabic rhythm. After the rise of the Mughal Empire it was much more beautiful than it had been before.

That it is very highly developed is shown by the rhythm also. There are rhythms of five and rhythms of seven, which are very difficult to keep. And there are songs in which no rhythm is apparent for some bars, but the musician keeps it in mind and after several bars comes in upon the right beat. There are rhythms which do not begin upon the beat, which always mislead the hearer. There are four different kinds of songs: the *dhrupad*, the *qawwal*, the *tumri*, and the *ghazal*. The *dhrupad* requires a special training of the voice, just as it is not everyone's work to sing opera music. The *qawwal* means imagination, the song of imagination.

THE EFFECTS OF MUSIC

Speaking now of the effect of music on animals, it is best to make experiments with those animals that are much associated with humans, such as the horse, the dog, the cows and oxen, and pet animals, such as parrots and cockatoos. By association with humans, these animals have some human qualities reflected onto them. The horse that is associated with humans has much more kindness, much more sympathy and understanding than the horse in the jungle. The dog that lives with humans becomes faithful, obedient. The wild dog is a very fierce animal.

I have made experiments with cows and found that they liked very much to listen to music. There was one old ox in particular which, when it heard an instrument played, would leave its fodder and come to listen. Birds are very fond of music. I have seen that a peacock, when music was played before it, would listen and spread out its wings and begin to dance; and then it would follow the player, and each day it would come a little nearer. It took such a delight in the music that it danced and quite forgot everything else. When I stopped playing it would come and tap the vina with its beak to get me to come back and play again.

Snakes, too, are easily attracted by music, by the Indian flute, a piece of bamboo, or by the vina, if they hear it. But the vina players are serious people, and would rather charm human beings than snakes. A special raga is used for charming snakes. The Yogis and the Sufis; in their meditations; have always had music. Music is the greatest mystery in the world. The whole manifestation is made of vibrations, and vibrations contain all its secret. The vibrations of music free the soul, and take from a person all the heaviness which keeps one bound.

There is this difference between the Sufis and Yogis and all other mystics: their ideas, their thoughts, and their life are quite the same, but you will see the Sufis sometimes in tears and sometimes in joy. Worldly persons think, "They are mad," and mystics may think, "They are on the surface. They are not on the same level." To the Sufi, self-pity—tears at what happens to the self—are *haram*, prohibited. But tears at the thought of the Beloved, at the realization of some truth, are allowable. Extreme joy for what happens to the self is not allowable. But joy in the thought of the Beloved is allowable. The heart is touched, it is moved by the thought of God. It is then that the dervishes dance. Sometimes the dance expresses the action of the Beloved, sometimes it is the face of the Beloved.

The Sufis have used music, not as an amusement, but as purification, as a prayer to God. The Chishti Order of Sufis especially uses music. This order exists chiefly in India, and has come from Russia.[1] *Chishti* in Russian means "pure," and *sufi*, *safa*, means "pure." There are different means of purification. According to our view, all seems good or all seems bad. The old Greek motto says, "Evil is to the one who thinks evil."[2] Music reaches the soul in a moment, as the telegraph reaches from here to New York. What may seem an amusement, something light, is a prayer to God. There are different ways of praying to God. In times when the world was most interested in music, art, science, and amusement, these were used to bring before people the idea of something higher. Music and plays have been used, and the churches have used some sort of show. If

1 At the time this lecture was given, Central Asia was a part of Russia.

2 "Shame to the one who thinks ill of it," or "*Honi soit qui mal y pense*," dates to a fourteenth century romance, "Sir Gawain and the Green Knight," and is the motto of the Order of the Garter.

you go among people of other occupations, you will find them cold. They will pay little attention, they will speak to you just one word. But the heart of musicians, who have to do with sound, is warmed by sound.

INNER AND OUTER RHYTHM

Music is the miniature of life's harmony in sound in a concentrated sense. The person who has no rhythm physically cannot walk well, and often stumbles. The person who has no rhythm in emotions falls easily into a spell, such as laughter, or crying, or anger, or fear. We should practice rhythm in our lives, that we may not be so patient and yielding that everybody takes the best of us; nor so carried away by our enthusiasm and frankness that we say things that are undesirable in the world; nor so meek and mild that we fall into flattery, timidity, and cowardice. Then, by and by, we may understand the rhythm of emotions, then the rhythm of thought, then the rhythm of feeling. Then a person comes into relation with the inner rhythm, which is the true meaning of the world.

DANCE AND MOVEMENT

The word *dance* has been so much debased because the dance has been taken up only by entertainers who have made of it an amusement, and we see that when a thing is made an amusement it always degenerates. When we come to Indian music we find that it has three parts: singing, playing, and dancing. The voice that comes from the lungs and abdomen cannot express itself fully without the bones of the head, the lips, the teeth, the tongue, the palate. So we see that this body is the instrument of sound. When the tree swings in the wind, each leaf gives a sound. The breeze alone cannot produce the full sound. The leaves of the trees rustle and become the instrument for the air. This shows us that the whole framework of this world is the instrument of sound.

If, while speaking to you, I remained as still as a statue, my words would have had much less effect than they can have when accompanied by the gesture. If a person says, "Go away from here," and does not move, those words will not have much expression. If that person moves the arms, the words will have more expression. In India, the pupil is taught to sing with gestures. These take the place of notation, and guide the pupil. A person might think, "Notation would be a much clearer method." But Indian music is so complicated that no notation can render it exactly. Then, too, the intervals are all filled up, and the movements of the hand and arm can express and guide more easily than any written signs.

The third part of music, the dancing, is not the made up dance, but the expression by movement. Mahadeva, the greatest avatar, himself danced. If you sing or play before a dervish, the dervish may begin to move the head and to move the hands. A great Indian poet, when speaking of what the singer must be, says:

> The singer must have a good voice,
> The singer must know the ragas,
> And be able to sing them.
> The singer must be a master of graceful movements,
> The singer must be calm, unaffected by the audience,
> The singermust impress the audience.

Our life is so full of occupations that we have little time to observe the animals. If we did, we should see that most of their language is movement. They speak little with one another, mostly they express by their motions. If you call a dog, the dog will at once begin to wag its tail; it will move its whole body to show its joy and affection. If you speak roughly to the dog, its whole body shows that its feeling at once by its movements. We waste much energy in useless speech. In the old races we see that a motion of the hands, an inclination of the head for many things takes the place of words.

As soon as a person comes into the room, we see by that person's movements, by the manner of walking, what that person is, how much refinement that person has. If we compare the horse whose price is five thousand guineas with the horse whose price is fifty guineas, we see what a difference there is in the movements. The horse of five thousand guineas has not been taught to move as it moves, but in every movement it is graceful. We see that the beauty given to the peacock has inspired in it graceful movements.

Dance is a very wonderful thing, and in itself a great proof of mysticism. We have each of us, in us, the nature of the bird and the nature of the animal. The nature of the bird is to fly; the nature of the animal is to jump. The tiger will jump from here to the top of the wall. If we cannot do this, it is because by eating, drinking, sleeping we have lost the power. If one sits in an armchair and to get up one pulls oneself up by the arm, then by eating, drinking, and sleeping one has become so heavy that one is not what one should be. That government is proper which knows what each of the governed is doing. Our mind governs the body. Our mind must have every muscle, each atom of the body under its command. When we move up, all must come up; when we turn to the right, all must turn to the right; when we turn to the left, all must turn to the left. In India there is a dance, the tiger dance. It is kept for the religious festivals. They paint themselves as tigers, and show the tiger dance. This dance has come to us from Egypt as a sacred dance.

THE RELIGION OF HARMONY

In speaking on the harmony of music, I should like to say that true harmony in music comes from the harmony of the soul, and that music alone can be called real which comes from the harmony of the soul, its true source; and when it comes from there, it must appeal to all souls. Every soul differs in its choice in life, in its choice of the path it should follow. This is owing to the difference of mind, but in their essence souls do not differ. Therefore, whatever means be chosen to bring the different minds of people together, there cannot be a better means to harmonize them than music. It would be no exaggeration if I said that music alone can be the means by which the souls of races, nations, and families which are today so apart may become one day united. Therefore, the musician's lesson in life is a great one. Music is expressed not by language, but by beauty of rhythm and tone reaching far beyond language. And the more musicians are conscious of their mission in life, the greater the service they can do for humanity.

Now as to the law of music which exists in different nations, there are, of course, differences of method; but in the conception of beauty there is no difference. The differences come when the music is human-made; there is no difference in the soul-made music. Suppose someone may come from the Far East, the extreme North, South, or West, but wherever one sees the beauty of nature, one cannot help admiring and loving it. And so music lovers, from whatever country come they come and whatever music they hear, if the music has soul and if the music lovers seek for the soul in the music, they will appreciate and admire all music. Furthermore, music has a mission not only with the multitudes, but with individuals. And its mission with the individual is as necessary and great as its mission with the multitude.

All the trouble in the world, and all the disastrous results arising out of it, all come from lack of harmony. And this shows that the world needs harmony today more than ever before. So if the musicians understand this, their customers are the whole world. When one learns music, one need not necessarily learn to be a musician or to become a source of pleasure and joy to one's fellow human beings. No—but by playing, loving, and hearing music, one must develop music in one's personality. The true use of music is to become musical in one's thoughts, words, and actions. We must be able to give the harmony for which the soul yearns and longs every moment. All the tragedy in the world, in the individual and in the multitude, comes from lack of harmony. And harmony is best given by producing harmony in one's own life.

There are different kinds of music, each kind appealing to certain souls according to their evolution. For instance, the children in the streets are very pleased by beating tins, because that rhythm has a certain effect upon them; but as people evolve so they long for a finer harmony. Why people like or dislike each other is owing to their different stages of evolution. For instance, one is at a stage when one appreciates a certain kind of music; another person whose evolution is greater wants music appropriate to that person's evolution. So it is in religion: some stick to certain beliefs and do not wish to evolve beyond. So it is possible that the lover of music may be tempted to keep to a certain sort of music, and will not rise further. The true way of progressing through music is to evolve freely, to go forward, not caring what others think, and in this way, together with one's development in music, to harmonize one's soul life, one's surroundings, and one's affairs.

During my travels throughout the world, I have heard the music of many different places, and always I have felt that intimate friendship and kinship existing in music. And I always had a great respect for music and for the devotee of music. And one thing I believe, and when in India was convinced of it time after time in meeting those who have touched some perfection in music: that not only in their music, but in their life one can feel the harmony which is the real test of perfection. If this principle of music were followed, there would be no need for an external religion, and someday music will be the means of expressing universal religion. Time is wanted for this, but there will come a day when music and its philosophy will become the religion of humanity.

THE DIVINE ART OF MUSIC

Why is music called the divine art and all other arts are not called so? Certainly we may see God in all arts and all sciences, but in music alone we see God free from all form and thought. In every other art there is idolatry. Every thought, every word has its form; sound alone is free from form. Every word of poetry forms a picture in your mind; sound alone does not make any object appear before you. All would rather hear music than a speech. By sound the world was created. In Vedanta it is called Nada Brahma, Sound-God.

A Persian poet says, "They say that the angels sang to the soul to make it become human, but really the soul was sound." The poets have said that by singing, the angels induced the soul to enter the human body. The soul that has always been free is unwilling to enter the body. Really, before its incarnation the soul is sound. It is for this reason that we love sound. The breath, the speech, the step, all have rhythm. Religions have all made music part of their worship. The Sufi especially loves music, calling it *ghiza-i ruh*, food of the soul.

THE DIVINE MUSICIAN

I gave up my music because I had received from it all I had to receive. To serve God, one must sacrifice the dearest thing, and I sacrificed my music, the dearest thing to me. I had composed songs, I sang and played the vina; and practicing this music, I arrived at a stage where I touched the music of the spheres. Then every soul became for me a musical note and all life became music. Inspired by it, I spoke to the people, and those who were attracted by my words listened to them instead of listening to my songs. Now, if I do anything, it is to tune souls instead of instruments; to harmonize people instead of notes.

If there is anything in my philosophy, it is the law of harmony, that one must put oneself in harmony with oneself and with others. I have found in every word a certain musical value, a melody in every thought, harmony in every feeling; and I have tried to interpret the same thing with clear and simple words for those who used to listen to my music. I played the vina until my heart turned into this same instrument. Then I offered this instrument to the divine musician, the only musician existing. Since then I have become God's flute, and when God chooses, God plays the divine music. People give me credit for this music, which in reality is not due to me, but to the musician who plays on God's own instrument.

God bless you.

Glossary

Akbar: Abu'l-Fath Jalal ad-Din Muhammad Akbar (1542–1605), Mughal emperor of India.

adharma (Sanskrit): lack of religion.

Amir Khusraw: Amir Khusraw Dihlavi (1253–1325), Sufi musician and poet of Delhi.

apsara (Sanskrit): beautiful celestial being.

Banda Nawaz: Sayyid Muhammad Husayni Gisu Daraz (1320–1422), Chishti Sufi saint.

Bernhardt, Sarah (1844–1923): popular French actress.

bodhisattva (Sanskrit): perfection of wisdom and compassion.

buddhi (Sanskrit): intelligence.

chauda tabaq (Urdu): fourteen planes of existence.

dervish: Sufi practitioner.

deva (Sanskrit): angel-soul, deity.

dharma (Sanskrit): duty, religion.

doa (Arabic): "prayer."

fana' (Arabic): annihilation.

fikr (Arabic): "thought," silent zikr.

gandharva (Sanskrit): musical heavenly being.

ghaws (Persian; Arabic: ghawth): "defender," level of the spiritual hierarchy.

ghiza-i ruh (Persian): "food of the soul."

hadith (Arabic): "tradition," a saying attributed to the Prophet Muhammad.

Hafiz: Khwaja Shams ad-Din Muhammad Hafiz Shirazi (d. 1326), Persian Sufi poet.

hamsadi: seeking beauty and goodness.

haram (Arabic): "prohibited."

Hatha Yoga (Sanskrit): school of Yoga based on physical and breathing exercises.

Indra (Sanskrit): Hindu deity, ruler of the devas.

jalal (Arabic): power.

jamal (Arabic): beauty.

kamal (Arabic): "perfect," state of suspended activity.

kibriya (Arabic): "divine grandeur," divine vanity.

Krishna (Sanskrit): Hindu avatar of Vishnu.

Mahadeva (Sanskrit): Shiva, "great god."

Mahmud Ghaznavi: Yamīn ad-Din Dawla Abu'l-Qasim Mahmud ibn Sebuktegin (971–1030), founder of the Ghaznavid empire.

manu (Sanskrit): prophet.

Maula Bakhsh (1833–1896): Indian musician and singer, grandfather of the author.

Muhammad Husayni Gisu Daraz: (1321–1422): Chishti Sufi saint.

Mu'in ad-Din Chishti: (1142–1236) Khwaja Mu'in ad-Din Hasan Sijzi. Sufi saint who established the Chishti Order in India.

murid (Arabic): "willing," a Sufi initiate.

murshid(a) (Arabic): "the guide," senior Sufi teacher.

nabi (Arabic): prophet.

Nada Brahma (Sanskrit): "Sound, the Creator."

nafs (Arabic): self, ego.

Narada: a sage, singer, and musician mentioned in Hindu scriptures.

namaz (Persian): prayer.

nazul (Arabic): "descent," ending of a cycle.

nur (Arabic): light.

Omar Khayyam: Ghiys ad-Din Abu'l-Fath 'Umar al-Khayyam Nishapuri (d.1131), Persian scientist and poet.

Parvati: Hindu goddess, consort of Shiva.

qutub (Urdu; Arabic: qutb): "pole," head of the spiritual hierarchy.

rajas (Sanskrit) obscurity, one of the three gunas in Hindu philosophy.

rasul (Arabic): "messenger," prophet

Rama: Avatar of Vishnu in Hinduism.

Rumi: Jalal ad-Din Muhammad Balkhi Rumi (1207–73), famed Persian Sufi poet of Konya and founder of the Mawlawi (Mevlevi) Order.

Sa'di of Shiraz: Abu Muhammad Muslih ad-Din Shirazi (d. 1291), Persian Sufi poet.

safa' (Arabic): "pure."

Shams-i Tabriz: Shams ad-Din Muhammad Tabrizi (d.1248), spiritual mentor of Jalal ad-Din Rumi.

Shiva (Sanskrit): Hindu deity of destruction.

sattva (Sanskrit): purity, one of the three gunas in Hindu philosophy.

sukradi: looking for the bad.

tamas (Sanskrit): darkness, one of the three gunas in Hindu philosophy.

Tansen: Miyan Tansen (c.1500–1586), famed north Indian classical musician.

Tulsidas (1511–1623): Hindu poet and saint.

Tumbara: a legendary celestial minstrel.

'uruj (Arabic): "ascent," beginning of a cycle.

vairagya (Sanskrit): path of indifference.

wali (Arabic): master.

zikr (Persian; Arabic: dhikr): "remembrance," Sufi ritual of divine remembrance.

Sources

Below are listed sources of the text within the volumes of *The Complete Works of Pir-o-Murshid Hazrat Inayat Khan, Source Edition* series.[1] Sources of other sections of the text are cited within those sections

Character Building	
Willpower	1923 vol. 2, 340–44
Music of Life	1923 vol. 2, 351–56
Self-Control	1923 vol. 2, 366–71
Relationship	1923 vol. 2, 390–94
Subtlety	1923 vol. 2, 402–7
Complaining and Smiling	1923 vol. 2, 419–26
Noiseless Working	1923 vol. 2, 433–35, 442–43
Inquisitiveness	1923 vol. 2, 444–46, 475–76
Gossip	1923 vol. 2, 480–81
Generosity	1923 vol. 2, 488–92
The Art of Personality	
Gratefulness	1923 vol. 2, 501–6
The Art of Personality	1923 vol. 2, 515–20
Gentleness	1923 vol. 2, 533–37
Persuasive Tendency	1923 vol. 2, 554–58.
Vanity	1923 vol. 2, 566–72
Self-Respect	1923 vol. 2, 579–83
Word of Honor	1923 vol. 2, 589–94
Graciousness	1923 vol. 2, 106–8
Economy	1923 vol. 2, 601–6
Justice	1923 vol. 2, 617–20
Ear Training	1923 vol. 2, 628–63
Attitude	1923 vol. 2, 639–42
Reconciliation	1923 vol. 2, 118–20

1 Omega Publications, Richmond, Virginia; www.omegapub.com. Free download available at www.nekbakhtfoundation.org.

Consciousness and Personality

Beauty	1922 vol. 2, 51–3
Are We Masters of Our Destiny?	1925 vol. 1, 37–42

Art and the Artist

The Divinity of Art	1922 vol. 1, 19–24

The Art of Music

Indian Music 1	1922 vol, 2, 197–201
Composition	1922 vol. 2, 314
Music, Astrology, and Alchemy	1922 vol. 2, 361
The Religion of Harmony	1922 vol. 2, 386–87

Biographical Note

Hazrat Inayat Khan was born in Baroda, India, in 1882. Trained in Hindustani classical music from childhood, he became a professor of music at an early age. In the course of extensive travels in the Indian subcontinent, he won high acclaim at the courts of the maharajas and received the title of Tansen-uz-Zaman from the Nizam of Hyderabad.

In Hyderabad Hazrat Inayat Khan became the disciple of Sayyid Abu Hashim Madani, who trained him in the traditions of the Chishti, Suhrawardi, Qadiri, and Naqshbandi lineages of Sufism, and at last blessed him to "Fare forth into the world."

In 1910, accompanied by his brother, Maheboob Khan, and cousin, Muhammad Ali Khan, Hazrat Inayat Khan sailed for the United States. Over the next sixteen years he traveled and taught widely throughout the United States and Europe, building up the first Sufi order ever established in the West.

In London Hazrat Inayat Khan married Ora Ray Baker. Four children were born to them, whom they raised in London during the First World War and afterward in Suresnes, France, where a little Sufi village sprung up around their home, Fazal Manzil.

The doors of Hazrat Inayat Khan's Sufi Order[1] were open to people of all faiths. Appealing to experience rather than belief, Hazrat Inayat Khan's discourses and spiritual instructions illuminated the twin themes of the presence of God in the depths of the human soul and the interconnectedness of all people. Numerous books were compiled from Hazrat Inayat Khan's teachings during his lifetime and posthumously. In September 1926 Hazrat Inayat Khan bade farewell to his family and disciples and returned to India. On February 5, 1927, he died and was buried in New Delhi.

---

1 Known today as the Inayati Order.

Index

A

Abu Al-Qasem Mansur, Firdausi 73
Abu Muhammad Muslih ad-Din Shirazi, Sa'adi 55, 84, 222, 263
Adam 84, 140
adepts 76. *See also* mystics.
adharma 112, 261
advancement, spiritual 67, 179
air 31, 125, 161, 233, 245, 253
Akbar, Emperor 18–19, 261
Alias 70
alif 202
Amir Khusraw 166, 261
ancestors 38–39, 240
angel 44, 49, 61, 64, 68, 88, 219, 240, 259, 261; angelic people 10; angelic plane 64, angelic sphere 110; angelic world 67. *See also* apsara, deva, gandharva.
animal 64, 88, 138, 157, 182, 198, 220, 222, 232, 247, 254; animal impulse 169; animal nature 34; effect of music on animals 249. *See also* individual animals by name.
annihilation 182, 261. *See also* fana'
apostles 99. *See also* Christ, disciples, fishermen.
appreciation 33, 58, 113–114, 127–128, 142, 166, 181, 195, 203, 223, 225, 226–227. *See also* gratefulness, thankfulness.
apsaras 62, 108, 261. *See also* angel, deva, gandharva.
Arabian Nights 21
Arabia 176; Arabic language 217; Arabic rhythm 248
architects 225. *See also* artist, architecture.
architecture 225, 233. *See also* art, architect.
art 6, 9, 26–28, 39, 45, 61–62, 64, 66–67, 76–77, 82, 83, 95, 103, 107, 112–113, 190, 196–200, 202–207, 209–211, 213, 215–230, 232–35, 240, 242, 244, 247, 250, 259; art becomes religion 216; art of arts 62; art of life 9; art of personality 61– 62, 66–67, 76–77, 82–83, 103, 107, 112, 218, 220, 228; art of reconciliation 27; art of the Creator 221; artistic spark 227; definition of art 215; divine art 61, 222, 224, 230, 259; dreams of art 211; God's art 222; language of art 211; love of art 62, 113, 222; mission of art 216–217; psychology of art 232; spirit of art 221, 225, 234, symbolic art 213. *See also* architecture, artist, beauty, color, composition, copying, creativity, dance, drawing, harmony, illusion, improvement, improvisation, literature, music, painting, poetry, sculpture, singing, symbol.
artist 6, 17, 28, 45, 62, 64, 105, 159, 186, 195–200, 202–219, 223–225, 227, 228, (*cont. overleaf*)

artist (*cont.*) 232–233, 240, 242, 243; artistic environments 196; artistic faculty 219, 221, 227; artistic impulse 198, 225; artists of ancient times 211; artistic temperament 18, 207, 214; changeableness of the artist 200; creative faculty of the artists 204, 207; God as artist 217, 222–224; heart of the artist 197, 212–213; imaginative artist 203; mind of the artist 171, 196, 200. *See also* architect, art, composer, conductor, dancer, illusionists, musician, painter, poet, sculptor, singer, writer.

ascetic 18, 63, 67, 69, 145, 150, 184. *See also* adept, asceticism, mystic, vairagya, Yogi.

asceticism 68–69. *See also* ascetic, fasting, indifference, renunciation, self-denial, solitude.

astral world 68

astrologer 80, 187. *See also* astrology.

astrology 29, 80, 245. *See also* astrologer, destiny, horoscope, planet, predestination, star.

atma 67–68. *See also* soul.

atom 117, 144, 174, 182; atom of the body 159, 163, 176, 196, 255

attitude 31–33, 35, 47, 105–106, 112–113, 132, 151, 196, 205, 224, 228; cheerfulness 33, 35; ever-complaining attitude 31; ever-smiling attitude 31–32; favorable attitude 106; friendly attitude 112; hopeful attitude 33. *See also* friendship, hope, optimism.

attraction 73, 146. *See also* love, magnetism.

avatar 254, 262. *See also* individual avatars by name.

awakening, spiritual 9, 30, 37, 101, 103, 135, 211, 222, 230, 235. *See also* realization.

Ayaz 56–57

B

babe 29–30. *See also* child.

baker 80–81

balance 14, 35, 40–41, 83, 98, 115, 128, 131, 201, 203; balance in breath 41. *See also* equilibrium, harmony.

Banda Nawaz *See* Muhammad Husayni Gisu Daraz.

beauty 5, 11, 13, 21, 26–29, 34, 40–41, 44, 55–56, 58–59, 60–62, 66–67, 76–77, 83, 90, 95, 97–99, 107–110, 113–114, 142, 152, 165–167, 169, 177, 179, 183, 189, 195–198, 200–201, 203–204, 208, 210, 216–230, 232–236, 242, 244, 248, 254, 256, 261–262; beautiful personality 113–114, 219; beautiful surroundings 196; beauty of feeling 166; beauty of lines and colors 166, 195; beauty of manner 197; beauty of rhythm and tone 256; desire toward beauty 169; divine beauty 109, 167, 235; fountain of

beauty 56; God's beauty and love of beauty 108, 165, 235, 224; goddess of beauty 235; insight into beauty 62, 200; intellectual beauty 166; love of beauty 62, 108, 113, 195, 201, 223, 227; ocean of beauty 203; path of beauty 230; spirit of beauty in all 234; symbolic beauty 235; worlds of beauty 166
Beethoven, Ludwig van 163, 218, 240
belief 16, 27, 50, 173–174, 186, 257; belief in God 109. *See also* religion, superstition.
beloved 22, 125–126, 142, 166, 250; curl of the beloved 29, 201; face of the Beloved 250. *See also* love, lover.
Bernhardt, Sarah 7, 261
bharjas 242
Bible 11, 16, 33, 47, 139, 144–145, 189, 220, 229, 231
bird 6, 36, 96, 220, 222, 232, 249, 254; bird of paradise 228. *See also* Hamsa, peacock.
blessing 94, 99, 152, 173, 228, 269; blessing of life 17
bliss 101, 122. *See also* ecstasy, happiness, joy, nirvana, samadhi.
bodhisattva 65, 261
Bonoparte, Napoleon 72, 168
Brahmins 175
brain 28, 140, 159, 161–162, 225
breath 13, 41, 63, 215, 259; balance in breath 41; breathing 41, 58, 63, 72, 114, 262; disorder of breath 41
Buddha 23, 235. *See also* bodhisattva.
buddhi 67–68, 261
business 39, 98, 130, 133, 223, 227. *See also* commercialism, money.

C

Caesar 11, 152
camel 39–40
Carter, Howard 74
celestial bodies 78. *See also* moon, planet, sun, star.
character building 3, 6, 8, 17, 20, 23–24, 38
chauda tabaq 63, 261
Chava 88
child 6, 12, 28–29, 35, 39–40, 43, 74–75, 80, 84, 89, 92, 96, 99–101, 105, 108–109, 127, 134–136, 140, 145, 175, 182, 186, 187, 222, 233, 240, 257, 269; child soul 8, 27, 35, 39; childhood 6, 44, 145, 157, 269; God's children 75, 105. *See also* babe, innocence.
China 113, 134, 235
Chishti Order 239, 250, 261–262, 269; Chishti, meaning in Russian 250. *See* individual Chishtis by name.
chord 239, 246
Christ *See* Jesus Christ.
Christian(ity) 3, 16, 33, 182. *See also* apostles, Bible, Jesus Christ, church, cross, fishermen, individual Christians by name.
church 16, 34, 235, 250. *See also* Christianity.
clairvoyance 176. *See also* revelation, vision.

clouds 55, 162, 164, 221–222; clouds of ignorance 111; clouds of illusion 5. *See also* illusion, veil.
color 6, 66, 72, 165–166, 176, 186, 195–196, 203, 206–208, 211, 216, 221–222, 233, 242; colors of the elements 176, 245; sense of color 196
commercialism 67, 132, 234, 241. *See also* business, materialism, money.
compassion 5, 26, 75; divine compassion 55, 58, 261. *See also* forgiveness, generosity, kindness, love, mercy, sympathy.
composer 70, 115, 242–244, 246. *See also* artist, composition, individual composers by name.
composition 195, 242, 244, 260, composition of God 232. *See also* composer, music.
concentration 7, 58–59, 99, 180, 195, 200, 202, 208–209, 211, 239, 252; concentration of the heart 225
conductor 9
consciousness 17, 36, 64, 157–158, 164, 172–173, 186, 222, 235, 239–240; consciousness of the soul 108; God-consciousness 16; ocean of consicousness 172–173; universal consciousness 127, 177. *See also* realization.
consideration 3, 12, 20, 26, 36, 66, 71, 82, 96–98, 122, 125, 128, 136, 138, 142, 234. *See also* graciousness, kindness, politeness, respect, thoughtfulness.
contemplation 69–70, 166–167; contemplation of the soul 59
control 8, 9, 14–15, 18, 40, 66, 76, 135, 164, 178, 200; control over oneself 9, 14, 66; lack of control 14, 66. *See also* mastery, self-control, strength.
copying 198–203, 213. *See also* imitation.
cosmos 78–79
creativity 39, 46, 162, 171, 179, 204, 211, 218, 226, 232, 235–236, 244, 246, 248; creative faculty of the artists 204, 207. *See also* art, Creator, expression.
Creator, the 28, 45, 64, 105, 141–142, 150, 198–199, 203–206, 215, 221–224, 232–233, 262; art of the Creator 221
cross 49, 82, 182, 205; kiss of the cross 183
crystal 78

D

dance 26, 29, 62, 108, 110, 233, 242, 249, 253–254; dance of the dervish 250; dance of the soul 28, 244; gesture 253; tiger dance 255. *See also* dancer, movement.
dancer 29, 225; dancers of the court of God 233. *See also* dance.
Daniel 179, 220
darkness 33, 110, 166, 263

death 29, 33, 50, 63, 77, 87, 106, 201, 218; death of honor 90; death of the mind 41
deity 217–218, 261–263; idea of divinity 166. *See also* Creator, divinity.
Delhi 18, 88, 261, 269
democracy 95
depression 36, 41, 49, 70, 72, 82, 159, 161, 164, 188. *See also* sadness, sorrow.
dervish 18–19, 94–95, 250, 254, 261
desire 29, 37, 62, 71, 75, 77, 91, 97, 109, 114–116, 129, 146–148, 150, 152, 183, 222; desire for beauty 169; desire for knowledge 42–43; desire of every soul 168; God's desire 108; plant of desire 77
destiny 185, 188, 206, 213. *See also* predestination.
deva 231, 261. *See also* angel, apsara, gandharva.
devotees 49, 61, 217–218, 258. *See also* devotion, worship.
devotion 50, 134, 169, 217–219; devotions 239, 247. *See also* devotees, prayer, reverence, service, worship.
dharma 20. 112, 261. *See also* duty, responsibility, religion.
dhrupad 248
dignity 70, 82–85, 98. *See also* honor, nobility, respect.
disciples 34, 50, 184, 269. *See also* apostles, initiates, murids, pupils.
disease 36, 124, 224; disorder of breath 41. *See also* illness, tuberculosis.
divinity 16, 169, 231– 234. *See also* deity.
doa 231. *See also* prayer.
dog 150, 184, 232, 249, 254
dome 46, 145
donkey 39–40, 49
drawing 66, 121, 225
dream 61, 69, 170–171, 211; heart dream 171; plane of the dream 170; soul dream 171; symbolical dream 171. *See also* sleep.
duty 11, 20–21, 42, 57, 83, 101, 112–114, 121–122, 126, 133, 148, 224, 261; duties of man 84; duties of womanhood 84; duty of the soul 9. *See also* dharma, obligation, responsibility, service.

E

ears 5, 42, 59–60, 107, 187, 247; ears of the heart 218. *See also* sound.
earth 5, 9–10, 16, 29, 31, 42, 44, 58, 61–62, 64, 70, 79, 88, 90, 95, 97, 135, 138, 144, 152, 161, 176, 180, 183, 185, 190, 202, 212, 216, 231–232, 234, 245; color of earth 245; earthly wealth 48; plane of the earth 86, 219; shadows of the earth 176
East, the 11, 39, 66, 146, 175, 228, 240–241, 246, 256
echo 46, 59; reecho 127, 145
ecstasy 233, 240. *See also* bliss, intoxication, joy, samadhi, wine.
ego 4–5, 69, 76, 79, 85, 123, 138, 240, 262; (*cont. overleaf*)

ego (*cont.*) blinded by one's own ego 123; egoism 69, 85; false ego 4–5, 56, 58, 79; intoxication of the ego 110; soberness of the ego 110; stages of the ego 69; true ego 5, 79. *See also* individuality, nafs, pride, self, vanity.
Egypt 74, 255
element 173, 242, 247; colors of the elements 176; elements of vibrations 245. *See also* air, earth, fire, water.
emotions 76, 178, 211; rhythm of emotions 252. *See also* feeling.
enemy 3, 18, 21, 31–32, 90, 122–124, 128–129, 134, 140–141, 162–163, 181; power of the enemy 123–124. *See also* enmity, foes.
energy 29, 72, 97–98, 254. *See also* fire, flame, magnetism, movement, vibration, vitality.
engineer 30, 188–189
English language 39, 67, 91, 94, 194
enmity 124, 129, 141, 163. *See also* attitude, enemy, foes, killing.
enthusiasm 39, 41, 150, 190, 252
equilibrium 15, 41. *See also* balance, kamal.
essence 75, 106, 168, 234, 256; essence of art 233; essence of beauty 108; essence of reason 68; essence of religion 137
evolution 10, 15, 23, 35, 58, 67, 91, 95, 99, 103, 105, 110–111, 122, 127, 144–145, 149–150, 166, 182, 186, 257; grade of evolution 61, 128, 140, 186, 225; wheel of evolution 157
exaggeration 40, 206, 215, 224, 226, 247, 256
eyes 57, 78, 94–95, 113, 117, 124, 131, 134–135, 138, 147, 159–160, 166, 176, 181, 187, 190, 196, 200, 204, 208, 211, 222–224, 233–234, 244, 247; developing the eyes 176; eye of God 79; eyes of the mind 239. *See also* clairvoyance, revelation, seer, vision.

F

faith 80, 131, 179; faithfulness 136, 142. *See also* religion, trust.
fana' 182, 261. *See also* annihilation.
fancies 3, 204. *See also* illusion.
fasting 12, 21, 48, 77, 184
fatalist 188
father 44, 73, 95–96, 105, 124–125, 140. *See also* parent.
faults 9. 46, 21, 23, 42–43, 45, 57, 71, 85, 104–106, 115, 122–123, 128, 130, 139–141, 175, 181, 183, 223, 228
fear 63, 111, 123, 131, 142, 161, 188, 215, 252
feeling 7–8, 15, 18, 26, 46, 48, 71–72, 83, 87, 94, 134–136, 140, 161–163, 171, 183, 188, 197, 204, 208, 211, 216, 221–223, 227, 229–230, 246, 254, 260; beauty of feeling 166; heart

as the organ of feeling 159, 161, 234; rhythm of feeling 252. *See also* emotion.
fikr 162, 261
Firdausi, *See* Abu Al-Qasem Mansur.
fire 117, 144, 161, 163, 184, 245, 247; love as fire 85, 141; test of fire 88. *See also* flame, torch.
fish 163; symbol of the fish 15–16
fishermen 61, 220
flame 103, 247; flame of the soul 27. *See also* fire, torch.
flower 33, 35, 55, 72, 137, 222, 229
foes 3, 31, 39. *See also* enemy, enmity.
foolishness 49, 65, 83–84, 112, 124–125, 137, 147, 151, 175, 186, 227
forgiveness 26, 35–37, 55, 96, 106, 124, 140–141, 180, 220; forgiveness of God 37; forgiving ourselves 37. *See also* compassion, mercy.
fountain 157; fountain of beauty 56
France 2, 7, 54, 269
frankness 27, 45, 252
freedom 13, 58, 71–72, 83, 125, 147, 149, 178, 181, 188, 196, 235, 239–240, 244, 250, 257, 259; freedom of God 259. *See also* independence, liberty.
free will 29, 42, 188
friend 12, 20–23, 26, 31–32, 39, 47, 61–63, 65, 75, 81, 83–84, 98–99, 101, 112, 122–129, 132–133, 136–137, 140–142, 145, 150, 152–153, 160, 162–163, 170, 180, 186, 217, 227; friend to God 65; heart of a friend 133. *See also* friendship.
friendship 20–22, 48, 65, 112, 122–124, 127–129, 132–133, 136–137, 141, 228, 258. *See also* friend, reconciliation.
fruit 28, 33, 77, 142; fruit of creation 231, 233
fulfillment 10–11, 21, 29, 43, 49, 62, 64–65, 83, 95, 100, 108, 112–113, 191, 195, 213, 215, 224; fulfillment of creation 189. *See also* satisfaction, success, victory.

G

Gaekwar of Baroda 243
gandharva 62, 107, 261. *See also* angel, apsara, deva.
generosity 47–48, 57, 122, 125, 148. *See also* compassion, generosity, kindness, mercy, unselfishness.
gentleness 39–40, 66–68, 71, 125, 127, 228. *See also* kindness.
ghazal 248
ghiza-i ruh 259, 261
ghost 81
ghaws 79, 261
goal 4, 17, 43, 48, 87, 149, 168, 226. *See also* purpose.
grace 98, 204, 248, 254
graciousness 94–95, 105, 127. *See also* consideration.
gratefulness 26, 50, 55–56, 59. *See also* appreciation, thankfulness.
greed 19, 147–148

Greeks 64, 250
guru 78. *See also* master, sage, teacher.

H

hadith 165, 224, 235, 261. *See also* Muhammad, the Prophet.
Hafiz *See* Shams ad-Din Muhammad Hafiz Shirazi.
Hamsa 228
hamsadi 228, 262
happiness 5–6, 11, 15, 18, 33, 77, 94, 111, 139, 141, 146–147, 150, 166, 176, 178, 183, 185, 191, 223; key to happiness 167. *See also* bliss, fulfillment, joy, pleasure, satisfaction.
haram 250, 262
Harish Chandra 88, 100–101
harmony 15, 20, 27, 36, 38, 129, 134, 165–166, 179, 196, 201, 208, 215–217, 219–220, 223, 229, 236, 239, 244, 246, 252, 256–258; harmonious atmosphere 107, 196; harmony of the soul 256; law of harmony 260. *See also* balance.
Hatim 88
health 32, 170–171, 245; healing 27. *See also* medicine, vaccination.
heart 8, 12, 14, 16, 25, 27, 32–33, 35, 37, 48, 59, 61, 72, 75, 81, 85, 88, 94, 100, 103, 105–106, 112, 117, 123–124, 129, 133, 135, 137, 140–141, 146, 153, 162–163, 166–167, 181, 218, 222–223, 225, 226–228, 244, 250, 260 aching of the heart 48; charity of heart 47–48; cultivation of the heart 162; ears if the heart 218; expansion of the heart 47, 142; heart as the organ of feeling 159; heart dream 171; heart inflamed by the spirit of art 234; heart of a friend 133; heart of musicians 251; heart of the artist 197, 212–213; heart of the universe 27; melting state of heart 162; opening of the heart 110; physical heart 161. *See also* love.
heaven 16, 33, 58, 132, 180, 202, 208, 211–212, 215, 221, 231, 234. *See also* angel, nirvana.
Hindi language 151, 183
Hindu 20, 62, 78, 88, 112, 228, 262, 269; Hindu poets 137, 201, 233, 263; Hindu teachers 34. *See also* Hindusism, individual Hindus by name.
Hinduism 173, 263. *See also* Hindus, Sanskrit, Vedanta, and individual Hindu gods by name.
Hindustani language 123, 187
honor 57, 70, 82, 90, 99, 122, 151; word of honor 87–88, 92, 100. *See also* dignity, duty, nobility, promise, respect.
hope 35, 41, 130, 150, 168, 223, 226; hopefulness 32–33. *See also* optimism.
horoscope 80. *See also* astrology.
horse 29, 232, 249, 254

humility 40, 49, 95, 135, 228. *See also* modesty.
hypocrisy 8, 27

I

Iblis 49
ideal 43, 75, 88–90, 92, 98, 100, 125–127, 132–133, 136, 147, 168–169, 220, 230; divine ideal 126; God ideal 142; spiritual ideals 191. *See also* inspiration.
idolatry 259; idolater 168
illness 43, 106, 188; plant of illness 32. *See also* disease.
illumination 33, 190, 269. *See also* light, radiance.
illusion 3, 5, 131, 185, 210, 211, *See also* cloud, fancies, illusionists, veil.
illusionists 204, 210. *See also* illusion.
image 25, 170, 235, 242; God's own image 28. *See also* picture, symbol.
imagination 17, 61, 128–129, 142, 159, 211, 216, 239; imaginative artist 203; song of imagination 248
imitation 198, 222. *See also* copying.
impression 7, 36, 83, 89, 100, 106, 113, 123, 161, 164, 171, 173, 180–181, 202, 222–223, 228–229, 239, 247, 254
improvement 108–109, 198, 203, 204–207, 213, 215, 224, 232. *See also* improvisation.
improvisation 198–199, 213, 232, 242, 246–248; God's improvisation 232. *See also* improvement.
impulse 8, 14, 66, 71, 83, 107, 123, 178; animal impulse 169; artistic impulse 198, 225; divine impulse 233
independence 15, 69, 110, 125, 134. *See also* freedom, liberty.
India 74, 100, 160, 162, 181, 234, 243, 247, 250, 255, 261–263, 269; India, music of 239–240, 242–243, 246–249, 253, 258; Indian poet 166, 254. *See also* Hindi language, Hinduism, Hindustani language, Sanskrit, individual Indians and places by name.
indifference 14–15, 69, 110, 152, 162, 182–184, 263. *See also* renunciation, vairagya.
individuality 17, 61, 108–109, 170. *See also* ego, self.
Indra 62, 64, 107, 262
inertia 40–41. *See also* kamal.
inheritance, divine 95, 138, 222, 224
initiates 241, 262; high initiates 78. *See also* disciples, initiation, murid, mystic.
initiation 79. *See also* initiates.
injustice 30, 69, 84, 127
innocence 97, 180–181. *See also* purity.
insanity 41
insight 9, 117, 181, 199, 203, 208; insight into beauty 62, 200
inspiration 25, 64, 74, 88, 90, 99–110, 171, 176, 196, 208, 211, 213, 216, 225, 232–233, *(cont. overleaf)*

inspiration (*cont.*) 242, 244, 254, 260. *See also* ideal.
instrument 7, 9, 64, 225, 239–240, 242, 246, 249, 253; God's own instrument 260. *See also* individual instruments by name.
intellect 195, 180–181, intellectual beauty 166. *See also* intelligence.
intelligence 25–28, 31, 68, 117, 128–129, 161, 178, 183, 210, 222, 231–232; divine intelligence 74; lack of intelligence 26. *See also* intellect, knowledge, wisdom.
intoxication 42, 67, 114; intoxicating drink 81; intoxication of life 112–113; intoxication of mastership 134; intoxication of the ego 110. *See also* wine.
intuition 75, 87
Islam 91. *See also* hadith, mosque, Muhammad, Qu'ran, individual Moslems by name.

J

jalal 40, 78, 177, 214, 262. *See also* power, strength.
Jalal ad-Din Rumi 22, 28, 43, 144, 163, 263
jamal 40, 78, 177, 214, 262. *See also* beauty.
Japan 160, 235
Jesus Christ 16, 23, 36, 43, 45, 49, 61, 95, 104–105, 139, 152, 220, 228, 235; law given by Christ 34; soul of Christ 231. *See also* apostles, Bible, Christian, cross, Sermon on the Mount.
jinn 61, 125; jinn plane 64: jinn sphere 110; jinn world 68
John, Saint 239
journey, of life 4, 12, 43, 48, 50, 56, 118, 150–152, 157, 187, 226. *See also* goal, path, pilgrimage, purpose.
joy 5, 11, 13, 17, 40, 57, 111, 123, 136, 159, 161–162, 176, 178, 183, 223–224, 232, 244, 250, 254, 257. *See also* bliss, ecstasy, happiness.
judge 83, 142. *See also* judgement.
judgment 45, 85, 95, 104, 127, 142, 145. *See also* judge, justice, law.
justice 30, 103–105, 127, 130; divine justice 104. *See also* judgment, law.

K

kamal 40, 41, 115, 177, 262. *See also* inertia.
karma 187
Kashmir 91
keynote 246
kibriya 76–77, 110, 262
killing 33–34, 73, 90, 163. *See also* enmity.
kindness 12, 21, 26, 34–35, 47, 55–57, 71–72, 74–75, 80, 83, 94, 105, 114, 124–128, 130, 132–133, 135–142, 220, 227, 249; over-kindness 114. *See also* compassion, consideration, generosity, gentleness, love, mercy, sympathy, thoughtfulness, tolerance.
king 19, 22, 26, 56–57, 73, 80–81, 89, 91, 94–95, 100–

101, 107, 168, 183–184; king of paradise 197; king of the universe 62. *See also* Indra.
kingdom of God 18, 33, 47, 62–63, 94, 138, 164, 183
kiss of God 22
knowledge 5, 9, 25–26, 42–43, 70, 73, 89, 144, 164, 169, 177, 190, 208, 213, 226, 244, 248; desire to know 43; divine knowledge 26, 183; knowledge of the world 180; perfect knowledge 117; self-knowledge 43; spiritual knowledge 25, 180. *See also* intelligence, wisdom.
Krishna 34, 235, 262

L

lamas, Tibetan 58
lamp 27, 231. *See also* light.
laughter 8, 72, 82, 89, 124, 162, 178, 252
law 33, 89, 103, 124, 127–128, 132, 136, 140, 144–146, 208; exceptional law 10; law given by Christ 34; law of harmony 260; law of music 256; law of nature 136, 148, 211, 245; law of perfection 209; law of relationship 23; law of the music of life 8; religious law 12; sacred law 12, 34; spiritual law 12, 21. *See also* judgment, justice.
liberty 29, 67. *See also* freedom, independence.
light 33, 41, 101–104, 110, 117, 125, 134, 168, 172, 174–176, 195, 215, 231, 250, 262; light of Allah 176; light of God 164, 175–176, 195, 231; respondent to the light 78. *See also* illumination, lamp, moon, radiance, star, sun, torch.
lightheartedness 82–84, 159
limitation 4, 18, 32–33, 44, 104, 191
line 4, 6, 66, 165–166, 186, 195, 216, 222; horizontal line 205; perpendicular line 20; straight 202, 205
lion 35, 67, 179, 220. *See also* Lion Gate.
Lion Gate 210–212
literature 73, 233. *See also* art, writer, poetry.
logos 76
loka 63–64
looking glass 175–176. *See also* mirror.
love 4–5, 16, 22, 31, 33–35, 57, 61, 72, 85, 103, 125–126, 129, 132–136, 142, 152–153, 162–163, 183, 197, 208, 220, 224, 229, 259; God's love of beauty 108, 165, 235, 224; love as fire 85, 141; love for beauty 113, 195, 197, 227; love for God 99, 142; love for gossip 45; love of art 62, 113, 222; love of beauty 62, 108, 219, 223, 227; love of power 80; love of self 4; love of solitude 69; love of subtlety 28; love of humanity 99; mother's love 75; service of love 75; (*cont. overleaf*)

love (*cont.*) source of all love 233. *See also* attraction, beloved, compassion, generosity, heart, kindness, lover, mercy, unselfishness.
lover 126, 143, 201; lover of God 22, 142–143; lover of music 256–257; lover of nature 201. *See also* beloved, love.
Lucifer 49

M

machine 8, 30, 175, 188–189, 227
magnetism 32. *See also* attraction.
Mahadeva *See* Shiva Mahadeva.
Mahmud Ghaznavi, emperor 135, 262
maitreya 65
manu 65. *See also* prophet.
manvantara 65
martyrs 34. *See also* self-sacrifice.
master 5, 26, 34, 39, 44, 49, 75, 78, 99, 101, 117, 127, 134–136, 185–186, 189, 201, 254, 263; master of life 63, 117; masters of nature 9. *See also* adept, guru, mastery, murshid, rishi, sage, wali.
mastery 3, 15, 149, 185–187, 189–190; intoxication of mastership 134. *See also* master, self-control, strength.
materialism 189, 191, 234. *See also* commercialism, money.
Maula bakhsh 243, 262
medicine 39, 70. *See also* health.
meditation 5, 58, 61, 64, 75, 180, 236, 239, 249; music and meditation 239–240. *See also* mysticism, spirituality, Sufism, Yoga.
medium 74
melody 58–59, 233, 239–240, 246, 260
mercy 55, 75, 195; divine mercy 130–131. *See also* compassion, forgiveness, generosity, kindness, love, sympathy.
message 35, 44, 190, 211, 213, 235, 241; message of Christ 34; message of Sufism 230; message of the master 34. *See also* messengers.
messengers 81, 263. *See also* prophet, rasul, individual messengers by name.
metaphysics 63, 75, 189, 224. *See also* religion.
mirror 57, 170; house of mirrors 46. *See also* looking glass, reflection.
modesty 12, 40, 148, 179. *See also* humility.
money 47, 74, 80, 98, 151, 163, 184, 186, 227, 234, 241. *See also* business, commercialism.
moon 36, 55, 77–79, 221
moral 109, 116, 125, 131, 142, 144, 147; moral of the ancients 135; moral principles 35; three stages of morals 145
Moses 22, 34, 235
mosque 49–50, 247. *See also* Islam.
mother 74–75, 105, 124–125, 240; mother's love 75. *See also* parent.
mountain 25, 40, 128, 147, 184, 220–221, 239
movement 6, 11, 41, 102, 124,

195, 222, 233, 253–254; gesture 253. *See also* dance, energy.
Mughal Empire 248; Mughal emperor 88, 219, 261. *See also* individual Mughal emperors by name.
Muhammad, the Prophet 48–50, 75, 88, 135, 144, 175, 235, 261; seal of prophetship 50; the Prophet's shadow 175–176. *See also* Islam, hadith, Qu'ran.
Muhammad Abu Hashim Madani 160
Muhammad Husayni Gisu Daraz 239, 262
Mu'in ad-Din Chishti 239, 262
murid 11–12, 117–118, 262. *See also* apostles, disciples, pupils, Sufis.
murshid 11–12, 78, 117–118, 160, 262. *See also* master, teacher, Sufis.
Musée Guimet 113, 194
music 6, 8–9, 16–17, 41, 58, 66, 107–108, 165, 190, 211, 216–218, 233–234, 239–242, 244–250, 253–254, 256–261, 269; divine music 259–260; Indian music 239, 242, 246, 248, 253; law of music 256; music of life 8–9, 107; music and meditation 239–240; music as a mystical practice 240; Persian music 248; Sufis and music 239, 250; true use of music 257; vibrations of music 250. *See also* art, chord, composition, conductor, harmony, improvisation, instrument, melody, musician, notation, notes, orchestra, pitch, raga, rhythm, singing, song, sound, symphony, tone, tuning.
musician 6, 9, 66, 216, 218, 225, 228, 233–234, 239–240, 242, 246, 248, 256–257, 260–263; divine musician 260; heart of musicians 251; musician's lesson in life 256. *See also* artist, composer, music, individual musicians by name.
mystery 25–26, 174, 250; mystery of life 26, 213. *See also* mysticism, secret, veil.
mystic 99–100, 144, 152, 176–177, 188, 202, 211, 239–241, 245, 250. *See also* adept, ascestic, dervish, initiate, mysticism, prophet, saint, seer, Sufis, vairagya, Yogi.
mysticism 75, 78, 146, 171, 208, 211–212, 242, 254; music as mystical practice 240; mystical development 246; mystical ideas 204; mystical practice 160, 177, 240. *See also* meditation, mystic, spirituality, Sufism, Yoga.

N

nabi 65, 79, 262. *See also* prophet.
Nada Brahma 239, 259, 262
nafs 176, 240, 262. *See also* self.
namaz 59, 262. *See also* prayer.
Narada 240, 262
nazul 213–214, 262
nervousness 7, 14, 26, 63, 66. *See also* impulse, restlessness.

night 16, 36, 67, 139, 164, 214, 223, 247
nirvana 23. *See also* bliss, heaven.
Noah 131
nobility 44, 47–48, 62, 83, 94–96; nobility of the soul 94, 113; noble manner of life 96; noble-minded 87–88; noble souls 90. *See also* dignity, honor, respect, self-respect.
notation 243, 246, 253
notes 107, 165, 216, 239, 242, 244–245, 247, 260–261; false note 115; higher note 8, 232; keynote 246; octave 247; patterns of notes 247; scales 242, 247. *See also* notation.
nur 176, 262. *See also* light.

O

obligation 20–21, 23, 112. *See also* duty, promise, responsibility.
observation 113, 179, 195–196, 199, 200, 202, 208
ocean 144; ocean of beauty 203, ocean of consciousness 172–173. *See also* sea.
Om 77
Omar Khayyam 29, 111, 151, 262
optimism 33. *See also* hope.
orchestra 9

P

Paderewski, Ignace 240
pains 8, 88, 139, 141, 148, 153, 169, 190, 213. *See also* suffering.
painter 196, 216, 219, 225, 228, 233–234. *See also* artist, illusionist, painting.
painting 66, 186, 200, 204, 216, 218, 220, 233–234, 255. *See also* art, color, copying, improvement, line, picture.
parents 23, 43, 92, 99, 105, 109, 130, 134, 136. *See also* father, mother.
Paris 113, 160, 194
Parvati 68, 263
pata loka 63–64
path 17, 25, 79, 125, 139, 152, 168, 190, 226, 256, 263; mystical path 212; endless path of interest 183; path of beauty 230; path of God 21, 47, 90, 131; path of renunciation 151; path of thankfulness 56; path of the improvers 204; path of truth 34; saintly path 23; spiritual path 56, 78–79, 99, 153, 180, 190. *See also* journey, pilgrimage.
patience 38, 40, 71, 96–97, 104, 109, 116, 123, 125, 129, 148, 180, 200, 206, 208, 252
Paul, Saint 36
peace 4, 15, 27, 38, 129, 134, 164, 224, 235, 236. *See also* reconciliation, solitude, stillness, tranquility.
peacock 110, 249, 254
perfection 30, 32, 44, 59, 62, 64–65, 86, 104, 126, 142, 144, 149–151, 168, 196, 198–200, 204–206, 208, 213–214, 216, 219, 221–222, 232, 244, 258, 261–262; human perfection 65; law of perfection 209,

258; perfect knowledge 117; perfection of wisdom 65, 198, 222; spiritual perfection 65, 200
Persia 73, 88; Persian music 248; Persian poet 22, 29, 222, 233, 259. *See* individual Persians by name.
philosophers 43, 233, 228. *See also* philosophy.
philosophy 6, 16, 67, 75, 105, 109, 150, 208, 215, 258, 260. *See also* metaphysics, philosophers.
picture 6, 27, 65, 139, 159, 162, 170–171, 174, 186–188, 196, 210–211, 216–218, 220, 259. *See also* color, image, line, painting, symbol.
pilgrimage 48, 132
pitch 8, 57, 107, 180, 225–226, 230
plane 12, 63–64, 68, 86, 139, 240, 261; fourteen planes of existence 63, 261; higher planes 58, 72, 100; jinn plane 64, 110: lower plane 64; physical plane 170; plane of the dream 170; plane of the earth 86, 219. *See also* sphere.
planet 10, 78–79, 187, 221, 242, 245; planetary influence 89
plant 35, 72, 157; plant of desire 77; plant of illness 32. *See also* flower, fruit, tree.
pleasure 8, 21, 27, 32, 62, 87, 111, 131, 139, 146–148, 153, 161, 178, 188, 229, 235, 257; pleasure of renunciation 147. *See also* fulfillment, happiness, satisfaction.
poet 6, 22, 28–29, 55, 70, 89–90, 137, 166, 190, 201, 216, 222, 228, 233–234, 239–240, 254, 259. *See also* artist, poetry, writer, individual poets by name.
poetry 16, 28, 41, 89, 139, 165, 190, 216–218, 225, 234–235, 242, 259. *See also* art, literature, poet.
point of view 19, 38, 106, 117, 138–139, 145, 151, 171, 172, 204–205, 215, 225
poison 63, 84, 122, 124, 153, 218
politeness 19, 71–72, 76, 105, 219, 234. *See also* consideration, gentleness, respect.
power 3–4, 8–9, 47, 59, 61, 66, 68, 75, 78, 82, 85, 89, 112, 117, 123–125, 128–130, 135, 144, 150, 160, 162–163, 169, 179–180, 185, 195, 200, 210–211, 216, 220, 248, 255, 262; divine power 80; God's power 150, 195, 210, 232; love of power 80; miraculous power 100; power of attraction 146; power of magnetism 32; power of mind 129, 196; power of music 245; power of the enemy 123–124; power of thought 163; power of turning wrong into right 33; power of water 68. *See also* control, mastery, strength.
prayer 3, 36, 49, 57, 59, 64, 180, 239, 250. *See also* devotion, worship.

predestination 186–187. *See also* destiny.
presence of God 45, 105, 113, 126, 269
pride 27, 69, 73, 76, 90, 108, 110, 126, 130, 133, 240; spiritual pride 18–19. *See also* ego, vanity.
promise 89, 91, 98–102, 128, 226; life's promise 191. *See also* honor, obligation.
Prophet, the *See* Muhammad, the Prophet.
prophet 26, 81, 85, 88, 187, 222, 231, 261–262; prophetic idea 75; seal of prophetship 50. *See also* messengers, nabi, rasul, revelation, vision, individual prophets by name.
psychology 35, 37, 80, 217; psychology of art 232
pupil 11–12, 63, 78, 201, 253. *See also* disciples, murids.
purgatory 41
purification 143, 173, 181, 250. *See also* purity.
purity 25, 126, 133, 174, 180–181, 233, 250; purest intelligence 68; purity of heart 197. *See also* innocence, purification.
purpose 42–46, 60, 62, 79, 83, 95, 112, 148–149, 163, 181, 223, 235. *See also* goal, path..
purusha 68
Purusha Shastra 174
putras 242

Q

qawwal 248
quiet 40–41, 49, 220; quiet working 39–40. *See also* silence, stillness.
Qur'an 125, 138, 144, 165, 224, 231, 235. *See also* Islam, Muhammad the Prophet.
qutub 79

R

radiance 98, 174. *See also* illumination, light.
raga 242, 245–249, 254; raga jogiya 247
raginis 242
rajas 40, 263
Rama 34
rasul 65, 79, 263. *See also* messenger, prophet.
realization 26, 56, 63, 108, 144, 145, 205, 207–208, 222, 250; self-realization 3. *See also* awakening, consciousness.
reciprocity 127–129, 140, 145
reconciliation 116–118; art of reconciliation 27
refinement 66, 103, 107–108, 254. *See also* subtlety.
reflection 2, 24, 27, 46, 74–75, 77, 115, 123, 166, 172, 174–176, 195, 208, 215, 249; reflection of divinity 233; reflection of the divine sun 78; reflections of the sun 78. *See also* mirror, looking-glass.
religion 6, 15, 20–21, 34–35, 75, 85, 88, 91, 93, 95, 98, 105, 109, 112, 144, 168–169, 174, 182, 215–217, 221, 224, 226, 230, 232–233, 235, 241, 255, 257–259;

essence of religion 137; mission of religion 217; religion of all religions 21, 98; religion of Christ 34; religious law 12; true religion 11; universal religion 258; world religions 215. *See also* deity, devotion, dharma, divinity, idolatry, faith, lamas, metaphysics, prayer, prophet, scripture, worship, individual religions by name.
renunciation 23, 77, 144–153, 163, 235; path of renunciation 151; pleasure of renunciation 147. *See also* asceticism, indifference, sacrifice, self-denial.
repetition 59, 96, 163, 171, 246, 248. *See also* echo.
resignation 5, 49, 185
respect 3, 26, 43, 50, 65, 70, 82, 98, 105, 125, 128, 130, 136, 142, 179, 206, 224, 258. *See also* consideration, dignity, honor, nobility, politeness, self-respect.
responsibility 9, 33, 42, 171, 223, 235. *See also* duty, obligation.
restlessness 39–40, 139; broken rhythm of mind 115. *See also* impulse, nervousness.
revelation 9, 25, 33, 176. *See also* clairvoyance, prophet, seer, unveiling, vision.
reverence 26. *See also* devotion, respect, worship.
rhythm 39, 107, 115, 166, 203, 244, 248, 252, 256–257, 259; Arabic rhythm 248; beauty of rhythm and tone 256; broken rhythm of mind 115; destructive rhythm 39; lack of rhythm 115; rhythm of emotions 252; rhythm of feeling 252; rhythm of the atmosphere 107. *See also* balance, nervousness, restlessness, stillness, tranquility.
rishi 100–101. *See also* master, teacher.
river 25, 123, 173, 221
rock 18, 68–69, 157; pebble 85; rocklike personality 25. *See also* crystal, stone.
ruler of life 48
Russia 160, 250
Rustam 73

S

Sa'adi *See* Abu Muhammad Muslih ad-Din Shirazi,
sacrifice 13, 16, 23, 34, 71, 87–90, 142, 145, 148, 260; sacrificing for humanity 16. *See also* asceticism, martyrs, renunciation, self-denial, self-sacrifice.
sadness 9–10, 13, 15–16, 33, 35–36, 43–44, 48, 82, 159, 161–162, 164, 183. *See also* depression, pain, sorrow.
safa 250, 263. *See also* purity.
sage 41, 114, 153, 163, 181, 184. *See also* guru, murshid, rishi, teacher, wisdom.
saint 22, 34–35, 48, 75, 78, 114, 166, 244; saintly path 23; saintly soul 32; senses of saints 166; way of the saint 5. *See also* individual saints by name.

samadhi 240. *See also* bliss, ecstasy, nirvana.
Sangam 173
Sanskrit 92, 182, 231, 246, 261–263
satisfaction 4, 6, 9, 43, 59, 62, 90, 108, 110, 117, 126, 149, 183, 196, 204, 213, 226; satisfaction of God 110, 183, 224. *See also* fulfillment, happiness, pleasure.
sattva 40, 263. *See also* purity.
science 6, 26, 39, 67, 174, 187, 190, 207, 233, 242, 245, 250, 259. *See also* machine, scientists.
scientists 159, 161. *See also* engineer, science.
scripture 48, 87, 169, 220, 229, 231; law of a scripture 34. *See also* individual scriptures by title.
sculptor 216, 219, 225. *See also* artist, sculpture.
sculpture 216. *See also* art, sculptor, image, statue.
sea 172–174, 221; sea of life 61, 83. *See also* ocean.
secret 20, 38, 43, 79–81, 103, 122, 124, 138, 218, 231, 250. *See also* mystery, veil.
seer 80–81, 111, 128, 233. *See also* clairvoyance, prophet, revelation, vision.
self 3, 18, 43, 46, 58, 69, 76–77, 87, 104–105, 126–128, 134, 136, 138, 140–141, 164, 176, 183, 190–191, 229, 250; false self 4; forgetting the self 4, 6; inner self 9–10; love of self 4; self of God 189; true self 4. *See also* ego, individuality, nafs.
self-confidence 7
self-control 9, 14, 66, 105. *See also* control, mastery.
self-denial 3, 21, 23, 118. *See also* ascenticism, fasting, renunciation, sacrifice, self-sacrifice.
selfishness 5, 34, 48, 69, 103, 122, 132–133, 138
self-pity 4, 111, 250
self-respect 82, 130. *See also* dignity, nobility, respect.
self-righteousness 141
self-sacrifice 16. *See also* asceticism, martyrs, renunciation, sacrifice, self-denial.
Sermon on the Mount 95, 228
serpent 63, 65, 74–75, 101. *See also* snakes.
servant 39, 49, 99, 101, 130, 134–136; God's sevants 144; servants of the mind 196; server 49. *See also* service.
service 12, 122, 133, 135, 148, 152, 215; service of humanity 16, 180, 256; service of love 75; serving God 21, 49, 180, 260. *See also* devotion, duty, servant, unselfishness.
shadow 110, 160, 174–176; shadows of the earth 176; the Prophet's shadow 175–176
Shakespeare, William 163
Shams ad-Din Muhammad Hafiz Shirazi 139, 262
Shams-i Tabriz *See* Shams ad-Din Muhammad Tabrizi
Shams ad-Din Muhammad Tabrizi 174, 263

Shiva Mahadeva 62–63, 67–68, 254, 262–263
sign 14, 16, 25, 32, 39, 43, 47, 49, 78, 162, 226, 228, 232, 253; sign of soul's unfoldment 108; sign of spiritual advancement 179; sign of spirituality 116, 181, 190; sign of the Sufi 116. *See also* symbol.
silence 26, 73, 222, 161; silent spheres 26. *See also* quiet, stillness.
singer 29, 151, 225, 228, 246–248, 254, 262. *See also* artist, singing, song, voice, individual singers by name.
singing 7, 17, 40, 59, 61–62, 108, 240–241, 244, 246–248, 253–254, 259–260. *See also* art, music, singer, song, voice.
sky 9, 10, 31, 67, 180, 221; mind as the sky 162. *See also* moon, planets, space, sun.
sleep 16, 22, 72, 80, 146, 188, 236, 240, 255. *See also* dream.
smile 8, 31–33, 47, 127; smiling forehead 159
snakes 74, 249. *See also* serpent.
soberness 114; soberness of the ego 110
solitude 21, 23, 69. *See also* asceticism, peace, quiet, renunciation, stillness, tranquility.
song 7, 59, 151, 233, 241, 243, 248, 260. *See also* qawwal, melody, music, singer, singing.
sorrow 5, 8, 48, 81, 84, 111, 162, 176, 178, 183, 190. *See also* depression, pain, sadness, suffering.
soul 9, 15–17, 20–21, 27–30, 32–33, 43, 46–48, 58–60, 62–70, 72, 74, 76, 79–80, 87, 90–91, 94, 97–98, 101, 104, 107–114, 117, 123, 125, 132, 135, 153, 157, 162–164, 166, 168–169, 172, 176, 181, 185–187, 196, 199, 215–219, 223–224, 226–228, 230, 232–233, 235, 240, 244–247, 250, 256–260, 269; bath of the soul 173; child soul 8, 27, 35, 39; consciousness of the soul 108; contemplation of the soul 59; dance of the soul 28, 244; flame as the soul 27; great souls 10; grown-up soul 27, 35; harmony of the soul 256; noble souls 90, 94, 113; old soul 8, 11, 21; purification of the soul 143, 173; saintly soul 32; salvation of the soul 55; searching of every soul 166; secret of the soul 43, 103; self-sacrificing soul 16; soul dream 171; soul of Christ 231; soul's unfoldment 103, 108; source of every soul 221; upliftment of the soul 58; young souls 11, 21
sound 8, 58, 76, 78, 229, 223, 239–240, 242, 244, 246, 251–253, 259. *See also* ears, echo, instrument, music, Nada Brhama, singing, vibration, voice.

space 9–10, 83, 176. *See also* vacuum.
spheres 17, 242; angelic sphere 110; human sphere 110; immortal spheres 146; jinn sphere 110; music of the spheres 260; silent spheres 26. *See also* astral world, plane.
spirit 50, 74, 76, 125, 144, 173, 198, 204–205, 213, 221–222, 226, 232, 235; spirit of the world 230; spiritual beings 81. *See also* angel, ghost, spirituality.
spiritual hierarchy 79, 101, 263
spirituality 6, 19, 27, 33, 58, 68–69, 75, 79–80, 87–88, 90, 114, 116, 147, 180–181, 190, 204, 213, 219, 224, 273; sign of spirituality 181; spiritual advancement 179; spiritual attainment, 147–148 spiritual economy 15; spiritual ideas 26; spiritual ideals 191; spiritual knowledge 25, 180; spiritual law 12, 21; spiritual path 56, 78, 79, 99, 153, 180, 190; spiritual perfection 65, 200; spiritual wisdom 152. *See also* angel, asceticim, meditation, metaphysics, mysticism, path, pilgrimage, plane, religion, soul, sphere, spirit, Sufism, Yoga.
star 79, 221
statue 69, 103, 217–218, 235, 253. *See also* sculpture.
stillness 41, 247, 253. *See also* peace, quiet, silence, tranquility.
stone 25, 79, 85, 139. *See also* crystal, rock.
strength 4, 10, 40, 71, 91, 123, 125–126, 130, 147–148, 160, 169, 177–178, 183. *See also* control, mastery, power.
struggle of life 3–4, 34, 76, 138, 149
subtlety 25–29, 110. *See also* refinement.
success 6, 15, 38–39, 63, 73, 148, 187–188, 200, 203, 206, 208. *See also* fulfillment, victory.
suffering 29, 44, 88, 90, 100, 131, 141, 189. *See also* depression, pains, sadness, sorrow.
Sufi message 190, 241
Sufi Movement 120, 190
Sufis 36, 63, 76, 88, 95, 105, 111, 117, 120, 125–127, 145, 149, 162, 170, 176, 182, 235, 239, 241, 249–250, 259; sign of the Sufi 116; Sufi poets 22, 29, 55, 142; Sufis and music 239, 250. *See also* dervish, murid, murshid, qawwal, Sufism, individual Sufis by name.
Sufism 59, 230; practice of Sufism 117. *See also* Chishti Order, meditation, mysticism, spirituality, Sufis.
sukradi 228, 263
Summan 123
sun 5, 55, 77–79, 162, 164, 174–176, 183, 221; divine sun 78; sunshine 33; reflections of the sun 78
superstitions 175

sword 34–35, 89
symbol 29, 182, 202, 204–205, 212–213, 217; symbolic beauty 235; symbolical dream 171; symbol of the cross 182, 205; symbol of the fish 15–16; symbol of wisdom 65. *See also* image, Lion Gate, sign, symbology.
symbology 49, 195, 211–213. *See also* symbol.
sympathy 26, 31, 48, 71–72, 105, 112, 121, 125, 132–133, 249. *See also* compassion, kindness, mercy.
symphony of life 8–9

T

Talmud 22
tamas 39–40, 263. *See also* darkness, restlessness.
Tansen 240, 247, 263, 269
teacher 34, 78, 130, 135, 139. *See also* guru, master, murshid, rishi, sage.
temptation 36, 127, 257
thankfulness 26, 55, 59, 122, 135–136; path of thankfulness 56. *See also* appreciation, gratefulness.
thoughtfulness 69, 84–85, 88, 91, 98, 127, 206, 215. *See also* consideration, kindness, politeness.
Tibet 58
tiger 67, 254; tiger dance 255
tolerance 18, 77, 84, 106, 123, 127, 140, 180. *See also* consideration, kindness.
tone 107, 166, 246,; beauty of rhythm and tone 256; microtones 242; semitones 242
torch 125. *See also* flame, light.
tranquility 15, 115, 180. *See also* balance, harmony, peace, quiet, solitude, stillness.
treasure 16, 56, 144, 213
tree 77, 81, 108, 157, 166, 231, 253
trust 20, 43, 56–57, 80–81, 104, 108–109, 126, 129, 143, 150, 179; trustworthiness 21, 88. *See also* faith.
truth 99, 102, 144, 162, 169, 190, 216, 232–233, 241, 250; path of truth 34
tuberculosis 63
Tulsidas 137, 263
Tumbara 240, 263
tumri 248
tuning 58, 179–180, 220, 226; tuning the heart 225; tuning the soul 20, 260

U

unity 181; divine unity 91
universalism 134; universal consciousness 127, 177; universal religion 258
unselfishness 5, 23, 103, 121, 127, 133, 150–151. *See also* generosity, love, service.
unveiling 5, 43. *See also* revelation, vision.
'uruj 213–214, 263

V

vaccination 62–63
vacuum 79. *See also* space.
vairagya 110, 182–183, 263; *See also* ascetic, adept, indifference, mystic, renunciation, silence, solitude, Yogi.

vanity 76–77, 90, 110, 129; divine vanity 110, 262; false vanity 126. *See also* ego, pride.
Vedanta 63, 67, 174, 239, 259; Vedantist 67. *See also* Hinduism.
veil 22, 26, 49, 114, 126, 153, 200, 231. *See also* cloud, illusion, mystery, secret, unveiling.
vibration 50, 58, 84, 159, 188, 244, 250; alchemy of vibrations 245; elements of vibrations 245; finer vibrations 247; vibrations from the mind invisible 161; vibrations of music 250. *See also* energy, movement, sound.
victory 123; victory in the battle of life 153. *See also* fulfillment, struggle of life, success.
vina 7, 235, 242, 247, 249, 260
violin 220, 225
virtue 13, 15, 21, 26, 40, 43, 45, 48, 71, 75–77, 81, 83, 87–88, 90, 92, 101, 103, 106, 110, 113, 116, 132, 138, 142–143, 148, 203, 229
vision 110, 116–117, 165–167, 171, 204, 223–224; vision of God 113, 135, 189, 200; visionary 69. *See also* clairvoyance, prophet, revelation, seer, unveiling
vitality 72. *See also* energy, vibration.
voice 8, 59, 107, 184, 196, 218, 239, 240, 242, 246, 248, 253–254. *See also* singer, singing.

W

wali 47, 79, 263. *See also* master.
water 10, 16, 25, 32, 63, 83, 123, 144, 157, 161, 172, 176, 179, 181–182, 195, 228, 245, 247; color of water 249; power of water 68; water of divine knowledge 183. *See also* fountain, ocean, river, sea.
West, the 17, 228, 239–240, 256, 269; Western world 230
will of God 118, 178
wine 56, 111, 139, 151, 233. *See also* ecstasy, intoxication.
wisdom 5, 13, 44, 83, 116–117, 129, 168, 179, 195, 198, 211, 235; perfection of wisdom 65, 222; sign of wisdom 49; spiritual wisdom 152; symbol of wisdom 65. *See also* intelligence, knowledge.
worship 78, 105, 221–222, 125–126, 168, 219, 259. *See also* devotion, prayer, religion, reverence, worship.
worshipers 142, 218. *See also* devotees, worship.
writer 159. *See also* literature, poet.

Y

Yoga, Hatha 62, 262
Yogis 249–250. *See also* adept, ascetic, Hinduism, mystic, vairagya, Yoga.

Z

zikr 162, 261, 263
Zoroastrians 88

Sulūk Press/Omega Publications is an independent publisher dedicated to issuing works of spirituality and cultural moment, with a focus on Sufism and, in particular, on the works of Hazrat Inayat Khan, his successors, and followers. For more information on the legacy of Hazrat Inayat Khan, please contact the Inayati Order at 112 East Cary Street, Richmond VA 23219. www.inayatiorder.org.